THE WORLD OF INDONESIAN TEXTILES

Line drawings by Richard Flavin

THE WORLD OF
INDONESIAN TEXTILES

Text and photographs by
Wanda Warming and Michael Gaworski

KODANSHA INTERNATIONAL
Tokyo • New York • London

Distributed in the United States by Kodansha America, Inc., 114 Fifth Avenue, New York, N.Y. 10011, and in the United Kingdom and continental Europe by Kodansha Europe Ltd., Gillingham House, 38-44 Gillingham Street, London SW1V 1HU. Published by Kodansha International Ltd., 17-14 Otowa 1-chome, Bunkyo-ku, Tokyo 112, and Kodansha America, Inc.

Library of Congress Cataloging in Publication Data
Warming, Wanda, 1947-
    The world of Indonesian textiles.
    Bibliography: p.
    Includes index.
    1. Textile fabrics—Indonesia. I. Gqaworski, Michael,
1950-   joint author. II. Title.
TS1413.I55W37   677'.09598   80-82526
ISBN 4-7700-1611-5

Contents

List of Illustrations

Maps

Color Plates

Figures

Introduction

Indonesians call their country *Tanah Air Kita* or "Our Land Water," a name that plainly expresses how, within the borders of the republic, there is more water than there is land. The 13,667 islands of the Indonesian archipelago stretch five thousand kilometers from the Malay Peninsula to Australia. Most of these islands are unnamed and uninhabited but they include Sumatra, Java, Sulawesi (formerly Celebes), most of Borneo (or Kalimantan to Indonesians), and half of New Guinea (known as Irian Jaya), as well as the smaller islands of Halmahera, the Malukus (the famous Spice Islands), and the Nusatenggara chain that includes the fabled island of Bali. Indonesia is home to more than 150,000,000 people, making it the fifth most populous country in the world. Ninety percent of all Indonesians live on Java, Sumatra, and Bali. These three islands contain some of the most densely inhabited regions on earth. Yet one could find few places in the world as sparsely settled as Borneo and New Guinea.

Indonesia is a land of contrasts and extremes. Tribes with a Neolithic culture live in villages of only a few houses while residents of giant metropolises like Jakarta lead a twentieth-century lifestyle. Three hundred tribal and ethnic groups speaking some two hundred languages coexist within its boundaries. Only in Indonesia are the four major religions of Islam, Christianity, Buddhism, and Hinduism represented, but many tribal peoples still adhere to animistic beliefs. This diversity is reflected in the arts and crafts—the variety of textiles in particular matches that of other aspects of the country. The motto of the republic is a hopeful "Unity in Diversity," but it is often the diversity that leaves the strongest impression on a visitor. From island to island, and often from region to region, the character of the people, their native dress, architecture, and language change.

When we first visited Indonesia in early 1972, we traveled over land and sea eastward through Sumatra, Java, Bali, Lombok, Sumbawa, and East Nusatenggara. Each island was a unique adventure. Going from Moslem Java to neighboring Hindu Bali is like entering another world, although the two islands are only an hour's ferry ride apart.

At that time, visitors were rare east of Bali and our trip eastward to Timor Island was a lesson in patience, a trait of utmost importance while traveling in Indonesia. Transportation became unpredictable at best; whenever possible we traveled by cargo boats that carry passengers on their decks, but to reach islands the cargo boats did not serve, we embarked on the single-masted sailboats that carry goods to the remote ports of Indonesia. Through the interiors of the islands most roads only exist in the dry season and to get from one village to another meant riding atop bags of onions or rice in the rear of a truck. These ancient vehicles broke down frequently in the rugged terrain, and where the trucks could not go, we walked.

In the isolated, less-developed East Nusatenggara islands of Flores, Sumba, and Timor, the locally made textiles captured our attention. From one region of East Nusatenggara to another, textiles show great differences and communicate the character of the people who weave them. Elsewhere we had seen the animal-patterned blankets of Sumba used as wallhangings, but arriving in Sumba we were amazed to see turbaned Sumbanese men actually wearing these cloths wrapped around their waists. The bold patterns decorating the cloths matched the flamboyant spirit of these rugged horsemen.

In outer islands like Sumba and Flores, inns are found only in a few towns. We often had to depend on the hospitality of village families and isolated Catholic missionaries. Staying in the countryside gave us an opportunity to see the

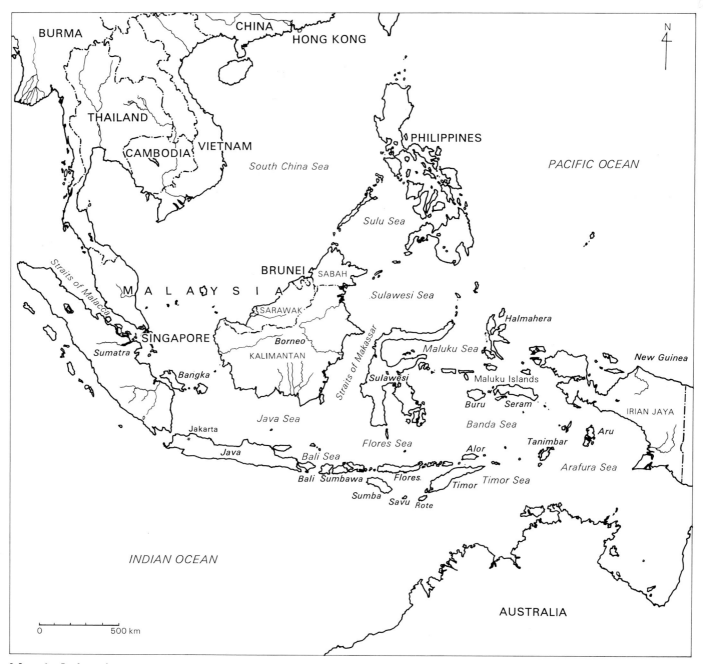

Map 1. Indonesia.

crafts, particularly weaving, at close hand. We often spent the days waiting for transportation studying Bahasa Indonesia, the official language of the nation, and talking to people—conversation is not a lost art in Indonesia. A motivation to learn more about the textiles, their production and motifs, was an incentive to visit out-of-the-way villages and get to know the weavers.

This initial introduction to the weavings of East Nusatenggara led us to a more in-depth study of the textile traditions of Indonesia. Subsequently, we returned to Indonesia five times and traveled to all the major islands to research textiles, their roles in each society, the techniques, and the meaning of the motifs.

For a land of its size and cultural richness, Indonesia is relatively little known outside of Southeast Asia. Textiles play an integral role in many Indonesian societies, and to understand this role, one must view them in the context of the different cultures that make them. But textiles must also be seen against the larger historical backdrop and to do this it is necessary to understand the forces that shaped the lives of the weavers. Indonesians have been greatly affected by various waves of migrations and by outside cultural influences, and these have all had an effect on their textile arts. Historical and cultural trends are covered in more detail in the text, but the following summary introduces the major sources of the rich diversity seen in Indonesian textiles today.

Fossils found in Java indicate that man first appeared in what is now Indonesia between 400,000 and 120,000 B.C. By 20,000 B.C. hunter-gatherers with Australoid features were living in the archipelago, and during the Mesolithic period (10,000 to 2000 B.C.) other groups of hunter-gatherers arrived. In approximately 2500 B.C. a substantial migration from the Yunnan area of southern China introduced a Neolithic culture to the islands. These Mongoloid peoples brought with them techniques of rice cultivation, animal husbandry, and pottery making, and probably at this time the islanders' indigenous bark garments were first decorated with simple motifs. Among certain peoples, this Neolithic culture later evolved into a Megalithic phase characterized by the building of large stone monuments that were connected to religious practices. Among the peoples where such Megalithic features survive today are the Bataks of North Sumatra, the Torajans of central Sulawesi, the inhabitants of Nias Island, and the Sumbanese.

Between the eighth and second centuries B.C., migrants from what is now northern Vietnam came to the archipelago, bringing with them a way of life referred to as the Dong-Son. The Dong-Son culture had a tremendous impact on many Indonesian peoples and its effects are still evident today. Most scholars believe that the backstrap loom and the dye-resist method of textile decoration called warp ikat were introduced into Indonesia during the period of Dong-Son influence. Until this time people had worn plain or simply decorated bark garments. The Dong-Son migrants also introduced metalwork, especially the technique of bronze lost-wax casting. They brought with them decorated bronze kettle-drums that were used in various rituals. Indonesian tribes borrowed many motifs that appeared on these drums, including the "tree of life" and "ship of the dead," and a characteristic style of geometric ornamentation.

Another culture, known as the Late Chou, had less of an impact on the tribes of Indonesia but had an influence on some tribes of Borneo, particularly on their nontextile motifs. The Late Chou designs tend to be asymmetric, while the Dong-Son patterns are geometric and symmetric.

The motifs brought by the Dong-Son people, and to a lesser extent the Late Chou, mixed with

Map 2. Sumatra.

the indigenous Neolithic-Megalithic animal and human figures to create a unique style of ornamentation that is still seen today on warp ikat textiles, particularly among the Torajans, the Bataks, the Timorese, and the Iban Dyaks of northwestern Borneo (now Sarawak, a state of Malaysia).

Indian civilization had a great impact on Indonesia, especially on Java and Sumatra. By the second century A.D., Indian traders had already made contacts with the coastal peoples of Java and by the fifth century they had established a Hindu kingdom there. In the seventh century, a Sumatran kingdom, Srivijaya, was beginning to assert itself. Srivijaya became a great center for the study of Mahayana Buddhism, which was the dominant religion of India at that time. Eventually, Srivijaya would extend its sphere of influence up the Malay Peninsula into northern Thailand. In the mid-ninth century, the kingdom of Mataram, which also owed much to India, was gaining power in Java.

What imprint this period of Indian influence left on the textiles of Indonesia is somewhat unclear. Some scholars argue that the technical knowledge needed to make batik cloth was introduced into Java from India at this time, but others dispute this point. The greatest legacy

Map 3. Sulawesi.

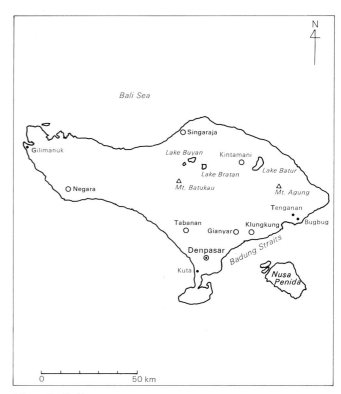

Map 4. Bali.

left by India was upon religion. Buddhism and Hinduism eventually blended with the native Javanese animism to form a unique combination. Temple architecture in Central Java, especially that of the temples of the Dieng Plateau, Borobodur and Prambanan, is testimony to the great civilization that flourished as a result of Indian influence.

From the tenth to the fifteenth centuries A.D., a succession of strong kingdoms in East and Central Java made their presence felt in the other islands of the archipelago. In the fourteenth century, the kingdom of Majapahit dominated many of the islands that are today part of the Republic of Indonesia. Again, the influence of these aggressive Javanese kingdoms on the arts and crafts of other islands is unknown. Local kings may have paid tribute to the Javanese, but the isolated tribal peoples were probably left in relative peace.

The next important influence on the archipelago was Islam. Islam originated in the Middle East in the seventh century A.D. and was brought to Indonesia in the fifteenth century by Indian and Arab traders. They were instrumental in spreading the faith in East Java. The remainder of Java, as well as many parts of Sumatra, later adopted Islam. Today Indonesia is more than ninety percent Moslem. These traders also introduced new techniques of fabric

decoration, such as weft ikat, supplementary weft weaving, and tie-dye along with sericulture. Because Islam discourages the portrayal of living things in the arts, the more naturalistic textile motifs of some areas, most notably Central Java, were modified and stylized.

In the early 1600s, the Dutch began to build an Indonesian colony that was to remain under their control for the next three hundred and fifty years. Their interest was primarily economic, and they generally did not interfere with the indigenous cultures they had contact with. Only a few areas of the archipelago, the Malukus and northern Sulawesi in particular, were profoundly affected by the Dutch presence. The Maluku islanders and the Minahassa of northern Sulawesi adopted Christianity and their cultures underwent radical change. But in most other areas of the archipelago, the Dutch stayed in the background and relied on Chinese middlemen to conduct their business. Although Dutch motifs were borrowed and adapted to the textile patterns of Java and East Nusatenggara, the Dutch policy of noninterference in local affairs generally tended, in the long run, to preserve native arts and crafts.

Certain traditional textiles are no longer produced in Indonesia, but most techniques, including the making of bark cloth, continue to be practiced. In this book we primarily cover the

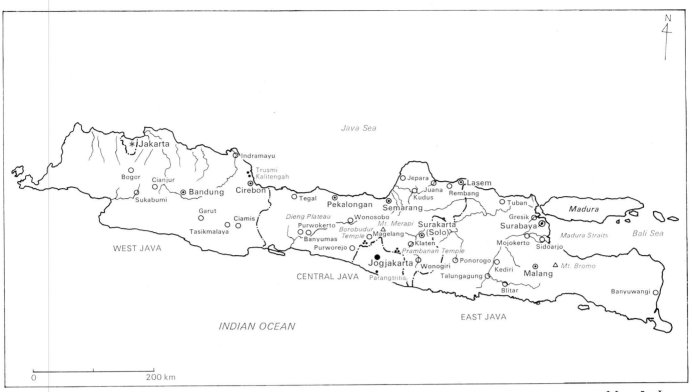

Map 5. Java.

techniques and motifs of contemporary textiles. But a few textiles that are no longer made are too important to ignore. The most notable examples are the woven ship cloths and the embroidered *tapis* skirts, both of which were once made in southern Sumatra. Also, the motifs and layout of the Indian patola cloth have been so widely adopted on Indonesian textiles of the past and present that we have devoted a section to this subject in chapter 3. Irian Jaya or New Guinea is culturally different from the rest of the archipelago and is therefore not covered in the text.

The important methods of contemporary textile decoration fall into two categories: dye-resist, in which a resist is used to block the dye and create the pattern, and woven techniques, in which the patterns are produced in the weaving process. Ikat-decorated textiles (the warp or weft threads are bound with fiber before dyeing to create the pattern), tie-dyed cloths, and batik (cloth patterned with wax) are all dye-resist techniques. Warp ikat and batik are perhaps Indonesia's most outstanding achievements in the field of textiles. Warp ikat textiles, which are made by certain tribal peoples, date back to Neolithic times and are covered in chapter 1 (technique) and chapter 2 (motifs and uses). Chapter 5 is devoted entirely to the important technique of batik and chapter 6 covers the different motifs that decorate batik cloth. Other dye-resist patterned textiles, such as weft ikat, double ikat, and tie-dyed cloths are described in chapter 3. Woven techniques such as supplementary weft decoration in which extra threads float over and under the background cloth to give the motif, supplementary warp, and specialized methods involving embroidery, tapestry weaves, and beading decorate some outstanding Indonesian textiles, and these are described in chapter 4.

No single volume could ever hope to deal with all the technical and design variations that make Indonesian textiles of such interest to both craftsman and collector. In our discussions of the different weavings, we have taken a middle road, providing both broad surveys of textile traditions and motifs, and basic explanations of techniques and materials. Our organizing the book by craft and not by region made the most sense, for techniques tend to show less regional variation than motifs and can therefore be dealt with without dragging in endless qualifications and exceptions. We have, however, tried to underscore the whole geographical picture, and within these chapters we rather freely island hop around the archipelago to present outstanding examples of textiles with a distinct local character.

Much as we wanted to, we were not able to go everywhere. But we were able to observe each major technique of textile decoration in at least

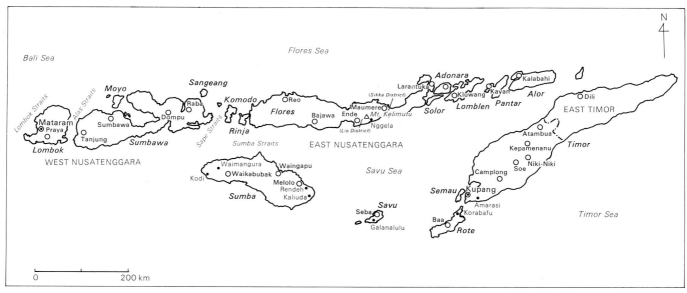

Map 6. West and East Nusatenggara.

one area of Indonesia, and the methods described here are generally those we saw. We stayed in small villages with weavers and their families, who never seemed to view our intrusion as a disruption of their daily lives. Between the social rituals of chewing betel nut, smoking clove-scented *kretek* cigarettes, and drinking glass after glass of hot tea, weavers would bring out their equipment and demonstrate how they made their dyes. Village elders were called upon to tell stories and show us their family heirlooms. Sometimes it was necessary to seek out the few remaining practitioners of particular techniques in larger cities. We talked to people in the marketplaces, stopped women in the streets, and boldly knocked on doors. To see certain techniques, we had to visit larger workshops. In West Sumatra, Java, Bali, and Sulawesi, factory owners interrupted their work to demonstrate how they made their textiles. The pride Indonesians take in their weavings coupled with their natural hospitality made our research easy.

A surprising number of textiles in Indonesia are still woven at home for personal use. In the islands of Indonesia, weaving is traditionally the work of women and textiles are considered to have a feminine nature. Only when cloths are produced in workshops do men begin to take a part in their creation. The techniques of textile production and the knowledge of the motifs are traditionally passed from mother to daughter.

The weaver creates her cloth from materials found in her surroundings and may produce textiles patterned with complex techniques using only simple tools. She may grow cotton in her backyard and spin it into thread herself. Her basic tools are made of readily available materials such as bamboo poles, the ribs of coconut leaves, and fiber from trees. Those implements that must be made are put together by her husband or the village carpenter. She gathers or trades for the dyestuffs and makes her own dyes. It is these textiles, wholly created by the weavers, that play the most important role in the life of the societies that make them.

However, as Indonesia progresses, the trend is for the production of these textiles to move from the home into workshops. Some types of cloth, such as batik, have long been made on a commercial scale as well as on the individual level, while other types of textiles such as weft ikat and supplementary weft weavings are just now moving to the cottage-industry level.

When the creation of a particular type of textile moves to a commercial level, undeniably much artistry is lost in the transition. The only alternative, however, is often that the technique will disappear altogether. We felt it was important to describe the textiles that are made in workshops, since a great deal of craftsmanship may go into their production and the techniques and tools employed are often not so different from those once used in the home.

The textiles of Indonesia are interesting not only for the richness of their patterns but for the meaning they often have in their society, particularly among tribal people. Their basic use is as a garment, but people view certain weavings as ritual objects that are necessary aids in carrying out their customs. Textiles may be required for burials, weddings, circumcisions, and other rites of passage. Not only are they worn by the participants in these ceremonies but they may also be displayed as an integral part of the ritual—wrapped around the corpse, placed over a ritual gift, or used in an exchange of goods. Some cloths are counted as wealth, and some may have magical uses.

Because of the social significance of the textiles, the designs are often strictly dictated by tradition. These motifs are in many cases more than just decoration—they are symbols representing deities and spirits, wealth, power, life-force, and fertility. The patterns take on greater importance when it is noted that in some societies textiles are the dominant visual art medium.

Since the textiles of Indonesia represent a great deal to those who make and use them, we have relied whenever possible upon people's own explanations of their motifs and customs. We have also tried to convey some idea of how Indonesians regard and value their weavings. In this way we want to show the textiles as they are used, and not as objects detached from the weavers, waxers, and dyers who create them. Through this we hope to give some glimpse of the character and life of these people.

Acknowledgments

During the course of our study we met many people whose information on textile techniques, motifs, or some aspect of a particular culture contributed to this work. In more than three years of research, we never came into contact with anyone who refused us his time, hospitality, or knowledge even though we arrived at homes or villages unannounced. So many people shared information with us, gave us food and shelter in isolated villages, or helped us when we ran into difficulties that there is not enough room to thank each person by name. But we would here like to acknowledge the considerable debt we owe to the weavers, dyers, and textile makers of Indonesia, without whose help this book would never have been written. Our thanks to them all.

We lived in Japan between visits to Indonesia and there are some special people we would like to thank, for without their help and guidance this book might still be a disjointed collection of miscellaneous information.

Professor Masakazu Utsumi, Dean of Students at Tama Art University in Tokyo, acted as our sponsor while we lived in Japan. Professor Utsumi made our problems his concerns and generally made our life as outsiders in Japan much easier. His valuable instruction and guidance in the conceptual and aesthetic guidelines needed to translate an idea into a cohesive unit will always be greatly appreciated.

We also owe a considerable debt to Professor Tomoyuki Yamanobe, former Curator of Textiles at Tokyo National Museum and presently Special Lecturer at Tama Art University and Director of the Toyama Kinenkan Foundation. As Director of the Design Research Institute at Tama Art University, Professor Yamanobe convinced us of the importance of our research through his boundless enthusiasm for every aspect of Indonesian textiles. He encouraged us to collect every scrap of information no matter how irrelevant it seemed, and taught us to view textiles not through our own prejudices but through the eyes of the people who weave them. For his valuable contributions to our work we remain eternally grateful.

Professor Yamanobe and his sister Harue Hashimoto, her husband, and their children also provided us with some stability in our chaotic lifestyle by opening their home and hearts to us, making us feel a part of their family. The periods that we spent with them contributed greatly to the positive attitude necessary to writing a book, and we look upon those times as cherished memories.

Many thanks to Richard Flavin for contributing the line drawings that accompany the text of this book. Mr. Flavin has a great feeling for tools, and his ability to work from photos and bring life into an otherwise lifeless object was a valuable contribution.

We would also like to thank Tama Art University, Toyama Kinenkan Foundation, and Professor Yamanobe for generously loaning examples from their collections to be photographed for this book.

Finally, we owe a special debt of gratitude to three people without whose help in the beginning we would never have been able to carry our research to its conclusion. We sincerely thank Sharon Rhoads Nakazato, Pam Takeshige, and Professor Kozo Sasaki, Dean of Art History, Waseda University, Tokyo. Our lives were greatly enriched by meeting these three people.

ABOUT INDONESIAN SPELLINGS

Indonesia's national language, Bahasa Indonesia, is written in roman letters and has undergone several spelling revisions from the Dutch period to the present. Spellings of Indonesian words and place names in this book follow the most recent revision of 1975. Vowels are pronounced in the Italian style and consonants are pronounced as in English, with the following exceptions:

$c = ch$ as in "cherry"
$h =$ silent or lightly aspirated
$r =$ rolled, as in Italian
$v =$ usually pronounced w

Major spelling changes incorporated into the new system are the use of c for old tj, j for dj, and y for j. These new spellings, however, have not yet been fully adopted, and older or variant spellings can still be found both in Indonesia and in foreign publications. Note that names for the batik tools *canting* and *cap* appear in this book as "tjanting" and "tjap," respectively, because they have acquired the status of English words.

Color Plates

Plate 1. Warp ikat *hinggi kombu* selimut with seahorse motif. Cotton; natural dyes; full cloth: 270 cm. × 142 cm. From East Sumba. Authors' collection.

Plate 2. Colorfully dressed vendors gather at a weekly market in Nita, Flores, near the town of Maumere.

Plate 3. Two East Sumbanese villagers wear traditional dress on a visit to the town of Waingapu.

Plate 4. Indigo stains on the hands of this dyer will last well beyond the dyeing season. Near Seba, Savu.

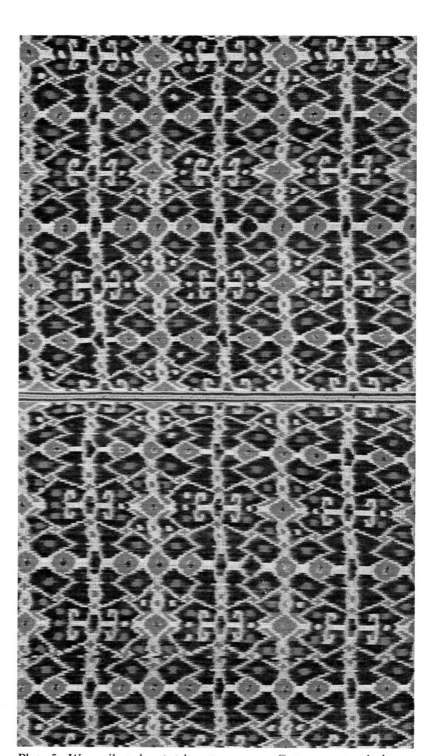

Plate 5. Warp ikat *lau patola ratu* sarong. Cotton; natural dyes; full cloth: 163 cm. × 62.5 cm. From East Sumba. Tama Art University collection.

Plate 6. Warp ikat *worapi* sarong with *makaba* motif. Cotton; natural dyes; full cloth: 191 cm. × 64 cm. From Savu. Authors' collection.

Plate 7. Warp ikat *wohapi* selimut. Cotton; natural dyes; full cloth: 184 cm. × 82 cm. From Savu. Authors' collection.

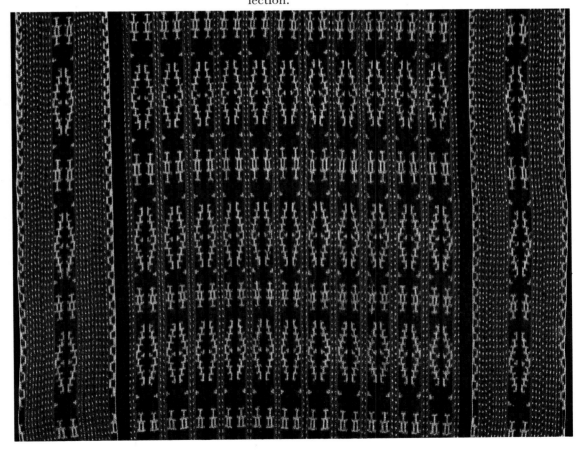

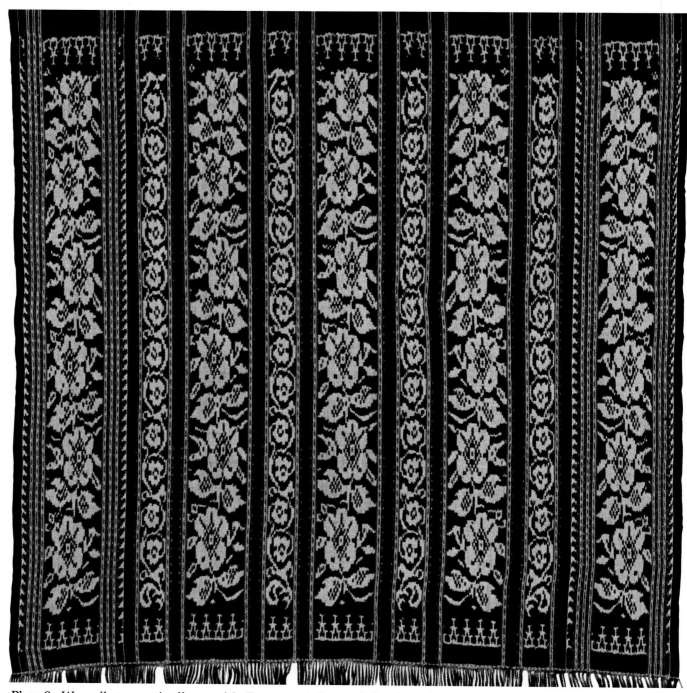

Plate 8. Warp ikat *worapi* selimut with European-influenced floral motif. Cotton; natural dyes; full cloth: 155 cm. × 76.5 cm. From Savu. Toyama Kinenkan Foundation collection.

Plate 9. Warp ikat sarong. Cotton; natural dyes; full cloth: 160 cm. × 59 cm. From Sikka, Flores. Tama Art University collection.

Plate 10. Warp ikat *lawo nepa mite* sarong. Cotton; natural dyes; full cloth: 196 cm. × 70 cm. From Lio, Flores. Tama Art University collection.

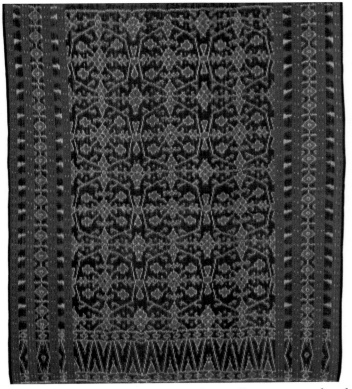

Plate 11. Warp ikat *selenda sinde* selimut. Cotton; natural and chemical dyes; full cloth: 160 cm. × 67 cm. From Lio, Flores. Tama Art University collection.

Plate 12. Warp ikat *lawo radu* sarong. Silk; natural and chemical dyes; full cloth: 174 cm. × 70 cm. From Lio, Flores. Tama Art University collection.

Plate 13. These men from central Timor are wearing their finest outfits for a trip to a weekly market. Niki-Niki, central Timor.

Plate 15. Warp ikat *natam koroh* sarong with bird ·motif. Cotton; natural dyes; full cloth: 160 cm. × 64 cm. From Amarasi, West Timor. Tama Art University collection.

Plate 14. Warp ikat woman's sarong with hook-and-rhomb motif. Cotton; natural dyes (for motif) and store-bought colored threads (for stripes); full cloth: 123 cm. × 74 cm. From central Timor. Tama Art University collection.

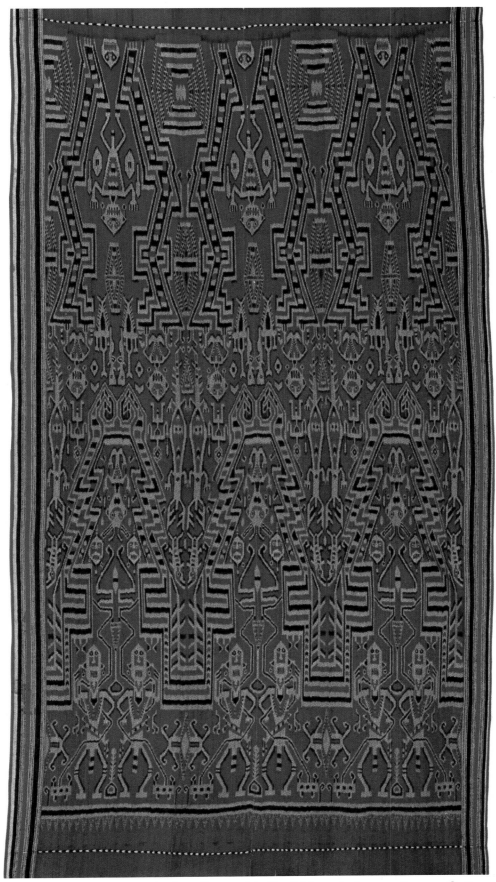

Plate 16. Warp ikat *pua kumbu* selimut with Neolithic-style human figures. Cotton; natural dyes; full cloth: 264 cm. × 140 cm. Made in the 1940s in Rajang River area, Sarawak, Malaysia. Authors' collection.

Plate 17. Warp ikat selimut. Cotton; natural dyes; full cloth: 147 cm. × 90 cm. Made in the 1930s on Rote. Tomoyuki Yamanobe collection.

Plate 18. Warp ikat *se'kon* selimut. Cotton; natural dyes; full cloth: 340 cm. × 75 cm. From Rongkong, South Sulawesi. Toyama Kinenkan Foundation collection.

Plate 19. Double ikat patola cloth with *jil-imprang* motif and *tumpal* border. Silk; natural dyes; full cloth: 444 cm. × 105 cm. Made in the nineteenth century in Gujurat area, India. Tama Art University collection.

Plate 20. Double ikat patola cloth. Silk; natural dyes; full cloth: 200 cm. × 82 cm. Made in the nineteenth century in Gujurat area, India. Tama Art University collection.

Plate 21. Double ikat gringsing selindang with *sanan empeg* motif. Cotton; natural dyes; full cloth: 216 cm. × 26 cm. From Tenganan, Bali. Tama Art University collection.

Plate 22. Double ikat gringsing selindang with *wayang putri isi* motif. Cotton; natural dyes; full cloth: 202 cm. × 50 cm. From Tenganan, Bali. Tama Art University collection.

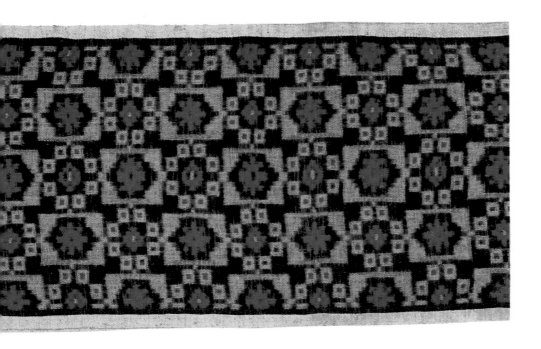

Plate 23. At the cremation ceremony of a high priest near Denpasar, Bali, a *baris tekok jago* dancer wears a double ikat gringsing selindang made in Tenganan village.

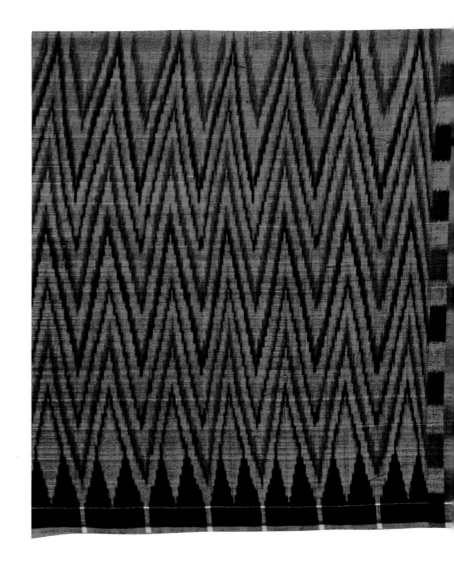

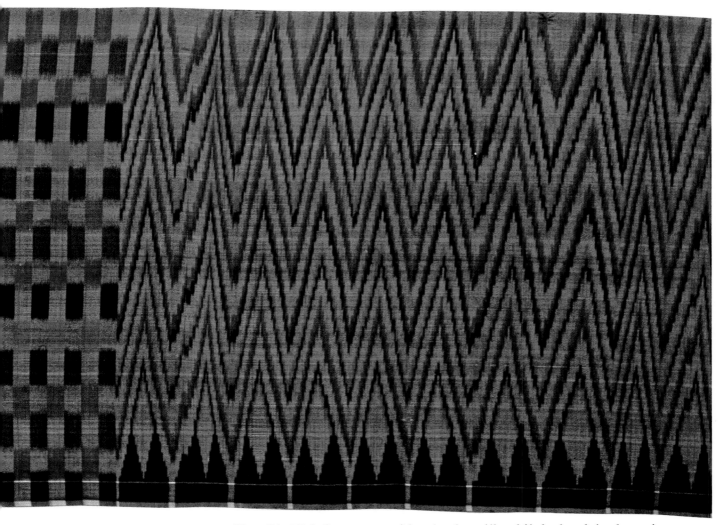

Plate 24. Weft ikat sarong with a *kepala* or "head," the break in the main pattern. Silk; chemical dyes; full cloth: 360 cm. × 54 cm. From Sempange, South Sulawesi. Toyama Kinenkan Foundation collection.

Plate 25. Weft ikat cloth with a warp ikat border pattern. Cotton; chemical dyes; full cloth: 118 cm. × 97 cm. From Gresik, East Java. Authors' collection.

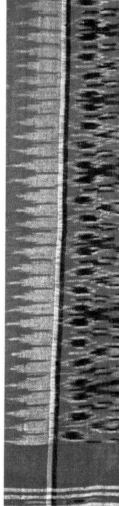

Plate 27. Weft ikat cloth. Silk; natural dyes; full cloth: 236 cm. × 81 cm. Made in the 1930s in Singaraja, Bali. Toyama Kinenkan Foundation collection.

Plate 26. Weft ikat *nduk* sarong. Silk; chemical dyes; full cloth: 175 cm. × 105 cm. Made in the 1930s on Bali. Authors' collection.

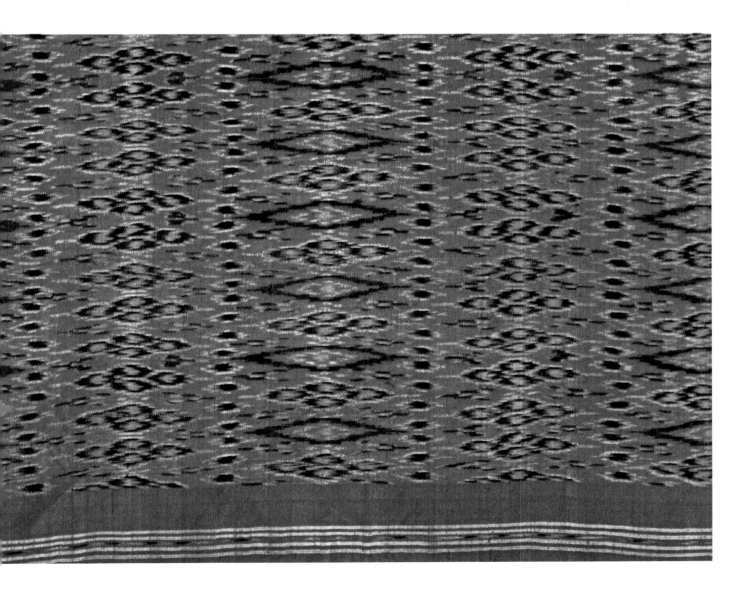

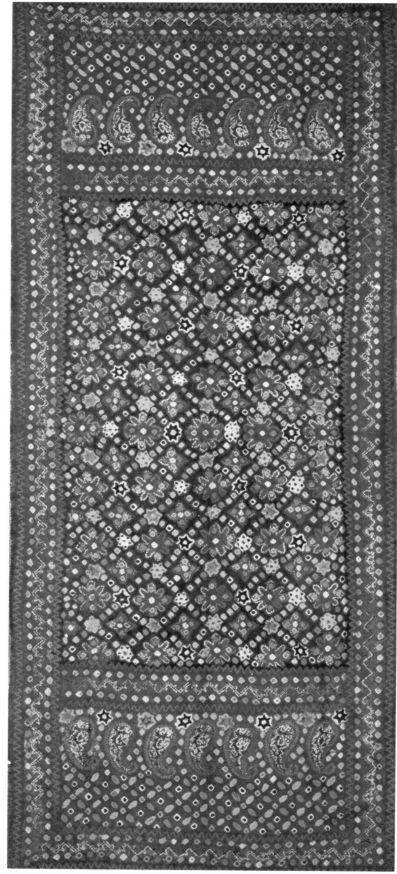

Plate 28. Tie-dyed cloth combining *tritik* and *pelangi* techniques. Silk; chemical dyes; full cloth: 280 cm. × 91 cm. From Palembang, South Sumatra. Toyama Kinenkan Foundation collection.

Plate 29. Selimut and sarong woven by the supplementary weft technique are still made by a few weavers in Palembang, South Sumatra.

Plate 30. Songket selindang with *tumpal* motif. Silver threads on a naturally dyed silk background; full cloth: 215 cm. × 79 cm. Made in the early twentieth century in Palembang, South Sumatra. Tama Art University collection.

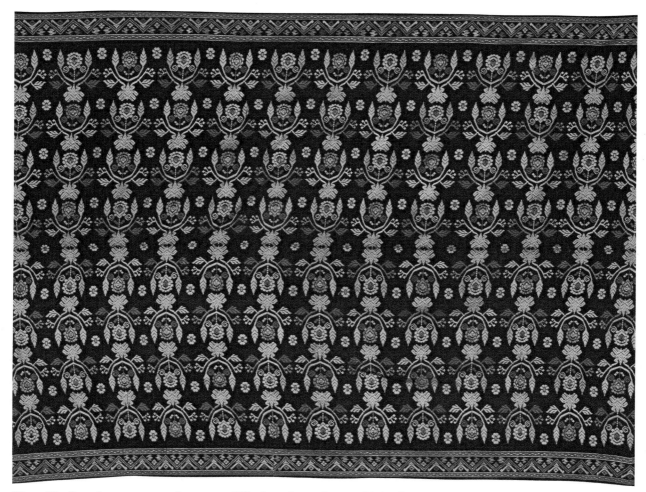

Plate 31. Supplementary weft sarong. Silk threads against a silk background; chemical dyes; full cloth: 150 cm. × 109 cm. Made in the mid-twentieth century in Klungkung, Bali. Authors' collection.

Plate 33. Two panels of a four-paneled supplementary weft *palepai*, or "ship cloth." Cotton; natural dyes; full cloth: 346 cm. × 75 cm. Made in the late nineteenth century in Kröe area, Sumatra. Tama Art University collection.

Plate 32 and detail. *Ragi hidup ulos* selimut combining supplementary weft weaving (see detail) and warp ikat. Cotton; chemical dyes; full cloth: 222 cm. × 105 cm. From Tarutung, North Sumatra. Toyama Kinenkan Foundation collection.

Plate 34. Supplementary warp *lau pahekung* sarong. Cotton; natural dyes; full cloth: 153 cm. × 61.5 cm. From East Sumba. Tama Art University collection.

Plate 35. Detail of warp pick-up weave. Cotton; chemical dyes; full cloth: 195 cm. × 109 cm. From central Timor. Tama Art University collection.

Plate 36. *Bidang* woman's skirt using *pilih* technique. Cotton; chemical dyes; full cloth: 108 cm. × 55 cm. From Rajang River area, Sarawak, Malaysia. Authors' collection.

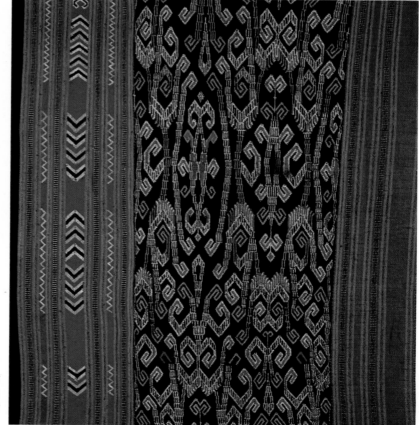

Plate 37. Detail of man's selimut using *sungkit* technique. Cotton; natural and chemical dyes; full cloth: 188 cm. × 122 cm. From central Timor. Tama Art University collection.

Plate 38. *Bidang* woman's skirt using *sungkit* technique. Cotton; natural and chemical dyes; full cloth: 104 cm. × 53 cm. From Rajang River area, Sarawak, Malaysia. Authors' collection.

Plate 39 and detail. Man's selimut using *kelim* technique (see detail) and warp pick-up weaving. Cotton; natural dyes; full cloth: 180 cm. × 117 cm. Made in the early twentieth century in central Timor. Tomoyuki Yamanobe collection.

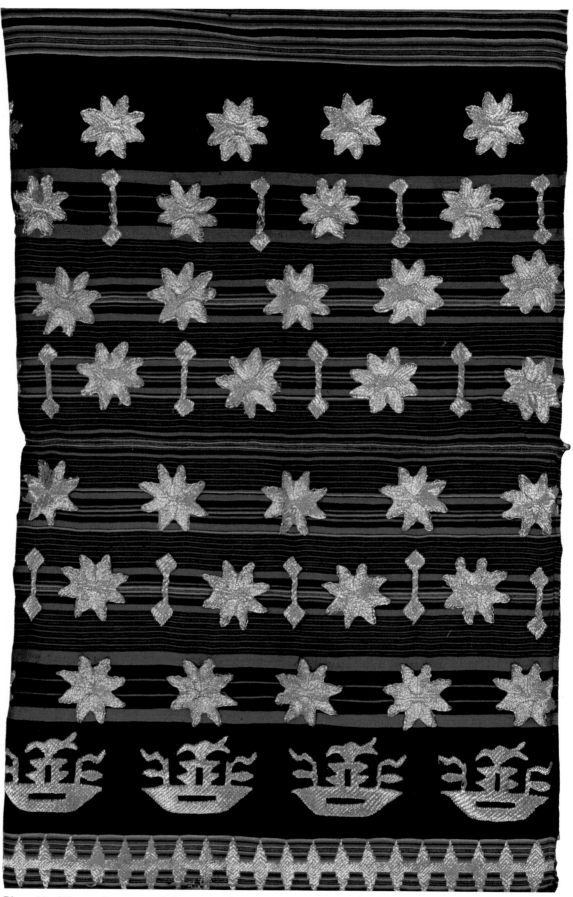

Plate 40. Woman's ceremonial sarong using embroidered gold thread. Cotton; natural dyes; full cloth: 108 cm. × 67 cm. Made in the 1920s in Lampung, Sumatra. Authors' collection.

Plate 41. Central Javanese women still wear traditional dress. The skirts are long wrap-around cloths called *kain panjang*; the tight-fitting blouses are called *kebaya*. Jogjakarta, Central Java.

Plate 42. Torajan *sarita* batik. Cotton; natural dyes; full cloth: 596 cm. × 20.5 cm. Made in the early twentieth century in South Sulawesi. Tama Art University collection.

Plate 43. Torajan *sarita* batik. Cotton; natural dyes; full cloth: 686 cm. × 33 cm. From South Sulawesi. Toyama Kinenkan Foundation collection.

45

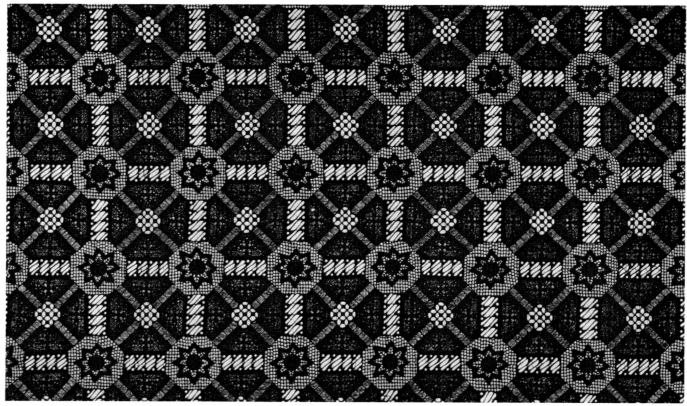

Plate 44. Batik with *ceplokkan* motif. Cotton; natural dyes; full cloth: 259 cm. × 105 cm. Made ca. 1930 in Jogjakarta, Central Java. Authors' collection.

Plate 46 and detail. Batik with *sekarjagad* or "flower of the universe" motif. Cotton; natural dyes; full cloth: 251 cm. × 103 cm. From Jogjakarta, Central Java. Authors' collection.

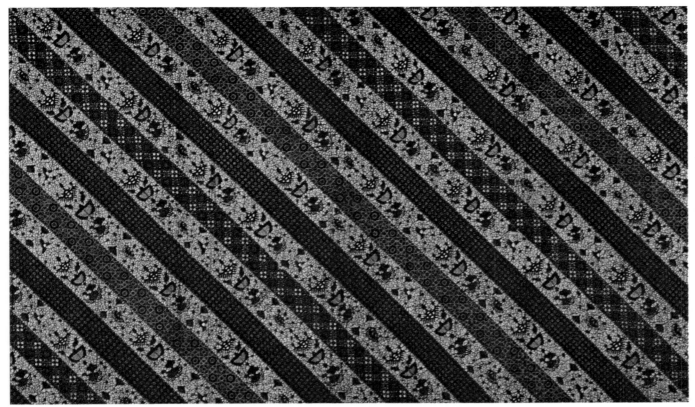

Plate 45. Batik with *garis miring* motif. Cotton; natural dyes; full cloth: 259 cm. ×
107 cm. Made ca. 1930 in Jogjakarta, Central Java. Authors' collection.

Plate 47. Batik with *luk cuan* birds. Silk; natural dyes; full cloth: 171 cm. × 100 cm.
From Rembang, northern Central Java. Authors' collection.

Plate 48 and detail. *Kapal kandas* or "ship run aground" batik. Cotton; chemical dyes; full cloth: 256 cm. × 105 cm. From Lasem, northern Central Java. Authors' collection.

Plate 50. Batik with *peksi naga sakti* motif. Cotton; chemical dyes; full cloth: 254 cm. × 105 cm. From Cirebon, West Java. Authors' collection.

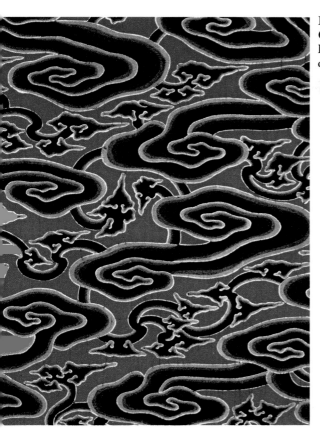

Plate 49. Batik with *megomendung* or "threatening clouds" motif. Cotton; chemical dyes; full cloth: 252 cm. × 105 cm. Made in Jogjakarta, but the pattern is originally from Cirebon, West Java. Authors' collection.

51

Plate 51. Batik with bird-and-flower motif. Cotton; chemical dyes; full cloth: 255 cm. × 105 cm. From Pekalongan, northern Central Java. Authors' collection.

Plate 52. Students and teachers wear batik with traditional patterns for the weekly dance practices held at the Sultan's Palace in Jogjakarta, Central Java.

1 Warp Ikat:
Craft of the Ancient Peoples

While staying in the town of Waikabubak on Sumba Island in East Nusatenggara, we met a local man who offered to take us to his village to visit some weavers. He led us on a short walk from town to the base of a tree-covered hill rising abruptly from a grassy plain, and then we followed him along a well-hidden path of worn boulders that wound its way up to the summit. Suddenly, the path opened onto a clearing, revealing the village of Tarung (see fig. 1). Spread out before us were thatched-roof houses eight to ten meters tall facing groups of table-shaped tombs. Dogs immediately began barking to signal our arrival; children stopped their play to cluster curiously around us and ask our guide who we were and what we were doing in their village. Most of the men of the village were out working in the fields, but the women stopped and stared at us for a few minutes before turning back to their chores. The heavy thuds made by someone pounding rice resumed. From under the eaves of a roof came the clacking sound of a woman weaving on a backstrap loom. The village elders, reclining under the overhanging roofs of the houses, broke out their betel nut and began talking about the strangers among themselves.

Tarung was one of the first traditional villages we visited in Indonesia. Looking around it, we felt as if layers of time had been peeled away and we had been transported into an earlier age. In the course of our travels, we stopped and stayed in many such places, but we never lost the feeling that in these small, isolated villages the connection between past and present was unbroken. The people of Tarung, surrounded by ageless stone tombs, refer to their forefathers of several hundred years back with an intimacy we reserve for our grandparents.

The Ancient Peoples

In the technique of warp ikat, threads are given a resist pattern before being dyed and attached to the loom for weaving. It is one of Indonesia's oldest methods of decorating textiles, and the people who practice it, like the weavers of Tarung, still live in a manner that is virtually unchanged from Megalithic times. Many terms have been used to describe these peoples, but perhaps they are best called the "Ancient Peoples"* because they continue to follow an ancient way of life. Sometime between the eighth and second centuries B.C., the Neolithic people who then lived in Indonesia came into contact with a bronze culture that had developed in what is now northern Vietnam. This Dong-Son culture, as it is known, introduced metalwork and advanced agricultural methods to many islands in Indonesia, and it is generally believed that the backstrap loom and warp ikat technique appeared during this period, although a direct connection between the Dong-Son culture and warp ikat has not yet been proven. The Dong-Son culture was also the source of a highly ornamental style of decoration that combined with the indigenous symbolic art of these early Indonesians. This combination of decorative and symbolic styles survives today among various groups, and can be seen es-

* A term used by Tibor Bodrogi in *Art of Indonesia* (Greenwich, Conn.: New York Graphic Society, 1972).

Fig. 1. Tarung village near Waikabubak, West Sumba.
The table-shaped stone formations are ancestral tombs.

pecially well in the motifs of their warp ikat
textiles. Another culture closely related to the
Dong-Son, the Late Chou, came from southern
China around the same time and also had some
influence in Indonesia, notably on Borneo Island,
but its impact was generally not as widespread
as that of the Dong-Son. After this period of
largely Dong-Son influence more than two
millennia ago, the Ancient Peoples were not
noticeably affected again by outside forces.
Buddhism, Hinduism, Islam, and, to a lesser
extent, Portuguese and Dutch colonialism helped
shape the art and beliefs of other peoples in
Indonesia but had relatively little impact on
the lives of the Ancient Peoples, with only a
few recent exceptions.

The Ancient Peoples of today live in hard-to-
reach mountainous regions or on remote islands;
their geographical isolation has served as an
important barrier against outside influences
and has been a significant factor in the preser-
vation of their cultures. Groups of Ancient
Peoples are found in widely scattered pockets
around Indonesia. Among the better-known of
these ethnic tribes are the Bataks of North

Sumatra, the people of Nias and Mentawai
islands, the Torajans of central Sulawesi, and
the Iban Dyaks of northwestern Borneo. The
inhabitants of most of the islands east of Bali
also once shared this traditional way of life,
and up to the present, peoples of East Nusatenggara and the island chain that includes
Kai, Leti, Kisar, and Tanimbar of the South
Malukus have kept alive much of the spirit of
Megalithic culture. Other Indonesian peoples
such as the Lampung people of southern Sumatra
and the Bali Aga of Bali are also closely related.
The peoples of the South Maluku islands of
Ambon and Seram (the fabled Spice Islands),
and the Minahassa of northern Sulawesi once
shared this culture, but their way of life changed
radically during the period of Dutch colonialism (1600–1949), and they no longer can be
grouped with the others.

Today is a time of great transition for the Ancient Peoples. The areas they inhabit, at one time
isolated, are opening up and now enjoy more
regular contact with other parts of Indonesia.
For the first time, many children of the Ancient Peoples are being educated in govern-

ment schools and introduced to new ideas and lifestyles. Naturally, these changes have had their inevitable effect on the traditional beliefs and tribal arts. Of course, change itself is not to be condemned, but all too often, instead of the Ancient Peoples evolving gradually in their own manner, they have abruptly abandoned their old ways; traditions that are the culmination of many centuries are rejected and forgotten in just a few years.

The erosion of traditional culture is occurring at widely varying rates among the Ancient Peoples, but the different tribes still share many characteristics and customs. Their traditional life is generally based on animistic religions and the division of society into rigid social classes. Ritual headhunting, which was connected with a life-force concept, was once widespread in the islands of Indonesia but ceased in this century. The Ancient Peoples' strong belief in an afterlife is expressed in elaborate burial ceremonies complete with animal sacrifices and grand feasts, and in the building of Megalithic tombs and monuments in memory of the dead. Sacred rocks, ceremonial house posts, and other objects are embodiments of spiritual or divine power. Before these holy stones, posts, coconut trees, and other spots where spirits are believed to reside, villagers make offerings as they request help in curing an illness or in increasing the prosperity of their village. Among these peoples, magic and supernatural forces are accepted as an integral part of daily life.

Although the villages of the Ancient Peoples are widely separated geographically and differ superficially in many details, there are many similarities. For example, in a Batak village in North Sumatra, a Torajan village in central Sulawesi, and a village on Sumba Island in East Nusatenggara, the grand, often intricately carved houses are invariably impressive and are arranged in formal rows or around tombs. The villages of the Ancient Peoples, even today, are often self-sufficient, growing their own food, building their own houses, and making their everyday utensils and clothing from materials gathered in their immediate surroundings.

The textiles of the Ancient Peoples also reflect their common heritage. As we shall see, motifs as well as techniques of textile decoration and dyestuffs are often remarkably similar, even though these peoples are separated by thousands of kilometers of open sea. Such similarities demonstrate how well the Ancient Peoples have held onto the legacy of their common Dong-Son background.

Bark Cloth

All Ancient Peoples share a history of making bark cloth, which their ancestors wore as an everyday garment and used for rituals and magical purposes. Bark cloth was eventually replaced by woven textiles in most areas. But a few tribes still make the older cloth, and these contemporary examples are probably very much like those worn by all Ancient Peoples before the development of weaving.

In a few very poor and isolated areas of East Nusatenggara men still wear simple, undecorated bark headcloths and loincloths although among the tribal people on these islands, using bark cloth is often looked down on as a sign of backwardness and poverty. While traveling in West Sumba, we saw a man planting corn with a pointed sick; he was dressed only in a bark loincloth. At another time while walking in the mountainous Lio district of southeastern Flores, our path crossed that of a man clad only in bark cloth and carrying a bow and arrow. When asked, he said that he was off to hunt paddy rats.

There are, however, still several tribes that actively make bark cloth and use it as part of their traditional costume. The Murut tribe of Borneo is one; they make vests and other garments of bark fabric. Several groups of people in Sulawesi, such as the people of the Palu district near Donggala in central Sulawesi and some of the more isolated Torajans, also have a tradition of making bark cloth.

The people of the Palu district are closely related to the Torajans and inhabit an overlapping region. The women of Palu make an unusual three-tiered skirt out of bark fabric. They also fashion a type of cape from undecorated bark cloth that is probably used as protection against the rain and sun. In addition to these unusual skirts and capes, they produce decorated women's blouses and brightly colored headcloths painted with geometric symbols.

The Torajan people brought the craft of making bark cloth to its highest technical and artistic level in Indonesia. It was their most important art form, and they made headcloths for men, headdresses for women, and poncholike garments that were brush-painted or stamped

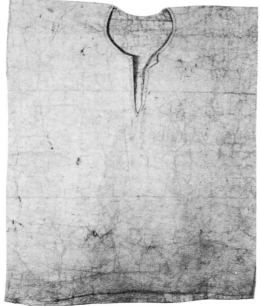

Fig. 2. Bark cloth shirt and trousers of a type formerly worn by the Torajans. Light brown; undyed. From central Sulawesi. Authors' collection.

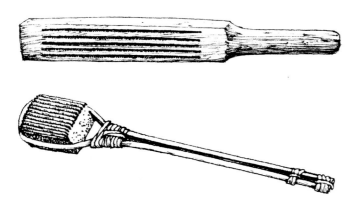

Fig. 3. The Torajans use stone and wooden beaters to make bark cloth. Central Sulawesi.

with decorations in four colors—natural pigments of red, yellow, purple, and green. Torajans today continue to make simple bark clothing (see fig. 2), but they no longer decorate the cloth. Some scholars believe the Torajans may have played an important role in the initial development of bark cloth in the entire Pacific region, including Polynesia, for the techniques used in central Sulawesi are very similar to those now used to produce the Polynesian bark fabric known as *tapa*, and there is some evidence that the craft began in Sulawesi and then spread to Polynesia. The trees, natural dyes, tools, and types of cloth, and often the names for these materials, are also similar in both places.

The Torajans make their bark cloth by boiling or fermenting the inner bark of pandanus, mulberry, or other local trees. The resulting pulp is then pounded into cloth with a stone beater on a wooden anvil (see fig. 3). Torajan bark cloth made in this manner is very soft and supple and suitable for clothing.

Warp Ikat

The gradual transition from making bark cloth to weaving with cotton took place at some indeterminate time in the past. At first, there may have been some experimentation with weaving plant fibers such as pineapple, agave, and *agel* (a fiber taken from a Malayan fan palm, *Corypha gebanga*)—all of these fibers are still woven into cloth in various regions. On the island of Mindanao in the southern Philippines, tribes like the T'Boli and Manobo, which share many characteristics with Indonesia's Ancient Peoples, weave warp-ikat-decorated cloth from abaca fiber. The T'Boli, especially, are noted for fine cloths that bear intricate ikat designs; these cloths are cut and sewn into clothing in the style of the bark cloth suit in figure 2.

When the Ancient Peoples first began to make cotton thread they probably used it only for part of the fabric, either the warp or weft. The people of the Sangihe Islands that lie to the north of Sulawesi produced an undecorated cloth with a fibrous warp and a cotton weft until recent times.* But cotton is also indigenous to the islands of Indonesia, and because of its superior properties eventually became the stan-

* Frits A. Wagner, *Indonesia: The Art of An Island Group* (New York: Crown Publishers, 1959), p. 48.

dard material for weaving among the Ancient Peoples.

The basic cloths made by the Ancient Peoples probably have changed little since the advent of weaving. They are the *selimut* (approximately 2.0 by 1.5 meters), a large rectangular cloth that can be worn around the waist or over the shoulders in a variety of styles, and the *sarong*, a piece of cloth sewn into a tube that is normally worn as a skirt by women. These garments could hardly be improved upon for their simplicity and utility. Smaller rectangles of cloth (approximately 1 meter by 50 centimeters) may be worn over one shoulder *(selindang)* or as a headcloth *(ikat kepala)*. These weavings, worn in differing fashions, make up the traditional dress of both the Ancient Peoples today as well as most other Indonesians. But like the decorated bark cloth they replaced, these cotton textiles serve as more than just ordinary clothing. They occupy a special place in the traditions of each group of Ancient Peoples and have assumed the important roles once played by bark cloth in rituals and ceremonies.

The single most important method of cloth decoration employed by the Ancient Peoples is warp ikat. As we have noted, warp ikat is believed to have been introduced to the Indonesian archipelago by the Dong-Son and Late Chou peoples, and in Indonesia the technique is found almost exclusively among Ancient Peoples.* Among these people all other means of textile decoration are secondary. The word *ikat* means "to tie" in the Malay language; warp ikat technique basically involves securely binding or tying areas of the warp (that is, lengthwise) threads before they are dyed and put on the loom for weaving. The bound areas appear on the finished cloth as a decorative, dye-resist pattern.

Almost all of the Ancient Peoples still make cloth patterned by warp ikat but the weavers of East Nusatenggara in particular use this technique to make some of the finest textiles found anywhere in the world. On the East Nusatenggara islands of Sumba, Savu, Flores, Rote, Timor, Alor, and Lomblen, weaving and other traditions are still handed down from one generation to the next and the old techniques are still very much alive. Carving, painting, and other art forms are not as common on these islands, so

* The Acehnese of northern Sumatra, though not classed as Ancient Peoples, use the warp ikat technique on silk.

weavings have become the main form of artistic expression. And since most of the themes and symbols that are important to each group of people appear in the motifs of the textiles, the cloths provide insight into particular cultures. In East Nusatenggara, textiles still retain a great deal of their ritual value, and here more than in any other area of Indonesia the homemade weavings continue to be the everyday dress for most of the people.

Other Ancient Peoples do produce fine ikat cloths, especially the Dyaks of Borneo and the Rongkong and Galumpang Torajans of central Sulawesi, but unfortunately, among some tribes, the textiles are losing their ceremonial role. Or, in many cases, the textiles have fallen out of daily use to be taken out only on festival days. Therefore, to see traditional weavings worn as everyday garments, in some areas it has become necessary to journey far from the towns.

Despite the geographic distances that separate the Ancient Peoples, we observed the same basic techniques and materials used for traditional weavings among the Torajans of central Sulawesi, the Bataks of North Sumatra, and the weavers of East Nusatenggara. In these areas we found that homemade tools differ only slightly, and that the backstrap loom used for weaving is fundamentally the same. The techniques of spinning thread, warping the threads, and arranging them for binding, and the processes of binding, dyeing, and weaving also show only slight variations from region to region.

Most weavers still gather the materials they need from their immediate surroundings, and one woman, working at home sometimes with the help of her family, completes an entire weaving herself beginning with the spinning of the thread. The following description of how warp ikat cloths are made is based on the most common methods that we saw among those Ancient Peoples weaving today.

Preparing the Thread

Machine-made cotton thread is now easily obtained almost everywhere in Indonesia. But especially in East Nusatenggara there are weavers who still, out of economic necessity or compliance with tradition, continue to spin their own thread from homegrown cotton. Sometimes, homespun thread is saved for special weavings that will be used for ceremonial occasions such

Fig. 4. As the first step in making thread, seeds are worked out of the raw cotton using a rounded stick on a piece of tortoise shell. Kolorai, Savu.

Fig. 5. A small hand-operated gin makes the task of cleaning raw cotton less tedious. Seba, Savu.

as a burial or a ritual gift, while manufactured thread is used to make weavings for everyday clothing or for eventual sale.

A weaver needs only a few simple tools to make her own thread from homegrown cotton, but the time and effort involved are considerable. A Savunese woman showed us how to clean raw cotton using just a flat square of tortoise shell and a smooth rounded stick; by rolling the stick over the fiber like a rolling pin over dough, she laboriously worked out the seeds, one by one (see fig. 4). This simple method works well but is slow and painstaking; most women prefer to use a small rough-hewn cotton gin built by a husband or the village carpenter to make this unpleasant chore easier (see fig. 5). The cleaned cotton is aired in the sun and then carded; that is, the weaver repeatedly pulls the fibers apart with her fingers alone or while holding a flat stick in one hand. In order to make the cotton as fluffy as possible before spinning, she uses a simple but effective tool—a bow with a bowstring of rattan. When the bowstring is plucked in a handful of cotton fiber, the cotton becomes downy and airy, and the weavers say that it can then be spun into a fine, even thread (see fig. 6).

Spinning smooth thread on a spindle always looks deceptively easy when demonstrated by an accomplished craftswoman. Resting a spindle with a clay or wooden whorl on a piece of broken pottery (sometimes a shard of a Ming bowl) or on a seashell, she twirls the spindle with one hand while with her other she draws the cotton fiber into a smooth thread (see fig. 7). If a woman is very skillful at spinning, her handspun thread may be as smooth as a manufactured one. In the space of a few minutes the spindle is filled with new thread, but it takes many times this amount before there is enough for a sarong or a selimut. A homemade spinning wheel (see fig. 8) is occasionally seen in some areas, but most women who make homespun thread continue to use the simple spindle, and they still teach their daughters to use this tool. Most girls are proficient at spinning thread by the time they are eleven or twelve since it is one of the first steps in their apprenticeship as warp ikat weavers.

Since the thread will be handled many times in the course of making a weaving, most weavers prefer to work with two-ply thread because of its greater strength. Thus, both homespun and purchased thread must be

Fig. 6. Fluffing the cotton fiber with a bow makes it easier to spin. Seba, Savu.

Fig. 7. Most weavers use a simple spindle to spin the cotton. Rendeh, East Sumba.

Fig. 8. Cotton thread is sometimes spun on a homemade wheel. Sikka, Flores.

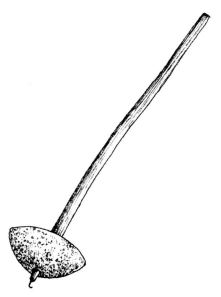

Fig. 9. The cotton is twisted together with a spinner to make durable two-ply thread. Sumba.

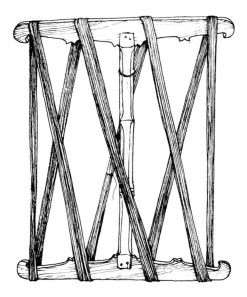

Fig. 10. Weavers use a tool called a niddy noddy to measure threads for the warp. Savu.

doubled by twisting two strands together, and this chore is usually passed on to the weaver's children. Both boys and girls are often seen walking along country lanes, plying threads with a hanging spinning tool that looks much like a spindle with a hook on the bottom (see fig. 9).

As the first step in the complex planning that goes into preparing the threads, the weaver must measure out enough yarn for the warp of the intended weaving. To do this, she wraps the thread (often directly from the spindle) around a tool called a niddy noddy, a bar with a perpendicular crosspiece at each end (see fig. 10). The number of times the thread goes around the niddy noddy is determined by the size of the weaving. The thread is removed from the niddy noddy in the form of a skein, and these skeins are then dipped in a starch made from water and either cassava, corn, or rice, which will make the yarn easier to handle. Later, the weft or crosswise threads will be measured and prepared in the same way.

Warping

For any weaving, the weaver must measure, count, and lay out the lengthwise threads for the loom. This is called warping. The first step in warping for warp ikat is to transform the skeins into balls, a task at which the entire family lends a hand. Some kind of tool is needed to hold the skein while the thread is being wound. The Bataks of North Sumatra simply use two bamboo poles, each elevated on one end by

a stand; these poles hold the skeins in the same way as two outstretched hands. Generally though, weavers place the skein on a standing or hanging tool such as those seen in figures 11 and 12. The circular frame revolves and releases the thread as the weaver or her helpers wind it into a ball by hand.

All warp ikat textiles are woven with a continuous circular warp: that is, the warp threads take the form of a circle around the poles of the loom. As the weaver works, she shifts the newly woven fabric to the bottom of the circle, simultaneously pulling unwoven threads to the top for weaving. In this way, the warp threads make one complete circuit around the loom as the weaving progresses (see fig. 88, chapter 4). In Sumba, the circular warp is laid out on a large rectangular frame with two adjustable parallel slats set for one-half the length of the finished cloth (see fig. 13). A little extra length is figured in to account for the fringe, the unwoven areas, and the length that will be taken up during weaving.

Warping is a job for two women, who usually set up the frame outdoors on a mat (see fig. 14). After placing two balls of thread in coconut halfshells so that they will unravel easily, the women form the circle of the warp by repeatedly passing the shells over the top of the warping frame, around one of the adjustable slats, back across the bottom of the frame, and up again around the other slat.

As the women lay out the warp, they mark off odd- and even-numbered threads by means of

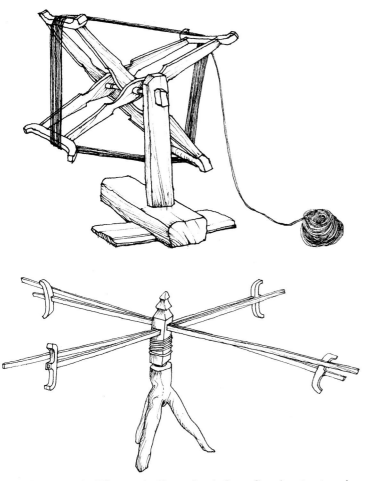

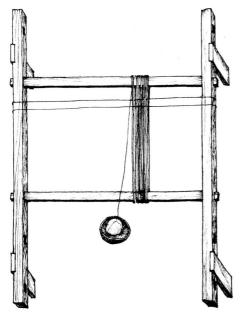

Figs. 11, 12. These winding wheels from Sumba *(top)* and Savu *(bottom)* hold the measured skein while its threads are wound into a ball.

Fig. 13. A warping frame from Sumba. The threads circle the adjustable slats, which are set for a little more than half the length of the finished weaving. Black cross-strings divide the warp threads into odd- and even-numbered sets.

Fig. 14. While laying out the warp, the weavers count and mark the threads that will be bound to resist the dye. Waingapu, East Sumba.

two black strings that are tied onto the frame perpendicular to the direction of the warp threads and about five centimeters apart.

These black cross-strings act as lease cords and are very important, for they will stay with the warp threads through the binding and dyeing to preserve their division into odd and even sets. When the patterned threads are finally woven on the loom, every other thread—for example, every thread that rests on top of the first cross-string—will be lifted so that a crosswise weft thread can pass through the slot that has opened up between the two sets of warp threads. Then the second set of warp threads will be lifted for the return pass of the weft. By repeating these steps, the over-under interlocking of warp and weft alternates on each line to create a plain-weave fabric.

Since the threads on the "bottom" of the circular warp will eventually become the "top" threads as the warp shifts around the loom during weaving, this counting off of odd and even threads during warping needs to be done only on the top of the circle of threads on the warping frame. As a warp yarn passes over the frame, it goes over the first cross-string, under the second, and completely around the bottom of the frame. On its next pass over the frame, the thread goes under the first cross-string and over the second. All of the following passes of the warp threads repeat this over-under alternation.

Warping serves an additional purpose for warp ikat textiles, because at this stage the weavers organize the lengthwise threads for the ikat binding process that will give the fabric its dye-resist pattern. The size, intricacy, layout, and degree of symmetry of the desired pattern all have a bearing on how the warping is done. And since the preferred patterns and layouts differ among the various groups of Ancient Peoples, warping is one stage of the warp ikat process with local variations.

Some warp ikat cloths, such as those from Sumba, have an ikat pattern across their entire warp (see plate 1), while others, such as those from Savu, are decorated with lengthwise bands of ikat-decorated threads alternating with plain-colored bands (see plates 7 and 8). On these Savu cloths, the ikat-decorated bands and the plain-colored ones are warped separately and combined at a later stage.

As the two women are warping the threads on the frame, one of them will also count and mark the number of threads that will make up the "ikat sections." Each ikat section consists of a group of warp threads, areas of which will be bound together as a unit to resist the dye. The bound area produces only an element within the total motif because the threads in a single ikat section account for only a narrow lengthwise portion of the fabric. The width of this portion will vary with the number of threads the ikat section contains, the tightness of the weave (how many threads per centimeter), and the overall complexity of the pattern, but it is usually less than one centimeter. Obviously, then, many different ikat sections will be needed to create a complete pattern, the actual number depending again on the intricacy of the motif as well as the width of the finished cloth. When the warping is finished, the weaver twists a piece of fiber around each ikat section so that it is clearly marked and separated from the others and will be easy to identify for the ikat work. Then she binds all the warp threads securely across their width to prevent tangling and make them easy to handle.

The width of a single piece of warp ikat cloth is determined by the width that a weaver can easily handle on her backstrap loom, usually a little more than the length of her forearm from elbow to fingertips. The length of the cloth is not as crucial, although a very long piece will be too heavy to work with on the loom. Larger textiles must be woven in separate pieces called panels, and these panels are sewn together to finish the weaving. For example, Sumbanese *hinggi* (the Sumbanese word for a selimut) are always two panels wide, as are the large selimut of Borneo and Sulawesi. Other weavings, such as the sarong of Flores and Savu, may be made of one large panel that is cut in several pieces and sewn together. Smaller headcloths and shawls are just a single panel.

Ikat weavings are decorated with patterns that repeat; one side of the weaving is usually a mirror image of the other, and the top is commonly a reflection of the bottom. This design makes it easy for a weaver to reduce the amount of repetitive work and ensure symmetry by doubling or quadrupling the number of threads that will be bound at one time in each ikat section. Keeping everything in order and proportion requires thorough planning and forethought on the part of the weaver, yet she usually achieves her goal without the help of a written diagram or any sort of sketch.

In most cases, each panel of a large weaving is warped separately; the alternate threads are marked with cross-strings, the different ikat sections are delineated with fiber, and the threads are secured at the top with cord. Then one entire panel's worth of thread is laid over another and their respective ikat sections, marked during warping, are matched up, combined, and treated as one unit for binding. Each combined ikat section now contains double the number of threads needed to create a particular portion of the motif. In this manner, the weaver can bind in the pattern once, and later when she separates the panels and weaves them, she has two identical pieces of cloth.

Mirror images on a single panel are produced by combining the top and bottom threads of the circular warp when they are on the ikat frame. The threads in each ikat section have been marked during warping and only need to be matched up on the top and bottom and bound together as a unit to produce perfect reverse images on the woven cloth.

Sumbanese weavers, for example, customarily make two identical animal-patterned hinggi at one time; each weaving consists of two panels that have been sewn together. Enough thread for each of these four panels is warped separately and is then combined, one circular panel on top of the other as described above. If a Sumbanese weaver has bound a horse motif across a certain number of ikat sections, when it is time to weave the cloth she undoes the bindings that hold the four circular panels together and separates the panels. Each panel is identical since the pattern was bound on all four simultaneously. Each circular panel is woven separately and then cut and opened up lengthwise. An identical horse thus appears at the top and bottom of each panel, for a total of eight times on the four panels. In actual practice, before she binds the threads, the weaver may combine them widthwise as well so that each vertical half-panel contains a repeated pattern. In this way, the horse pattern will, in the end, appear not eight but sixteen times on the four panels.

Ikat weavings like the sarong and selimut of Savu (see plates 6, 7, and 8) that alternate ikat-decorated bands with plain-colored bands are more complex in the warping. For this type of weaving, all of the ikat-decorated bands that will have the same pattern are warped separately; each one is divided into ikat sections and secured with cord. Then the bands are combined, one on top of the other, in the same way as the panels for a Sumbanese cloth. The ikat sections of the bands are matched up and bound as one; later, after dyeing, the bindings are removed and the threads are separated into the individual bands. These bands are not "ready to weave" as a simple Sumbanese panel is, for they must first be arranged in the order they will appear on the woven cloth; this step will be discussed in more detail later in this chapter.

Binding

After the threads have been warped, divided into ikat sections, and combined, they are ready to be bound. Weavers in Savu believe that interrupting the work at any point from now on brings bad luck. Our desire to obtain a sample of bound threads caused a commotion that we could not at first understand; then the weaver and her family explained that they would have to sacrifice a chicken to dissipate any harmful effects of stopping the work before it reached its natural conclusion. Once the offering was

completed, there was no problem removing the threads from the frame.

The ikat frame that is used to hold the threads while they are being wrapped with fiber varies according to the size and type of weaving. In Sumba, the frame is quite large since it holds warp threads that are a little longer than one-half the length of the large finished weaving. In Savu and Rote, the frames are smaller, not only because the finished weavings are not as large, but because often only a single band is bound at one time. In addition, for binding, Savu and Rote weavers may double the threads in a band by folding it to one-quarter the length of the finished weaving. In this way, the same pattern bound on the ikat sections of a particular band will appear four times when that band is opened up to its full length. The frame used to hold these small bands need not be too large (see fig. 15).

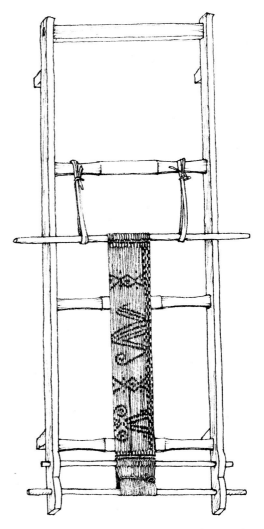

Fig. 15. In Savu, ikat-patterned bands are bound individually on a frame.

Fig. 16. In East Sumba, the threads are bound with a natural fiber such as palm-leaf thread. Waingapu, East Sumba.

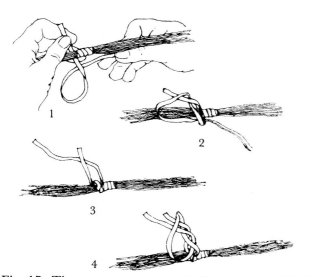

Fig. 17. The weaver wraps each ikat section with fiber and then secures the binding with a tight double knot.

Fig. 18. Detail of bound threads.

To create a dye-resist pattern, the weaver tightly wraps fiber around small lengths of each ikat section (see fig. 16). This binding will enable these areas to resist the dye, thus forming the separate elements of a pattern in negative. Sometimes these patterns are recorded on paper or on leaves of the *lontar* palm *(Borrassus flabelliformis)*, but more often than not the weaver knows by heart which areas of each ikat section need to be bound. She rarely needs to consult a drawing when she begins to work, nor does she sketch the design onto the threads. Occasionally, a weaver may draw a few rough guidelines on the threads, but usually she measures the distances and checks the straightness of the pattern with a piece of her binding fiber.

With amazing speed, the weaver deftly wraps the fiber around each part of the ikat section that needs to be protected from the dye and ties a double knot, pulling it tight to secure the binding (see fig. 17). The completed knot stands up from the threads so that when the time comes to open the bindings after dyeing it can easily be cut off (see fig. 18).

A variety of materials can be used as binding fiber; the fiber need not be completely waterproof, for it is the tightness of the binding that blocks out the dye, and not any characteristic of

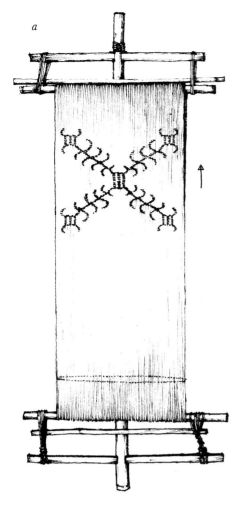

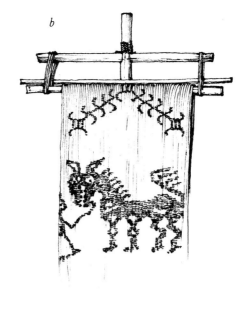

Fig. 19. (*a*) In Sumba, a center design is first bound on the top of the circular panel of warp. (*b*) These bound threads are then shifted over the top of the frame, and the top and bottom of the circle of warp are bound together with a different pattern, such as a horse. The horse thus appears twice on the finished panel, while the center design appears once to prevent a gap in the middle of the cloth. The unbound area at the bottom of the panel is cut and becomes the fringe of the finished fabric.

the material as such. The most commonly used material, at least in East Nusatenggara, is *agel,* a fiber taken from the leaves of the *gebang* palm. However, mountain grasses, cotton threads, or coconut-leaf fibers are also satisfactory, and if they can obtain it, weavers are happy with colored plastic string.

Among most Ancient Peoples, weavers bind together the top and bottom of the circle of warp threads between the bars of the ikat frame, leaving an area of thread secured around the bars (see fig. 15). This area around the bars cannot be bound and patterned, and on these weavings a break appears in the continuity of the patterns (see plate 17). This gap is often emphasized and set off with an ikat-decorated spearhead pattern.

On the weavings from Sumba, however, as we have noted, the entire surface of the cloth is covered with ikat decoration. The weaver accomplishes this by first binding in the entire center motif on the top threads alone while the warp is still in a loose circle on the ikat frame. When she has finished the central motif, she

shifts it over one of the bars and then binds the top and bottom threads together in the usual manner for the remainder of the pattern (see fig. 19).

Dyeing

Throughout Indonesia most warp ikat weavings are dyed two colors, first blue and then red; other colors such as yellow and green appear only as accent. Occasionally a monochrome scheme is found, often on a weaving that is to be worn for working in the fields and other everyday activities, but most traditional weavings combine the two basic colors. Where the blue and red dyes combine on the cotton, a third color, ideally a shade of black, should result; but in reality the color blend usually ranges from rust to purplish brown to black. Because the combination of red and blue dyes produces this third color, the weaver must first bind the parts of the motif that she desires white or red so that these areas can be protected from the blue color of the first dyebath. After the weaver has dyed the threads blue, she then puts them back on the ikat frame, removes the fiber-resist bindings from the areas to be colored red, and, conversely, binds the parts of the pattern that will remain blue. Only then is she ready to dip the threads into the red dyebath. Some weavers will use one type of fiber, *agel* for example, to ikat the white areas and another material, such as waxed string, to tie off the red parts of the motif so that they can easily distinguish which knots need to be opened between dyeings. However, most weavers are so thoroughly familiar with their motifs and color schemes that they bind with a single type of fiber throughout the ikat process; when they put the dyed threads back on the ikat frame, they can rearrange the bindings by eye.

To achieve light and dark shades of a single color, a detail which gives East Sumbanese textiles a depth and variety of shade that is an essential part of their appeal, the weaver alters the bindings part way through a single dyebath. After the blue dyeing is partially completed, for example, the weaver may return the threads to the ikat frame and remove some of the bindings. At the end of the dyeing these newly opened areas will have taken on a lighter shade of blue than those areas of the threads that have been through every dyebath.

Preparing the natural blue and red dyes is time-consuming work, and achieving good results demands a lot of skill. Weavers in Indonesia take great pride in their dyeing mainly because exceptional color is one of the most important criteria by which local people can judge weavings. In many instances the clarity of the ikat work and the tightness of the weaving are of secondary importance to local judges. Villages or areas that have a local reputation for fine weavings invariably make weavings with a strong rich color, but the other qualities of the fabrics are not always exceptional. Cheap and easy-to-use chemical dyes are available to village weavers nowadays, and though they are sometimes used for cloth that is made to be sold, most weavers refuse to use them for weavings they will keep in their family. Thus, because of the value many weavers place on naturally colored fabrics, the dyeing process is in many cases secret, surrounded by taboos and superstitions.

The color most admired and the shades considered ideal are entirely a matter of local preference. Often, human nature being what it is, the rarer the dyestuff and the more difficult the dye is to make, the greater the value placed on that particular color. In lush, green Flores, fields of indigo plants flourish, but the blue dye obtained from indigo is used only as a secondary color; deep shades of red, which can take years to achieve due primarily to the scarcity of the dyestuff, are the favorite colors among people on the central and eastern parts of the island. Nearby on the small dry island of Savu, weavers are judged on the depth of black color they obtain although the main component of the dye, indigo, is usually in short supply.

Indigo Blue

Indigo is one of the most widely used natural dyes in the world. It was known four thousand years ago and was used by the early Egyptians, Greeks, and Romans. It is a vat dye, which means that there are two steps necessary to the dyeing process; first, the dye compound must be made soluble in water, and second, in order to produce the color, oxidation must take place when the dye is on the fabric. The indigo plant *(Indigofera tinctoria)* yields a dye substance called indigo blue, which is insoluble in water. Natural vat dyes such as indigo need to be reduced by fermentation to produce the soluble dye, which in the case of indigo is a compound known as indigo white. The threads pick up the indigo white during the dyebath; when the threads are hung up and exposed to air, the indigo white turns back into indigo blue and colors the fiber.

All over Indonesia, the blue dye for warp ikat cloths is made with the same basic ingredients: indigo plants, lime, and lye made of wood ashes leached in water. The lime and the lye are alkalis that aid in the solubility of the dye compound. The steps in combining these three ingredients vary, and other plants and additives are introduced to the basic mixture by individual dyers. Even when the same ingredients and methods are used, the results may vary from one dyer to the next, and the same woman may have trouble achieving exactly the same results each time she dyes a bundle of threads. The organic ingredients often differ in strength, and the dyer, rather like an experienced cook, uses a certain amount of instinctive judgment in preparing the dye, adding a dash of this and a handful of that after glancing at the color in the pot.

Many dyers are reluctant to reveal their personal dyeing methods in their entirety since the procedure may include not only the actual ingredients but certain rituals they follow to ensure success. In Sumba today, the enclosure where the threads are dyed blue is forbidden to all men. In many areas, menstruating women may not dye cloth or approach the dyeing compound because their "impure" state might disrupt the process. Dyers in Rote once believed that evil spirits attracted to the dye would dip their hands into the solution and ruin its color. To protect the dye, Rote dyers hung a magical symbol over the dyeing area; now that most Rotenese are practicing Christians they believe the sign of the cross protects the dye. As far as the dyer is concerned, the magical steps taken with the dyeing and other processes of making a warp ikat can be as important as the practical mixing of the basic ingredients.

The women of Savu are admired even by other East Nusatenggara weavers for the excellent indigo color of their cloths. Savu was therefore a good place to study the traditional methods of indigo dyeing. The widow of the last king to rule Savu, Ibu C. C. Rame Haoe* is an authoritative lady when it comes to questions about Savunese weavings. An ample figure and a quick sense of humor do not hide her forceful personality; she was, after all, once a queen, and although the system of royal rule has been phased out since independence in 1949, she is still highly respected throughout the island. Often when most people have forgotten the legends and local history, the members of the upper classes still remember the old lore. They also retain the best weaving techniques because women of the royal family made weavings and were expected to produce the best. Once, Ibu Haoe related, only the upper classes of Savu knew the complicated formulas for making good-quality dyes. However, they began to hire outside women to help them with the work of weaving, gathering the raw materials, and performing other tasks. Inevitably, these helpers learned their secrets and were able to copy the dyeing methods followed by the noblewomen. Over the years, the knowledge has spread all over the island and now many Savunese women of all social classes are skilled dyers.

* *Ibu* is a word meaning "Mother" in Indonesia and is used as a term of respect in addressing all older women. Elsewhere in this book, the word *Pak*, which means "Father," appears for older men.

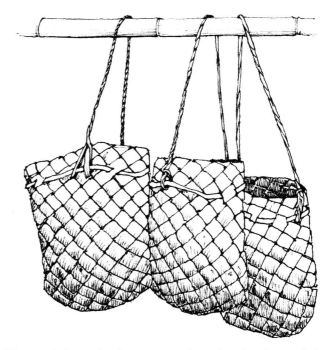

Fig. 20. Woven baskets are used on Sumba for straining an indigo solution to produce a ready-to-use blue dye.

Ibu Haoe still makes warp ikat cloths herself following the traditional Savunese methods and her variation of indigo dyeing is described here. Behind Ibu's house there is a small field of indigo plants, a luxury in dry Savu, and grouped beneath her back porch are large clay pots like those used by other weavers on the island. When it is time to make the dye, Ibu Haoe's daughters gather as many indigo leaves as possible, usually a small armful, and Ibu soaks them overnight in water. As she removes the partially fermented leaves the next day, she works a small handful of lime into each bunch, and while dipping them in and out of the water, she wrings out the maximum amount of color. After stirring the water until the "rotten smell" disappears and leaving the liquid to settle for a short time, she pours off the top water until only the concentrated liquid on the bottom remains.

Ibu Haoe makes a batch of dye when she has collected enough indigo leaves, but even though she has her own patch of indigo, she must save the batches and combine them until there is a sufficient amount for a dyebath. Indigo is also scarce on the island of Sumba. There, the dye is made by soaking indigo leaves in water, removing them, and adding lime to the indigo water; this mixture is then strained through a tightly woven basket (see fig. 20). A blue foam of indigo remains in the basket and is left to dry for several days; it can be used as a kind of "instant indigo" after the weaver mixes it with lye made from wood ashes and water. As on Savu, several lots of dye must be combined before there is enough to produce good color.

When a large clay pot of indigo water is ready, Ibu Haoe adds several heaping coconut halfshells of ashes directly to the dyepot. These ashes are made from the husk of the fruit of the *kalumpang* tree (*Sterculia foetida* L.), but not all dyers are particular about the type of ashes they add; some use common kitchen ashes. Other dyers insist on using ashes from the wood or bark of a particular tree. In Sumba, for example, ashes made from the bark of *Cartamus tinctoria* trees are preferred. Wood ashes of any kind when leached in water yield lye, which is needed to help the indigo blue dissolve in water. Most dyers mix ashes and plain water, let the ashes settle to the bottom, and pour off the top water to use in the dye, but in Savu the ashes are mixed directly into the indigo water.

Once the basic dye mixture of indigo leaves, ashes, and lime is prepared, each woman has special substances such as palm sugar or local plants that she adds to the dyepot in hopes of producing a superior shade. Ibu Haoe mixes in a powder containing betel nut (*areca* nut), *sirih* (a fruit chewed with betel nut), turmeric root, and *loba* bark (from a type of symplocos tree often used in natural dyes in Indonesia). The exact chemical function in the dye of these extra ingredients is difficult to ascertain, but some, for example sugar, aid in the fermentation process. Other additions may play a magical role rather than a practical one. For example, betel nut, chewed with *sirih,* is a very important part of Savunese life; it is often used as an offering to holy rocks and to the dead. Its juice is red and this may have some desired effect on the color of the dye. Or betel nut may just be symbolic, at one time added to invoke the aid of good or friendly spirits. For whatever reasons, Ibu Haoe adds her powder and leaves the dye to rest. She also adds a local root that she says keeps the dye free from insects and worms as it ferments.

After several days of fermentation, Ibu begins checking the color of the dye on her fingers. When the dye is ready, it stains the skin dark blue; so hard is the dye to remove that women with blue hands are seen long past the dyeing season has ended (see plate 4). At this stage, some fine adjustments to the dye can still be made. If Ibu feels that the dye is not staining her fingers properly, she adds more ashes to make the liquid more alkaline. If the dye has a greenish cast, she adds more of her powder of betel nut, *loba, sirih,* and turmeric. Volcanic sulfur and *gambir* leaves (*Uncaria gambir* Roxb., also chewed with betel nut) are among some of the other substances that can be added to help the dye develop properly.

When the dye meets Ibu Haoe's strict standards, she wets the bound warp threads with plain water so that they will absorb the dye evenly and immerses the bundle in the indigo solution overnight. All the next day the threads are hung up and aired so that the dye can oxidize. After three days of repeated overnight soakings and daytime airings, the threads are rinsed and hung in a windy place for several days. Ibu Haoe repeats this cycle of soaking and airing in the same dye until the color is satisfactorily dark; this takes at least a month and often longer in Savu. If the final color has not taken well or if it runs, the threads of the finished cloth can be washed in the sea to help fix the color (in Rote the fabric may be buried in salty sea sand).

Fig. 21. Bound threads are dyed blue by immersing them in an indigo solution. Nggela, Flores.

The length of time needed to complete the dyeing does not bother the weavers for they know that the traditional methods cannot be hurried. The indigo dyeing process takes only a very quick three days in Flores (see fig. 21) where the supply of indigo is abundant, but usually it takes a month or more on other islands. When the Bataks of North Sumatra follow their traditional methods, the blue dyeing can take more than one year.

After the threads reach a satisfactory shade of blue, the bound threads are returned to the ikat frame so that the bindings can be altered. Bindings on those ikat sections that are desired red must now be cut away so that the red of the next dyebath can penetrate them. At the same time, those sections of the threads that will appear blue on the finished weaving must be wrapped with fiber to protect them from the red dye and preserve their color. Anywhere the red dye covers the blue will be a third color, which, as mentioned above, ideally is black; actually it will range from purplish brown to rust to black depending on the strength and number of blue and red dyeings.

Mengkudu Red

The red dyeing is somewhat more complicated than the indigo dyeing because it requires that the threads be pretreated. Weavers stress that the thread will not absorb the red dye unless it has first been soaked in some kind of oil. This oily mixture is usually made by crushing either *kemiri* nuts (from the candlenut tree) or *kalumpang* fruit and combining the pulp with lye water made from wood ashes. The alkaline lye water helps to eliminate excess oil. The particular type of oil used in the pretreatment does not seem to be crucial; the Bataks like to treat their threads with a mixture based on animal fat, while the southern Balinese at one time used coconut oil. However, *kemiri* or *kalumpang* oil is the most commonly used.

Varying the secondary ingredients added to the pretreatment oil mixture will later produce different shades of red when the cotton is dyed. A variety of local barks, as well as leaves and other organic materials, are common additions. It is quite likely that some of these barks, most of which we could not identify, contain some form of tannic acid, a substance which is commonly used as a mordant, a chemical agent that fixes the dye and makes it insoluble on the fabric.

Weavers in each area of Indonesia may follow different methods of mixing the oil bath, but the importance of the presoaking cannot be overstressed and most dyers take as much care with this step as they do with the actual dyebath. In Amarasi, West Timor, for example, the composition of the presoaking oil is considered to be the key to obtaining the strikingly deep reddish maroon color prized there (see plate 15). West Timor weavers claim, too, that they can produce specific color variations when the threads are dyed by varying the proportions of the secondary materials they add to the oil. They may add the leaves of two different types of pomegranate trees, hibiscus bark and leaves, leaves from a tree they call *pacar* (probably henna), and several other types of local bark to the *kemiri* nut oil.

When the the oil bath is prepared the threads are soaked and squeezed in it repeatedly and then aired in the sun for a period of time ranging from just a few days up to three months.

The red dyeing that follows the pretreatment of the threads is often the most time-consuming step in making an ikat weaving, taking from a matter of months in some places to as long as ten years in Flores and Bali. This red dyeing process is, like that of indigo, also a closely guarded secret in many areas. In Sumba, walls were once built around the red-dyeing compound to shield the work from onlookers.

Today, many women may still prefer to keep their special tricks to themselves, but the primary ingredients of the dye are widely known: the red dye is made from the root of the *Morinda citrofolia* tree (or *mengkudu* as it is called in Indonesia), from *loba* bark, and from lye of wood ashes. The *mengkudu* dye is a mordant dye; that is, it needs a substance (usually a metallic compound) to fix the pigment onto the fiber. In this case, the *mengkudu* root contains the red pigment and the *loba* bark contains one or more aluminum compounds that act as the mordant. The ashes, which give lye when leached in water, make the liquid alkaline and probably improve the solubility of the pigment as in the case of indigo.

The predominantly red animal-patterned weavings of Sumba are the best known of all Indonesian ikat cloths, and their vibrant red color is certainly part of their appeal. The

Sumbanese call them *hinggi kombu* (*kombu* being the Sumbanese name for the *mengkudu* root from which the dye is derived). That the cloths are named for the dyestuff used to make them is an indication of the importance placed on their color by Sumbanese (see plate 1).

Hinggi are an important trade item for East Sumbanese weavers these days as they are often sold to tourists and exported. But this activity is nothing new—hinggi were being sent abroad in the 1920s and possibly earlier. At that time, quite a few women in the vicinity of the small town of Waingapu, Sumba's main port, wove cloths to meet the demand. It was during this period that many hinggi weavers began using purchased cotton thread, but on the whole they continued to employ the natural dyes and followed the old methods of production. This foreign trade has had its ups and downs, periods when outside interest slackened and the weavers turned to creating weavings only for their families and for ceremonies. At other times, such as the present, many weavers have been able to support their families by the weavings they sell.

In recent years, this source of outside income for East Sumbanese weavers has been threatened by a few factories that have been set up in Java and Bali to mass-produce copies of Sumba hinggi—usually only the blue and white cloths called *hinggi kaworu*. These imitation hinggi are recognizable by their inferior colors and shoddy workmanship.

In East Sumba, weavers like Ibu Hina from Preliu village continue a tradition of fifty years by making hinggi for sale; this is an unusual situation among the Ancient Peoples. Especially among older women like Ibu Hina, pride in craftsmanship is still a strong motivation even though most of the weavings are sold to visitors. Ibu Hina is a strong matriarch whose grown daughters help her with some of the dyeing and weaving while her son helps to sell the finished cloth. Many of the weavers in East Sumba continue to use natural dyes of indigo blue and *mengkudu* red to dye their hinggi. Ibu Hina's sources of dyestuffs are found mostly near her house: a small patch of indigo plants, a tree whose bark provides ashes for lye, and a single *mengkudu* tree.

A common problem facing dyers, not only in Sumba but in many parts of Indonesia, is the scarcity of the *mengkudu* tree whose root is the source of the red dye. Each tree can only give

Fig. 22. The weaver crushes *mengkudu* root with a mortar and pestle as one of the first steps in making red dye. Rendeh, East Sumba.

up so much root at one cutting, so the dyestuff is usually collected over a period of time and saved until there is enough for dyeing. Large roots of the tree are stripped of their outer bark and crushed with a large mortar and pestle of the same kind used to hull rice (see fig. 22). Ibu Hina mixes the crushed *mengkudu* root with a little lye water and shapes the pulp into balls that fit easily into her hand. When dry, these balls can be stored and saved for dyeing.

When it is time to make the dye, Ibu Hina dips ten or twelve of these *mengkudu* balls, one at a time, into a pot of water and squeezes the color out of them (see fig. 23). A hand's length of dried *loba* bark and some *loba* leaves are crushed into powder and stirred into the dyepot. Some lye water is then poured into the dyepot, and the *mengkudu* dye is ready to be used.

Ibu Hina takes the threads which have been previously treated with oil and kneads them in the dye until they are thoroughly wet. She then leaves them in the liquid overnight. The next day, she airs them in the sun, which she says is an important part of the process. If Ibu Hina has enough of the *mengkudu* root she can produce the

Other Natural Dyes

Fig. 23. The color from balls of crushed *mengkudu* root is squeezed into a pot to make the red dye solution. Nggela, Flores.

bright red color favored in Sumba in just three dyeings, but each time she must make a fresh batch of dye; consequently, a large quantity of *mengkudu* root is necessary to dye a pair of *hinggi kombu*.

Weavers elsewhere in East Nusatenggara generally favor shades of red deeper than the brighter color popular in Sumba; weavings on islands like Flores vary from warm rust to maroon and usually require more than just three dyeings. Often the partially dyed threads must be stored away for many months between dippings and the entire dyeing process may go on for years.

The mixing of the red dye, which is comparatively simple in Sumba, takes on more complicated forms in these areas. In the Sikka district of eastern Flores, for example, two mixtures—one containing the *mengkudu* root, the mordant bark *(loba)*, and the lye water, and the other consisting of ground roasted tamarind seeds—are prepared separately. These two solutions are then stirred together just before the threads are put into the dyebath. This produces a pleasing shade of red (see plate 9).

Throughout Indonesia, *mengkudu* red and indigo blue are the principal dyes used to color warp ikat cloths, but various other natural dyes may be used to tint small amounts of thread that will be added to the warp as accent stripes. In a few cases, dyes may also be painted directly onto the woven cloth to accentuate a portion of the motif. Colors other than indigo blue and *mengkudu* red are not used as a dye for bound threads, nor do they comprise a large portion of any warp ikat weaving found in Indonesia. These dyes are generally not as colorfast as indigo or *mengkudu*, and they are not available in large quantities.

The most common of these secondary natural dyes is derived from turmeric root (*Curcuma domestica* Val.), a root commonly used as a cooking spice throughout Asia. Yellow turmeric is a direct dye; that is, it contains a pigment soluble in water that directly colors the cotton fibers. No mordant is required, nor is oxidation or fermentation necessary. The process of mixing a direct dye is very simple; fresh turmeric root is crushed and soaked in water until the yellow pigment has dissolved. Occasionally, a pinch of lime may be added to the liquid, probably to help improve the solubility of the pigment and thus obtain a darker shade of yellow. Threads for accent stripes can be dipped in the resulting yellow dye, or the dye can be daubed directly onto the woven cloth with a frayed stick. To help improve the color fastness of the dye, weavers sometimes rinse the threads in citrus or tamarind juice.

Most other natural dyes are found only in localized regions of Indonesia. We were shown other yellow dyes, most of which seemed to be direct dyes if the weavers' descriptions of their methods were accurate. In fact, for direct dyes, yellow is the most common color found in natural substances. A yellow wood (which might well be cudrania wood, the *soga tegeran* of batik dyeing discussed in chapter 5) gives a yellow dye that is used in the Sikka district of eastern Flores. The wood is shaved into boiling water, and after a little lime is added it is ready to use. In Sumba, the bark of a tree (unidentified) found in the highlands is the source of a yellow dye that is not used for dip-dyeing but is painted directly onto the woven cloth. Yet another yellow dye found in East Nusatenggara is obtained from the bark of the mango tree. These secondary dyes, found only in particular areas, show how the dyers use and experiment with the plants they find in their vicinity.

Another accent color, green, is most often produced by dipping turmeric-dyed yellow threads in a weak indigo blue solution, but there are several other interesting methods of producing green. The sarong of the Sikka district are often accented with narrow warp stripes of a beautiful shade of green, the color of new leaves. To produce this color the threads are soaked in a solution containing cotton plant leaves and another type of leaf (unidentified) which brings out the green color. In central Timor, weavers make a green dye from the leaves of a species of bean plant.

One more natural dye worth mentioning is found in Amarasi, West Timor. In this region, the usual method of dyeing over indigo blue with *mengkudu* red to produce black is not followed. Instead, Amarasi women boil the bark of the wild mango tree, which probably contains tannin, and the leaves of a local plant (unidentified). They soak the threads in this liquid overnight and then bury the threads in the mud of a nearby mountainous lake for a day; when the threads are removed from the mud, they are a deep black color. The mud probably contains an iron salt that acts as a mordant. This method of utilizing natural tannic acid and ferrous mud to produce black is a primitive form of mordant dyeing found widely throughout the world.

Weaving

When the dyeing of all the threads is completed, the weaver slices off the ikat knots with a sharp knife and removes all the binding fibers. At this point the pattern appears as confused patches of white and colored areas on the threads, but to the practiced eye of the weaver her design is clearly recognizable. Just before the binding process, panels or bands of threads were combined so that the weaver only needed to bind a repeating pattern onto the threads once. Now these groups of threads (which are still in the form of a circle) must be separated so that the warp threads can be arranged as they will appear on the loom and on the finished weaving. For example, Sumbanese hinggi are woven in pairs containing two panels each. The four panels were overlaid one on top of the other for the ikat process so that the pattern could be

bound onto all of them simultaneously. Now that the dyeing is completed, the threads must be separated back into the four individual panels; there is no risk of tangling or confusing threads here because the threads of each panel are still held together with the cord that was tied on before they were taken off the warping frame.

The panels of Sumbanese hinggi feature an unbroken ikat pattern, and once the panels are separated their warp threads are in the proper order for weaving. But if a weaving features bands bearing ikat motifs alternating with bands of solid colors like the weavings of Savu, the weaver is faced with the additional chore of putting the bands of thread into the order in which they will appear on the finished cloth (see plates 7 and 8).

Because the threads of each identical ikat-decorated band were bound together, the weaver must first separate the bands that were bound as a unit into the individual bands. One selimut may combine a large motif with a red and white pattern against a black background, an auxiliary band with a simple white ikat motif against a red background, and another secondary band with a white design against a blue background, plus various solid-colored stripes. The major motif band may repeat four to eight times across the width of a weaving with the other bands interspersed in between.

To put these different bands into their proper order, the weaver begins by draping the circles of warp threads loosely around a couple of bamboo poles that, when propped up against a porch or wall, serve as a makeshift frame. First, the major pattern bands are slipped over the bamboo poles and then the smaller auxiliary ikat-patterned bands; finally the solid-colored bands are fit into their correct order. On many weavings from Rote, Flores, and Savu, the exact arrangement of the bands is strictly decreed by tradition. Savunese weavers have names for each band all the way down to ikat-decorated stripes consisting of only a few threads.

After all the warp threads have been properly arranged in a loose circle around the bamboo poles, the weaver then lashes the threads between three or four split sticks (see figs. 24 and 25). This important step immobilizes the warp threads and prevents them from shifting and thus blurring the ikat pattern as the threads are woven into cloth. These sticks will remain bound into the

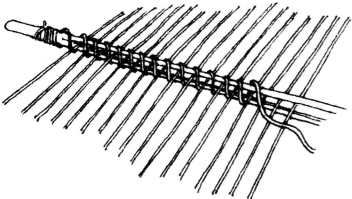

Figs. 24, 25. Weavers bind the dyed warp threads onto split sticks to keep them from shifting on the loom and blurring the pattern during weaving. Seba, Savu.

warp until they are removed one by one as the weaver comes to them on the loom.

The warp threads, now secured between the split sticks, are stretched for several days. They are put on a simple frame, or they are hung over a bamboo pole while a second piece of bamboo, weighted with stones, is placed at the bottom of the circular warp (see fig. 26). As the threads stretch, the weaver makes them easier to handle by treating them with a starch derived from corn (or cassava or rice) mixed with water. The starch may be applied with a special rattan brush (see fig. 27) but just as often a handy corn-cob is adapted to do the job. This stretching and

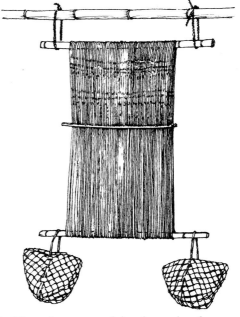

Fig. 26. Threads arranged in the order for weaving are hung and stretched with a weighted bamboo pole before being put on the loom. Flores.

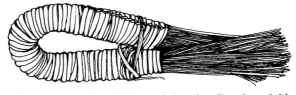

Fig. 27. A rattan brush is used by the Bataks of North Sumatra to apply starch to the warp threads as they stretch.

WEAVING 73

Fig. 28. The dyed, ikat-patterned threads are woven into cloth on a backstrap loom. Danali 'di, Savu.

starching process completes the preparation of the warp; the threads are now, finally, ready to be transferred to the loom.

Warp ikat textiles (and all other fabrics made by the Ancient Peoples) are woven on a simple backstrap loom. This loom basically consists of two poles that are held together by the warp threads, and has devices to lift the threads so that the crosswise weft can be inserted. Since the warp is circular, the weaver just slips the two main poles of the loom into the circle of threads to "set up" the loom. She then ties the pole farthest from her to a couple of posts and attaches the closest beam to a strap that goes around her back. A typical backstrap loom is pictured and its parts and how it works are described in detail at the beginning of chapter 4.

When the yarn was first warped, the odd- and even-numbered warp threads were marked with black cross-strings, and these were left in place throughout the binding and dyeing steps. Now, since the alternate threads are clearly marked, it is easy for the weaver to loosely attach a rod to every other thread (the odd ones, for example) with loops of a continuous length of string. Each loop connects the rod to a thread, so when this rod, in weaving called the string heddle rod, is raised, all the odd threads lift with it and a slot for the weft thread to pass through is opened. The even-numbered threads are lifted by a pole, the shed roll, for the return pass of the weft thread. Lifting these two devices alternately for the passes of the weft results in what is called a "plain weave."

It is important to note that the plain weave of warp ikat cloths is given a "warp face." This means that the warp threads are spaced very closely together while the weft threads are not beaten in too tightly as the cloth is woven; the result is that there are more warp threads than weft threads in every square centimeter of cloth. Thus, the patterned warp threads are visually predominant. The weft threads are usually dyed the same color as the primary background of the weaving so that even if the weft does show through slightly, it will blend in as much as possible and not distract from the warp pattern.

Most weavers set up their looms in the shade of the porch or underneath the raised floor of the house (see fig. 28). For the weavers of

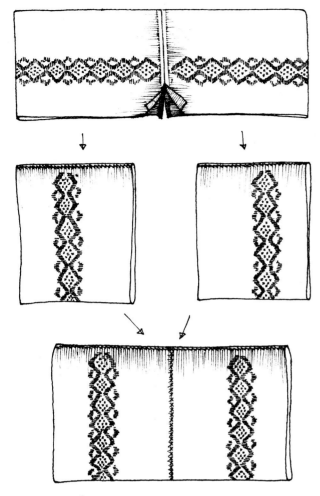

Fig. 29. To make a sarong, weavers cut a long, circular woven piece and then resew the smaller pieces into a tube.

When the weaving is finished, the circle of woven cloth is taken off the loom, the string heddle rod and all the other weaving aids are removed, and the fabric is cut across the warp where it is unwoven. The unwoven threads become the fringes on the top and bottom of a selimut. Often the cloth must also be sewn into the desired shape, since the width of the fabric, as we have mentioned, is limited by the reach of the weaver on the loom. Large selimut such as the *hinggi kombu* from Sumba are woven one-half at a time, and the two panels are sewn together. A sarong is woven in a long circular piece that is cut into two to four pieces which are then sewn together into a tube (see fig. 29).

The last step on a selimut or selindang is finishing off the fringed edges. A line of chain stitching is applied to the edge of the selimut just above the fringe to prevent unraveling. In Sumba, a border five to ten centimeters deep may be woven onto the edge of the weaving once it has been sewn (see fig. 98, chapter 4). The fringe threads are often corded; that is, groups of threads are twisted first in one direction and then pairs of these groups are twisted together in the reverse direction. These neat cords are knotted at the ends or dipped in wax so that they will not unravel.

The Rhythm of Warp Ikat

The making of warp ikat weavings must follow the rhythm of nature. Indonesia has only two seasons: a dry season extending from about March to October and a rainy season falling roughly between November and February (this schedule varies somewhat from one island to another). The amount of rainfall differs greatly from island to island, but even in arid regions like parts of East Nusatenggara, rain may fall for only one or two months in a year—the humidity stays high for much longer. When the air is damp, it is difficult to spin cotton fiber into thread, so the spinning must be saved for the dry season. Ikat work is not affected by either dry or humid weather and can be done at anytime. In the households of many weavers across the archipelago, the long afternoons of the rainy season are passed warping and binding; in this way, the threads will be ready for dyeing by the end of the rainy season, when indigo plants are most plentiful and the blue dye can be made. During the next few months, if possible,

warp ikat cloth, the actual weaving is the most difficult step of all, more trying than the complicated ikat, warping, and dyeing processes. A mistake in the weaving may be impossible to correct and can waste all the careful effort put into preparing the threads. Since the weaving process is the culmination of so much effort, often one or two years of work, it is inevitable that many superstitions surround it. Once it was customary for weavers to make offerings invoking the aid of friendly spirits before commencing work, and this practice is still observed by women who continue to follow the traditional animistic religions. In Flores, it is believed that a jealous woman can use magic to ruin her rival's weaving while it is on the loom. Weavings used for burials or as shrouds for the dead must sometimes be woven following special rituals. In Savu, one such cloth is woven at the gravesite, and when it is completed a pig is sacrificed and blessings are invoked.

the *mengkudu* red dye is mixed so that work can progress on the threads. Weaving, like spinning, must also be done in the driest part of the year because the cotton threads stick together in damp weather and will tangle and break easily. A weaving made according to the rhythm of the seasons will take at least one full year or more to complete.

Learning is also a natural process. Girls begin to take an active part when they are young, helping their mothers with simple weaving chores and gradually absorbing the intricate motifs and the processes. Most girls learn spinning early and can ikat by the age of twelve or thirteen. But the weaving technique itself is not mastered until the girl has become a young woman of seventeen or eighteen. Being able to weave ikat cloths, from beginning to end, is a sign of womanhood and a prerequisite for marriage. Among Ancient Peoples, every girl learns to weave. Since the cloths are often used for ceremonies, as well as for clothing, weaving skills take on an even greater, almost ritual importance. The weaver puts something of her "spirit" into the cloth, and it is commonly believed that the weaver's character is revealed in the cloth she makes. A prospective mother-in-law will scrutinize the weavings made by a possible bride for her son before the marriage is arranged, since she believes that they reflect the true nature of the woman who made them.

2 Warp Ikat: A Myriad of Motifs

The day begins early in Indonesia. The small town of Nita in eastern Flores holds one of the weekly markets that add excitement to the humdrum routine of village life, and by sunrise the marketplace is already alive with people. Some villagers walked through the night many miles over rugged country, carrying chickens, vegetables, clay pots, and baskets. Others, like ourselves, set off long before dawn packed into the back of one of the vintage trucks that bring in marketgoers from nearby villages. Such weekly markets are found throughout rural Indonesia, and the scene varies little whether it is South Sulawesi, North Sumatra, or Flores in East Nusatenggara (see plate 2). Women display the mangoes and betel nut they have for sale on woven rattan mats and exchange the week's gossip with friends while their husbands gather at the edge of the market field to drink palm wine and inspect livestock. A standard attraction at most markets is the traveling medicine man. Crowds listen in rapt fascination to his stories of magic and faraway places that inevitably end in a pitch for his particular brand of remedy. Vendors circulate selling treats like sweet bean porridge and ices. Wide-eyed country people move slowly through the goods and produce, occasionally stopping to haggle good-naturedly over a pot or a chicken.

To many villagers who live in relative isolation most of the time, the market is the big social event of their week. They prepare for the occasion by dressing in their finest clothing as if they were on their way to a festival rather than just a trip to town. Besides the local holidays or traditional ceremonies, which we saw only by chance, the weekly markets regularly provided us with a fascinating display of local costumes, as well as a good place to meet people.

The Significance of Traditional Costume

We were dazzled by the variety of traditional weavings that could be seen, since people from more than one district or tribe attend the larger markets. A native of each area, however, can tell a lot about a person just by his or her dress. In a region like East Nusatenggara where many different ethnic groups live closely together, the weavings serve as a way of identifying the home of a stranger. Traditional dress acts as a kind of introduction, announcing a person's tribe, clan, or district, as well as giving clues to status within the tribe. In eastern Flores, for example, certain sarong patterns are worn only by women of one or two villages, although other patterns are more widespread. During a journey by foot in the Lio district of eastern Flores, we accompanied a native Catholic priest who knew the weavings of this area very well. As we would meet a woman along the path, he would say, "She must be from Copu village because she is wearing a *nepa* patterned sarong" or "That woman is from the village of Tenda because the pattern on her sarong is a *weko wenda.*"

On the island of Rote in East Nusatenggara a very orderly system of identification was once based on the motifs of the tribal weavings. The island was divided into eighteen kingdoms and each claimed particular variations in the textile motifs that revealed, to a Rotenese, the kingdom a person lived in. Over the past few generations, however, the motifs of Rote have gradually blended, the weavers of one kingdom freely borrowing designs from another, and many of the local distinctions have disappeared. Nowadays, it is only possible to make a guess as to which kingdom a particular weaving was made in. Unfortunately, this trend has been followed to some extent in other parts of East Nusatenggara.

The town of Kupang on the west coast of Timor Island is the provincial capital of East Nusatenggara and boasts a large daily market that draws not only people from nearby towns but visitors from other islands as well. Here the islands of East Nusatenggara appear in microcosm as people from Rote, Savu, Flores, and many districts of Timor wander through the market. Many villagers in this area of Indonesia still take pride in their background and tribe, an attitude they demonstrate by wearing the homemade weavings of their group. The cloths themselves are simple in form; the basic pieces are the tube worn as a skirt (the sarong) and a rectangle that can be worn in a variety of styles (the selimut).

A clue to the character of each group of people can be seen in its manner of dress. Savunese women always look dignified and command respect in their well-tailored blouses and somber-colored sarong, neatly doubled and folded at the waist. In contrast, the women of Flores look casual, just holding an edge of their loose sarong over one shoulder. Men from Rote Island wear store-bought plaid cotton sarong and white shirts, a common fashion of men's dress seen throughout Indonesia. But they proclaim their identity by carrying a folded Rote selimut over one shoulder. Even in Kupang, on Timor, some Rotenese men wear their unique plaited hats that feature a single woven horn rising from the crown. Men from the various tribes of Timor are the most eye-catching, wearing two or three elaborately draped selimut at a time. Floral patterns decorate the weavings worn by villagers from the vicinity of Kupang while geometric motifs identify men from the Amarasi district to the south. Men from the central highlands of Timor are resplendent in cloths with rainbow-colored stripes and bold stylized patterns. A native Timorese could, of course, make finer distinctions and tell you which person came from the town of Niki-Niki and which from Kepamenanu. Only in East Nusatenggara can one see

such a display of traditional costume at affairs like the daily market in Kupang. The variety of weavings and their continuing importance to the people is unique today in Indonesia.

One of the many characteristics shared by the Ancient Peoples is the division of society into classes of royalty, nobility, commoners, and, at one time, slaves. Textiles sometimes echo this class structure. Not surprisingly, the most exquisite textiles are owned by the kings and nobles. The scarcity of materials, especially dyestuffs, needed for making warp ikat cloths is one factor that naturally limits the number of people that can weave good-quality cloth. The upper classes, by virtue of their wealth and status, have access to the best materials, and this shows in the superior color of their weavings. The women of the royal families and the nobility also have time to devote to weaving since they do not have to work in the fields. They use this time to experiment and refine their skills, and if the need arises, they can call on the most skillful weavers in their area to help them make their cloth. Generally, then, the textiles made by the upper-class women are technically finer than those of the common people.

Certain textiles are sometimes reserved for the exclusive use of a particular class of people. For example, sarong decorated by the supplementary warp technique (see chapter 4) are worn only by royalty and noblewomen in Sumba, and at one time there were similar restrictions on ikat-decorated cloth in East Sumba. In general, however, the use of ikat-decorated cloth was not an exclusive privilege of the upper classes among the Ancient Peoples, and it is surprisingly rare for certain motifs to be reserved for them. But the size of their motifs may be larger—the sarong of Savunese noblewomen sometimes feature main motif bands that are twice as large as those on sarong of other women. High-quality cloths, with rich colors and finely executed motifs, were necessary for the upper classes to indicate their status, but in other respects many of the royal textiles were just very well made versions of weavings worn by commoners.

Occasionally, the signs of rank are subtle and arbitrary. In the Amarasi district of Timor, the number of narrow red lengthwise stripes that appear on the weavings is a sign that denotes rank; a person of royal birth uses one stripe while commoners use two.

Some types of ikat-decorated cloth in East Sumba were reserved for specific people. In this area, the power and prestige of the tribal king were stronger than in other areas of East Nusatenggara. Until the early part of this century, only the kings and the men in his service (even if they themselves were slaves) could wear the red, black, and white animal-patterned cloth known as *hinggi kombu*. However, any man could wear a monochrome blue and white version of the same cloth known as *hinggi kaworu* (*kaworu* is the Sumbanese word for indigo). Actually, a king did not always wear the colorful *hinggi kombu*; for daily affairs he often wore plain black cloth, which is a symbol of authority among Sumbanese. Since the beginning of the export trade in East Sumbanese weavings in the 1920s and the gradual erosion of the power of the kings, the wearing of *hinggi kombu* has become widespread among men of all classes.

In Sumba we also saw an unusual example of a warp ikat cloth known as *rohubanggi*, which was once worn only by Sumbanese kings. A king wrapped this long, narrow textile (seven meters by seventy-five centimeters) around his waist before going into battle, believing it would give him extraordinary strength. *Rohubanggi* are no longer made today but the family of the late King Baba Hunggu of the Tabundung district in East Sumba showed us a family heirloom that was woven over a century ago by the grandmother of the last king.* The ends of this *rohubanggi* cloth were decorated with an elaborate tapestry weave technique (called *kelim*; see chapter 4) and a bird figure produced in warp ikat. An unusual aspect of the design was found in the center of the cloth—the red, white, and blue stripes of the Dutch flag, perhaps copied as a charm to tap the strength of the ruling colonialists. A few other special-purpose weavings used only by the upper classes will be mentioned later in this chapter.

Warp ikat textiles in the societies of the Ancient Peoples serve as more than local costumes and status indicators for the upper classes. The unique story of these cloths is that among many Ancient Peoples they have a ritual and spiritual

* When King Baba Hunggu died, the rule of kings was discontinued in the Tabundung district. Since Indonesian independence in 1949, as the ruling tribal kings pass on, their "offices" have been discontinued. Those kings that still rule are highly venerated, and respect is given as well to the surviving royal families, though they no longer rule officially. In this way the government is gradually phasing out the old system of tribal rule and replacing it with offices of the government.

value that extends beyond the mere physical object. Textiles are required for ceremonies, but not just as traditional dress for the participants. The cloths themselves are a necessary part of the ritual. Warp ikat cloths act as burial shrouds, as part of the exchange of gifts before a marriage, and as a way of preserving local history and legends. Some textiles are also believed to have magical powers such as the ability to protect their owners against evil spirits and illness. Like many of the other characteristics of the Ancient Peoples described in chapter 1, such as their animistic religions and ancestor worship, the close relationship between textiles and culture began in Neolithic times and has continued up to the present.

Neolithic patterns, like the human and animal figures that appeared on bark cloth, were symbolic or magical in intent, rather than strictly decorative. Some of these motifs have survived until today (see fig. 30). Generally, Neolithic motifs are thought to have been greatly changed by the influence of the Dong-Son culture. Spreading out from Indochina from the eighth to second centuries B.C., the Dong-Son culture had an enormous impact on the traditional art of many peoples in the Indonesian archipelago. Especially influential were the motifs found on bronze kettle-drums, examples of which can be found on the islands of Alor in East Nusatenggara and Bali. Purely ornamental patterns of a rhythmic, repeating nature are an important Dong-Son contribution. The hook-and-rhomb

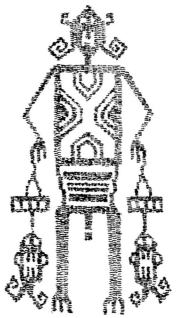

Fig. 30. Neolithic-style human figure. Iban Dyak region, Sarawak, Malaysia.

designs such as those found on the textiles of Timor are Dong-Son elements that have survived on the weavings of the Ancient Peoples. Another motif taken from the bronze drums, the "ship of the dead," is particularly important in the textiles of Sumatra. The Neolithic symbols gradually blended with the ornamental designs and symmetrical style of the Dong-Son to create many of the contemporary patterns that decorate the warp ikat cloths of the Ancient Peoples.

Today, the cloth woven by the Bataks of North Sumatra, the Torajans of central Sulawesi, the Iban Dyaks of Borneo, and the people of Timor show distinct similarities in their motifs. All of these people were particularly isolated after the Dong-Son period of influence, and they have preserved the older patterns in a pure form. The textiles of many other Ancient Peoples, especially those in East Nusatenggara, were later markedly influenced by imported textiles, in particular by the Indian patola cloth (discussed in chapter 3), and their motifs underwent further development.

Like the textiles themselves, the motifs of each tribe of Ancient Peoples—whether in their pure or developed form—reveal some of the tribe's individual characteristics. Especially in East Nusatenggara, where warp ikat weavings are the main art form, the motifs reflect the matters of greatest concern to the tribe. In some areas, they are mainly religious in nature, representing beliefs connected with the afterlife, important deities, or death rites. In other areas, the patterns are connected with different facets of life, such as the tribe's class structure, clan divisions, historical contacts, or marriage customs.

East Sumba

The best known of all warp ikat textiles are the hinggi cloths made along the coast of East Sumba. Their motifs are particularly expressive and reveal a great deal about the character and life of the people who live in this area. Hinggi are patterned with easily recognizable animal and human figures that are quite unlike the geometric and stylized motifs characterisic of other warp ikat weavings. The symbolism of the figures is often relatively straightforward, and a review of these motifs helps to paint a picture of life on the island since the motifs symbolize

Fig. 31. A horseman poses in traditional dress. Waimangura, West Sumba.

aspects of the complex animistic religion, the social structure, and the once absolute power of the kings.

Sumbanese are unique among the Ancient Peoples in that they are horsemen who are most at ease galloping across the countryside (or through the towns for that matter). Horses are their wealth: in East Nusatenggara, a man's fortune is measured by the number of heads of livestock he possesses. Sumbanese horses, known as sandalwoods, have long been famous as far away as China. Centuries ago the Sumbanese were trading their horses to the Chinese for ceramics, and Chinese export ware of the Ming and even earlier periods was once commonly found in Sumba. Like many horsemen, Sumbanese have a reputation for being fierce warriors. They certainly look the part (see fig. 31). Men wear long knives tucked into their belts and would not consider leaving their village without them. A long knife offers a Sumbanese horseman protection as well as completes his distinctive dress. He wraps his hinggi around his waist and holds it up with a wide leather belt, letting the fringed ends of the cloth dangle down between his legs. Today, many men wear khaki-colored military-style shirts with epaulets that, along with the jaunty turban, enhance the rakish effect. For more formal occasions, a second hinggi—the second of the pair woven at the same time—is laid over one shoulder (see plate 3). Most men wear the blue and white *hinggi kaworu* or a hinggi of a solid color for daily use, but on special occasions they put on the colorful *hinggi kombu* once reserved for the kings.

Hinggi kombu and *hinggi kaworu* are patterned with a great variety of animals, birds, and human figures, but the most common motif is the horse, and this of course reflects its importance in Sumbanese daily life. Horses shown standing, prancing, and in a variety of other poses are generally quite lifelike.

Fig. 32. *Andung* or "skull tree" motif on a warp ikat *hinggi kombu*. Red, rusty black, blue, and white. From East Sumba. Tama Art University collection.

Another prominent motif is the "skull tree" or *andung* (see fig. 32). Sumbanese, like other tribes of Ancient Peoples, had a long history of ritual headhunting, an important part of their culture that died out in the 1930s. Warriors used to make raids in search of valuables and slaves, and many traditional villages of Sumba (like Tarung village, chapter 1) are hidden on well-fortified hilltops as a protection against such attacks. Warriors would retrieve the heads of their fallen enemies, and when a victorious king returned from a raid he would have these heads mounted on a "tree" that was then placed at the entrance to the village. This skull or head tree was meant to serve the dual purpose of frightening away enemies and of bringing the village prosperity. For the warriors, not only in Sumba, there was a great deal of prestige in-

volved in the taking of heads, and among Ancient Peoples the concept of a life-force was closely connected to this skull cult.

There are usually eight heads on the Sumbanese skull tree, one for each of the eight stages the dead must pass through in the afterlife. Sumbanese say that there are also eight legendary places that their ancestors stopped at on their initial migration to Sumba. The "skull tree" motif can also be connected to the "tree of life" motif, a fertility symbol that is found in many areas of Indonesia.

Many warp ikat motifs are associated with the power of the kings, a subject which surfaced again and again in conversations with Sumbanese. East Sumba is divided into eight kingdoms, but only two kings are still alive and ruling today. The power of these royal families, before the system of kingship was phased out, was absolute. Some motifs, such as the deer, were symbols of royal privilege. The kings of East Sumba used to organize great deer hunts, particularly in the kingdoms of Kapunduk and Kanatang; no one but a king was allowed to hunt deer, so this animal naturally became a symbol of royalty. At one time, the deer motif was believed to be found only on the hinggi belonging to kings of Kapunduk, but like other motifs that were once specific to a particular area, it has been borrowed by weavers in other parts of East Sumba.

Since each hinggi features several animals, the question arises as to whether or not the various figures on a single weaving are related to each other. Does the weaver mean to tell a story or is there an underlying symbolism that ties all these figures together?

One village elder told us that when the kings were at the height of their power, they would order hinggi to their own specifications. If a king had just been on a hunt, for example, he would ask his weavers to make a hinggi depicting the animals that he had killed or seen to commemorate the event; since deer was the principal game animal, it would logically be the predominant motif on such a "representational" piece.

But on East Sumbanese weavings today, we found that the weaver herself uses her knowledge of traditional decorative elements to choose the animal motifs that decorate her cloth. She arranges the figures within the horizontal bands of the hinggi to create what she feels is a pleasing design, rather than to tell a particular story. Throughout East Sumba, each figure in itself has a fairly standard and clear meaning to Sumbanese, but it does not necessarily have to relate to the other motifs on the cloth.

Another motif regarded as a symbol of royal power is of relatively recent origin. The pair of standing lions often seen on hinggi was derived from the coat of arms of the Netherlands, probably as it appeared on Dutch coins. Perhaps the motif was originally chosen to please the Dutch when hinggi first found favor as an export item in the early part of this century. Although the lions at first may have been seen as a symbol of colonial power, as they came into common use they gradually became a symbol of the authority of East Sumbanese kings.

The most dangerous animal found on Sumba, the crocodile, is also connected with royalty and with the afterlife. Since the king was considered all-powerful, he could be as brave and dangerous as the crocodile when provoked. Courageous warriors are often compared to crocodiles in East Nusatenggara. In West Sumba, for example, a legendary albino warrior is said to have been fathered by a crocodile. The reptile is also dangerous in the afterlife because, according to Sumbanese beliefs, the last obstacle a soul must overcome before reaching the land of gods is a river infested with crocodiles. If the proper arrangements have been made by the family of the deceased, the soul may safely cross this river. But if the customs have not been followed exactly, the soul will fall into the river and be eaten by the crocodiles.

Too many motifs are depicted on Sumbanese weavings to cover all of them here, but there are a few more commonly seen figures. A shrimp symbolizes longevity because it drops its shell and is thus "reborn" when it grows a new one. The snake is widely believed to possess magical powers among the Ancient Peoples; because it sheds its skin like the shrimp, it also signifies rebirth and long life. The Chinese dragon, a popular motif, was borrowed from the Chinese ceramics imported into Sumba and is believed to possess magical powers. Roosters are associated with masculinity and dogs represent warriors. Frontally viewed human figures, a motif characteristic of the Neolithic period, are an occasional feature of hinggi although standing figures are more common on the woven sarong of Sumba and on the warp ikat textiles

of Timor and Borneo. Other figures include monkeys, lizards, fish, insects, seahorses, cockatoos, and other local birds.

These animal figures are arranged on the hinggi in horizontal bands of alternating background colors (see plate 1). This is an unusual arrangement for warp ikat cloths, for most of these fabrics, like those in plates 7 and 8, are designed with warpwise bands, a logical outcome of the warp ikat technique. Each hinggi has three to five bands arranged to the top and to the bottom of a single center band. Sumbanese say these horizontal bands in which the animal and human figures appear represent the layout of the traditional Sumbanese village. The king lives in the center of the village, surrounded by his nobles, who are in turn encircled by the commoners, while slaves live on the outer edge (slavery of course no longer exists in Indonesia). The center section of a hinggi, like the center of the village, is thus reserved for royalty, while the bands on both the top and bottom (beginning from the center band) represent the other social classes—nobles, commoners, and, near the fringe, slaves. Many of the older hinggi have only three bands on either side of the center, which strengthens this analogy. A king must achieve balance in his kingdom, we were told, by being fair and impartial in settling disputes and dispensing wealth. The top and bottom symmetry of the hinggi is designed to express this balance. When East Sumbanese men wear the second hinggi of a pair they are careful to keep the center at the highest point over their right shoulder to show respect for their king.

Animal figures almost always appear in the top and bottom bands but the choice of animal has no relation to the class the band represents. The motifs of the central bands, however, are usually associated with royalty by Sumbanese. Occasionally, hinggi from the early 1920s feature human figures in the central band, but virtually all contemporary hinggi display geometric designs here. The number of center motifs is limited and the few that are described below are the ones that appear on most hinggi seen today.

One of the most common center motifs is called *kanduhu* and consists of six-pointed stars and diamond shapes. We were told that because the stars are the highest objects in the sky, they represent the highest authority in the kingdom. This pattern was once a speciality of the Kaliuda

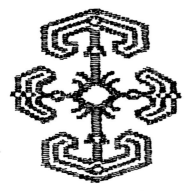

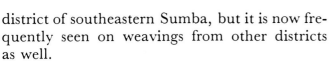

Fig. 33. *Habak* motif. Sumba.

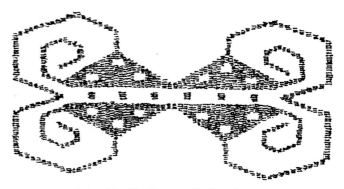

Fig. 34. *Karihu* motif. Sumba.

district of southeastern Sumba, but it is now frequently seen on weavings from other districts as well.

Habak is a symbol of royalty that was once associated with the Kanatang district (see fig. 33). With four branches, it resembles a symbol that was used on bark cloth made by the Torajans of central Sulawesi. It is also similar to the characteristically Dong-Son patterns found in Timor.

Another pattern found in the central band is a peculiar figure called *karihu,* said to represent an open shellfish (see fig. 34). When we asked what could possibly be the similarity between a shellfish and royal power, we were informed that the shellfish, though small, will dare to snap shut on a man's fingers, just as a king will not fear to punish a man who oversteps the boundaries of traditional law.

One of the most important center patterns is a complex geometric design called *patola ratu (ratu* means queen in Indonesian). This motif was borrowed from the silk patola cloths imported from India (see plate 20). In the past it was most commonly found in Kanatang kingdom, the area where Sumbanese say the Indian patola cloth first entered Sumba, but today it is an important pattern on hinggi made all along the east coast. These Indian patola cloths, as we shall see in chapter 3, were highly prized possessions that were owned only by kings in Sumba.

The *patola ratu* pattern that appears in the central band of many hinggi is also found on the only noteworthy ikat-decorated sarong made in East Sumba, *lau patola ratu* (see plate 5). *Lau* is the Sumbanese word for sarong—the weaving is thus named for its motif. Most women in East Sumba wear sarong that are decorated with very simple arrowhead or diamond ikat patterns in a monochrome color scheme, or black sarong with embroidered motifs; these contrast with the visually exciting hinggi that women weave for their men. For ceremonial occasions, however, noblewomen may wear the *patola ratu* sarong or a sarong decorated with supplementary warp techniques.

Savu

Within a small area like East Nusatenggara differences in the weavings from one island to the next are often dramatic. The bold designs and bright colors of the Sumbanese weavings are quite a contrast to traditional Savunese cloths, although the islands are only two days apart by sailboat.

The weavings of Savu feature delicate geometric or floral motifs, and the colors of the fabrics tend to be somber, predominantly blue-black combined with touches of rusty red. Even the mostly red cloths have a subdued tone compared to the bright Sumbanese hinggi. The individual motifs of Savu are not as expressive as those of Sumba, nor are they linked directly to legends or local customs. Also, Savunese weavings do not show regional variation, probably because the island itself is very small—it only takes a few days to walk completely around it—and its population is homogeneous. However, one of the most important aspects of Savunese weavings, along with their refined beauty, is that they work as a system of clan identification. Savunese elders say that sixteen generations ago (if we take one generation to be 20 years, this would be 320 years) the people of Savu were divided into two clans. At that time there were two sisters, Majibabo and her younger sister, Lobado. The matrilineal descendants of Majibabo became the Hubi'ae clan (the larger clan) and the descendants of

Lobado became the Hubi'iki (the smaller clan). Today, there is less significance attached to the clans in regard to customs such as marriage. But Savunese still know which clan they belong to, and each group wears particular types of sarong and selimut.

The sarong Savunese women wear to denote their clan are said to be unchanged from the time when the clans came into existence. These sarong are ikat-patterned in white against red backgrounds with a few black and white accent bands. Each band needs to be dyed in only one color, an effect that is easier to achieve and probably earlier in development than the more complex two-colored weavings. The sarong worn by women of the larger clan, the Hubi'ae, is called *raja* and features small bands of woven decoration in a type of warp pick-up weave (see chapter 4) between some of the ikat bands.

Both the *raja* sarong and the sarong worn by the women of the smaller clan, the Hubi'iki, feature one major motif band that appears on the top and bottom of the finished sarong. The main motifs for these traditional sarong are chosen from only a few native patterns. The larger clan, which wears the *raja* sarong, is broken into three subclans, each one entitled to wear a different motif. One of these patterns is *tutu*, a motif of stylized birds and flowers (see fig. 35). But all the sarong worn by women of the smaller clan always feature the same motif,

a geometric pattern called *le'do*; *le'do* is also the name by which the sarong itself is known (see fig. 36).

These monochrome sarong that indicate clan membership are now less popular than a newer variety of sarong among women of both clans. Called *worapi*, these newer sarong are decorated in red and white against a black background, a development that allows the weaver a greater range of artistic expression than the single-color scheme (see plate 6). Thus, like Sumba hinggi, the threads of these sarong are dyed in two colors and the ikat bindings are rearranged between dyeings. In Savu, the weaver binds the white parts of the motifs with *agel* fiber and the red parts with a different fiber so that she can easily tell them apart. Savunese refer to this method as *pararapi*, from which they derive the name *worapi* for both sarong and selimut that feature motifs with two colors.

Men of Savu may also wear a designated type of selimut to show their clan affiliation. Men of the smaller clan wear a unique weaving which they call *wohapi* (see plate 7). Savunese believe it has been used for at least twenty generations and they say it is the oldest style of weaving still made in Savu today. Originally, this weaving was only indigo blue and white with an ikat pattern; contemporary examples feature a light blue color and narrow red accent stripes. The *wohapi* motif (from which the cloth derives its

Fig. 35. *Tutu* motif. Savu.

Fig. 36. *Le'do* motif. Savu.

name; see fig. 37) always dominates the pattern scheme, and the same precise layout, motifs, and colors are found on *wohapi* cloths all over Savu. Because the *wohapi* has such a long history, it is considered very suitable as a burial shroud. This selimut is generally not worn everyday, unlike most of the other Savu weavings, and there are comparatively few of them produced. Men of the smaller clan save the light blue *wohapi* selimut for their burial.

Our questions concerning the significance of traditional motifs often caused surprise and consternation in the villages of East Nusatenggara, and Savu was no exception. When we asked a difficult question, the old women of the village would gather together; before any answer could be given, there would be an animated discussion in Savunese. Most people who weave and wear the textiles are not accustomed to talking about the motifs they create and found it odd that we should be interested in what the motifs "mean."

According to Savunese custom, men of the larger clan (the Hubi'ae) wear two-colored *worapi* selimut decorated with several traditional motifs. One common pattern is called *boda*, and Savunese often refer to it with pride as the "Savu Flower," although it has no actual counterpart in nature (see fig. 38). Another simple motif consisting of several zigzagging lines, similar to lightning, is called *kekamahaba*

and is said to portray the accordion-folded leaves of the *lontar* palm, an essential tree in Savu. The *lontar* palm is a source of palm sugar, an important staple food, and one of the raw ingredients for making palm wine and liquor. The leaves of the tree can readily be converted into baskets, plaited into mats and sandals, or even dried out and cut into cigarette papers.

An old and mysterious motif used by men of the larger clan is *dula* (see fig. 39). If this symbol appears on a selimut, the men consider the weaving a fitting burial shroud, although the cloth can still be worn at other times. Among all Ancient Peoples, certain motifs and types of weavings are preferred for such rites but this does not necessarily mean that they are exclusively for that purpose. It may be difficult to discover the exact reason why a certain pattern is linked by the people to burials, but often it seems that it is the oldest motifs which are associated with this most important ceremony. This seems to be the explanation with the *dula* motif. All Savunese we asked agreed that it is very old and important, but no one could quite express a clear idea of what this strange figure represents. One Savunese thought it was a "tray with something on it" while another said it was a tomb. The *dula* motif resembles some of the stylized "ship of the dead" motifs found in other parts of Indonesia, particularly Sumatra. This "ship of the dead" motif dates from the period of Dong-Son influence, and the idea that a ship carries the souls of the dead to the afterlife is a part of Savunese lore. Whether the *dula* motif portrays a soul ship or not is immaterial; what is important is that it once represented something of great significance to the Savunese people.

Savunese wear their sarong and selimut in a characteristically refined and elegant manner. In the past, women of Savu wore their narrow sarong belted at the waist, then pulled up and

Fig. 37. *Wohapi* motif. Savu.

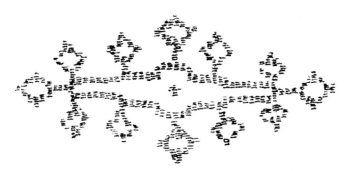

Fig. 38. *Boda* motif. Savu.

Fig. 39. *Dula* motif. Savu.

folded or pinned around their breasts (see fig. 40). Today, many women wear tight-fitting blouses and tie their sarong with a sash, folding the upper part down over their hips and back up to the waist where the fabric is tucked in—the effect is that of a two-tiered skirt (see fig. 41). Over their shoulders they wear a smaller-sized weaving, a selindang, to complete their dress. Women working in the fields may wear plain indigo sarong, as do their children (see fig. 42). Men wear two large selimut, one draped around the waist and the other one draped over the right shoulder. A small woven rectangle of fabric is tied as a headcloth. Out in the countryside men continue to wear the woven selimut although trousers and shirts have replaced the traditional costume in the island's main village of Seba. Many Savunese women, however, continue to wear their sarong even when they migrate to neighboring islands.

Some of the most striking Savunese weavings do not feature the strictly traditional patterns described above. A pattern called *makaba* or *makassar* (named after the large seaport in Sulawesi, now Ujung Pandang) is similar to Dong-Son hook-and-rhomb designs typical of other Ancient

Fig. 40. These Savunese are dressed for a festival. Seba, Savu.

Fig. 41. These young Savunese are in traditional dress for a ritual dance. The baskets on their feet are filled with dried peas that, when shaken, will provide a rhythmic accompaniment. Seba, Savu.

Fig. 42. A young shepherd girl wears an undecorated sarong. Galanalalu, Savu.

Peoples (see plate 6). Savunese say that before World War II they traded pots of their palm sugar for raw cotton with Bugis sailors from Makassar, and that they learned this motif from the boatmen. But the motif might have been copied from textiles brought to the island from Timor, for it is not found among the Bugis.

Other Savunese patterns have been inspired by Portuguese and Dutch sources. Of all the Ancient Peoples, Savunese have been the most artistically successful in adapting new motifs to their own weavings. The *worapi*-type sarong and selimut with the two-color ikat motifs are often decorated with European-derived patterns (see plate 8). Deep red and white motifs such as realistically portrayed roses have exceptional depth against the dark background of the cloth. Other motifs found on the selimut include grape vines, meandering flower patterns, and Western-style birds in various combinations. Sarong may feature lions from Dutch coins (as in Sumba), cherubs, and flower vases with bouquets, among other patterns. Some of these motifs may have been inspired by Dutch crochet work. Indonesian women took up this craft and now make exquisite crocheted bed decorations with figures similar to those that appear on these weavings. Savunese draw a clear distinction between "their" motifs—*boda, kekamahaba, dula,* and so on—and these European-influenced patterns. On other islands in East Nusatenggara, the old tribal motifs and newer ones are often not so sharply differentiated.

Savunese who still follow the native animistic religion still prefer to wear the traditional designs that have special significance. In Seba, however, the main "town" on the island—it has one street, a few shops, no electricity, and no motor vehicles—many people have converted to Christianity. Here we most often saw people wearing the foreign-influenced designs. But on our second visit to Savu, we arrived in Seba in the midst of preparations for the burial of an acquaintance's mother. Then, even these progressive Christian townspeople brought out weavings with the traditional *boda, kekamahaba,* and *dula* patterns, and many of the mourners appeared in the traditional red sarong of their clan.

Eastern Flores

The motifs of eastern Flores demonstrate how the textile patterns evolve as the people themselves adopt new concepts. As changes come about in the lives of the people through more contact with outside influences and the introduction of new religions, these events are often recorded in the motifs. Because the traditional motifs are often so closely related to the animistic religions among Ancient Peoples, the introduction of a new religion especially is bound to have an impact on the tribal art.

This type of development can clearly be seen in two areas of eastern Flores, Lio and Sikka, and also in the nearby area around the port of Ende. Today, several religions exist side by side among the people of these three areas. Before the period of European colonialism, they shared similar religions and customs, and their textile motifs —also similar—were closely connected with the native religion. Today, however, the people of Sikka are Catholic Christians, those around the town of Ende have embraced Islam, and the people of the more isolated mountainous district of Lio still follow the old animistic beliefs. The textile motifs of these three districts have diverged and now reflect the changes that have taken place in the lives of the people.

In the Sikka, Lio, and Ende districts, the sarong is the principal type of ikat weaving; ikat-decorated selimut are less common. The women of Flores wear their sarong in a casual manner, draping a corner over the shoulder and holding it in place with the hand or tucking an end under one arm (see fig. 43). Men of the lowlands are rarely seen in homewoven sarong.

Fig. 43. A young girl wears her sarong in the casual manner of the Lio district. Mone Koanara, Flores.

But men from the mountains of Sikka often wear coarse homespun sarong of plain blue, and in the highlands of Lio they wear attractive sarong made of store-bought silk or rayon in gradiated shades of rich indigo blue.

In this eastern part of Flores, weavings are a trade item and also serve ritual functions as gifts between clans, as exchanges between families at a marriage, and as burial shrouds. Weaving is done primarily by coastal women who trade their surplus sarong, along with fish and salt, to the inland mountain dwellers for agricultural products. Flores is one of the few areas of East Nusatenggara where woven textiles regularly appear in the weekly markets to be sold and traded among local people. On Savu, Rote, and Timor, weavings are generally made for the weaver's own family or for ritual exchanges, and not to be sold. In Sumba, the weaving of hinggi for export is another case altogether.

ENDE: Ende, a port on the south coast of Flores, is the perfect scene for a picture postcard. The town hugs a bay marked by active volcanoes that make their presence known with ominous rumblings and puffs of smoke. Sailboats ranging in size from single-masted ships to an occasional three-masted schooner anchor in the harbor. These boats belong to the Bugis people who handle much of the trade between the small islands of East Nusatenggara. Bugis are devout Moslems, and their settling in the Ende area was an important factor in converting many of the indigenous people to Islam (most Ancient Peoples tend to embrace Christianity if they give up their traditional religion). Before conversion to Islam, weavings made by the native people around Ende were decorated with realistic animal figures that were important in the old animistic faith. Since that time, the patterns have been modified because Islam discourages the lifelike representation of living creatures. Consequently, the once realistic animals have become very stylized or have evolved into geometric designs (see fig. 44). A common indigenous pattern in pre-Islamic Ende, for example, was the horse; today it appears as a figure resembling a chair with two legs and a hooked back. The elephant is another motif that has been simplified; local people describe this figure today as looking like two chairs. Elephants are not native to Flores but ivory, brought in by the Portuguese from Africa, is very important in

Fig. 44. Warp ikat sarong. Cotton; rusty red and black using natural dyes; 138 cm. × 71.5 cm. From Ende, Flores. Tama Art University collection.

the economy of eastern Flores, especially as part of the brideprice. The elephant also appears as a motif on some of the Indian patola cloths that were an important influence on the area's textiles, and these may have been the original source of the elephant motifs.

SIKKA: From Ende to Maumere, the port on the northeast side of the island and the largest town in the Sikka district, it is a day's trip by jeep through spectacular mountainous country cut by deep gorges filled with dense vegetation. Flores ("flower" in Portuguese) was not misnamed; its scenic beauty is unsurpassed in the East Nusatenggara chain.

The people of Maumere and the surrounding Sikka district have been Catholic for several centuries. Legend has it that several hundred years ago, a tribal king traveled north to the Malukus where he met Portuguese priests and was converted to Catholicism. When he returned to Sikka, the king spread his new beliefs throughout his domain. At that time, some people of Sikka took Portuguese names, as well as adopting Christianity. The last king to rule Sikka, Tomtomas (from the Portuguese Don Tomas), on

ceremonial occasions wore seventeenth-century dress complete with a conquistador-style helmet, an indication of the lasting effects the Portuguese had on this area.

Because of this strong European influence in the background of Sikka, it is not surprising that many traditional motifs connected with the pre-Catholic culture have disappeared. The old patterns that remain today are purely decorative, their tribal significance long forgotten. New motifs, such as flower bouquets, Western-style birds, Indian-derived patterns, and other designs introduced by the Europeans caught the fancy of the Sikka weavers. Unlike the weavers of Savu, the women of Sikka do not make a distinction between motifs that are traditional, that is, patterns that reach back to pre-Catholic times, and motifs that are clearly derived from European sources. Winged cherubs cavorting around a flower vase may seem an incongruous sight on a warp ikat sarong, but nevertheless, the women of Sikka are still enthusiastic weavers. They have not abandoned their handwoven sarong in favor of Western-style dress, as has sadly occurred in many areas where European influence was strongly felt, like parts of the Malukus. On any Sunday, when the doors of the Catholic churches open after mass, the women file out in their very best ikat-patterned sarong (see plate 9).

LIO: From the sea to the mountains between Sikka and the port of Ende lies the Lio district, an area where the old religion is alive and the native motifs and their meanings are still remembered. The Lio district is difficult to reach and was thus less affected by outside influences than either Ende or Sikka. In fact, many of the customs and motifs once common in Ende and Sikka can now only be found in Lio. Occasional visitors may pass through a few Lio villages on their way to climb Mt. Kelimutu, but otherwise the area sees few outsiders. Lio villagers themselves shun the area of Mt. Kelimutu, a volcano with three crater lakes—one blood red, one turquoise green, and the other milky chocolate in color—since they believe the area to be the resting place for the souls of the dead.

Some villages in Lio, like Nggela on the south coast, can only be reached by boat or by a steep path through the mountains and have had little contact with foreigners. But Nggela village is well-known in this part of Flores because of its strong adherence to the old ways and its reputation for making the best weavings in the

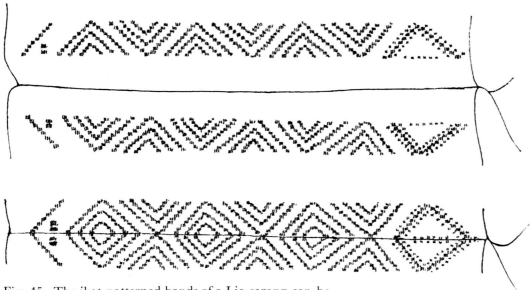

Fig. 45. The ikat-patterned bands of a Lio sarong can be folded together to form a snake.

area. Our visit precipitated a near riot of excitement, but once the initial surprise at seeing two foreigners had passed the villagers were generous with their stories and legends.

The oldest patterns in Lio portray snakes, lizards, and birds. The snake, or *naga,* is an important cult figure in the animistic religion of Flores and is the subject of many myths. Local people believe that in the beginning a snake brought the tenets of the traditional religion to Flores, and even today the snake is considered a harbinger of good tidings.

The most meaningful motifs in Lio are said to be images of snakes or copies of the patterns that appear on snakeskin, which is considered to be very beautiful. Often sarong that are appropriate for burials or other ceremonies bear snake patterns such as the *naga lala,* a wavy-line motif said to represent a crawling snake, or the *naga sawaria,* a pattern inspired by python skin. Sarong bearing *naga* motifs may be used for protective and productive magic. A sarong with a motif consisting of snakeskin-patterned bands, called *nepa mite* (see plate 10), is worn in Lio by pregnant women who believe it will ensure that their babies are born healthy. Sometimes the complete image of a snake is hidden in the layout of this sarong, so that when the sarong is folded a snake with a head and a tail appears (see fig. 45).

A Lio sarong called *lawo gamba* (*lawo* is the word for sarong in Lio) features a wide range of motifs that are not confined within bands; this makes it unusual, for all other sarong in eastern Flores enclose the motifs inside bands.

The motifs on the *lawo gamba* include important traditional symbols as well as some newly acquired patterns. The snake, of course, appears in many guises, sometimes hanging in the branches of a "tree of life," the symbol of fertility and life-force that is widely found in Indonesian art. Sometimes the snake is portrayed as coiled and ready to strike. A variety of birds, animals, and human beings may also decorate these sarong and often appear alongside figures that attempt to express the modern world outside the villages. Alongside traditional magical symbols with a long history we have seen steamboats, automobiles (although none pass through Ngela), and people seated at a table drinking from teacups.

Motifs that act as charms to bring good fortune or keep away evil often have complicated backgrounds, and it is sometimes difficult to understand just why such powers have been attributed to them. A manlike figure, called *pundi,* as it appears on the *gamba* sarong is believed to bring the wearer good luck (see fig. 46). Originally, the word *pundi* meant a small

Fig. 46. *Pundi* figure. Lio, Flores.

bag of rocks that was carried by men when they went to war to ensure their safe return. Today some women still wear a similar bag of stones as a protective charm. The textile motif which now bears the name *pundi* represents those original bag-carrying warriors, and over the years the motif itself has gained the reputation of bringing good fortune.*

OTHER AREAS: Women of the Larantuka area on Flores's far-eastern peninsula weave warp ikat sarong similar in layout to those of the Sikka area but with spidery human and animal figures. To the west in the Bajawa district, weavers make a cloth called *kain hoba*, which is notable for its rough vitality. Simple arrowhead motifs appear in white on wide warpwise bands of rusty red or indigo blue. The texture of this textile, quite at odds with the detailed ikat work and complex patterns of most Flores weavings, is another reflection of the diversity of peoples on this island. The islands immediately to the east of Flores—Lomblen, Alor, Adonara, and Solor—show strong influence of the Indian patola cloth in their weavings.

Timor

Animal figures are important motifs on some of the ikat weavings on other East Nusatenggara islands and on the remote South Maluku islands of Kisar and Tanimbar where ikat cloth is still woven. Many Ancient Peoples place special significance on the lizard though it may appear to us an unlikely candidate for so much attention. The Bataks of North Sumatra say the lizard represents wisdom, while the Iban Dyaks of Borneo believe that when they die their souls enter a lizard. Like the snake on Flores, the lizard plays a vital role in the religion and textile motifs of central Timor, and the sarong and selimut of this area are often patterned with ikat or embroidered lizards (see fig. 47), as well as with other animals, birds, standing human figures, and complex geometric designs. Lizard motifs are also painted and carved on the ceremonial houses used for rainmaking and other rituals.

The people living in the highlands of Timor are the earlier inhabitants of the island; over the

Fig. 47. Lizard motif. Timor.

years, they have been pushed up into the eroded mountains by surrounding tribes. It is very hard to eke out a living in these inhospitable highlands. The traditional dwelling is, for example, a round frame covered with thatch, a crude shelter compared with the elaborate houses of other Ancient Peoples. In terms of textiles, however, the area is rich and produces a wide variety of weavings. In addition to warp ikat technique, the weavers of central Timor are skillful at several of the most intricate types of weaving found in Indonesia, such as the embroidered warp technique called *sungkit* and the tapestry weave called *kelim*. Sometimes several of these methods will be combined on a single selimut to present a virtuoso display of technique, color, and design (see plate 39).

Timorese follow a strict etiquette for wearing the traditional cloths, and the proper manner of dress in the central highlands is quite complicated. A man wears one selimut wrapped loosely around his waist and held up with a woven belt that must be tied in an intricate knot. He then drapes another cloth around his shoulders, and to properly complete the traditional costume he wears a second selimut over the first waist cloth (see plate 13). Timorese women wear ikat-decorated sarong, and they too must wrap a second cloth over the first. Often we would meet women with the bottom of what looked like a beautiful homemade sarong peeking out below a piece of cheap printed cloth. Usually, they were too shy and embarrassed to remove the outer wrap to show us the sarong beneath.

Today the weavings of the highlands are characterized by narrow warpwise stripes of red, yellow, orange, and other bright colors. The colored thread used for these weavings can be purchased in the weekly markets held in the area, but before this manufactured thread was available the stripes were in the more subdued natural colors of *mengkudu* red, indigo blue, natural green, and yellow. The plain-woven striped panels usually appear on either side of a central panel that can be decorated by warp ikat or several different woven techniques. An ikat-

* Most of the information on textile traditions in the Lio district of Flores was received in personal conversations with Father Piet Petu of Ende, Flores.

patterned center is often made of coarse home-spun cotton and dyed in natural indigo, in contrast to the gaudy stripes on either side (see plate 14).

Hook-and-rhomb geometric motifs are widely seen in a pure Dong-Son form on the textiles of many parts of Timor in both ikat and woven techniques. Central Timorese say these patterns began with a stylized lizard head, a kind of arrowhead shape, and developed into a four-branched motif similar to the *habak* motif of Sumba (see fig. 33). This figure, Timorese say, then gradually evolved into the elaborate patterns found on textiles today. The real significance of this explanation, however, is that it takes a design which can be traced back to the Dong-Son period of influence in Indonesia more than two thousand years ago and links it to the local Timor mythology surrounding the lizard cult.

AMARASI: These hook-and-rhomb motifs are virtually the only patterns found on the weavings of the Amarasi district of West Timor. The people of Amarasi raise cattle and many have moved from their isolated villages to houses near the main roads so that they can have better access to the cattle markets in Kupang. In spite of their wealth and relative sophistication, they continue to weave and use their tribal textiles for ceremonies and festivals. Ibu Koroh, the widow of the last king, is making an effort to preserve the traditional Amarasi patterns. When we visited her one dark rainy night, she showed us a notebook in which she had drawn page after page of detailed schematic diagrams of Amarasi motifs; we thought if only every area of the archipelago were fortunate enough to have someone with such foresight more traditional patterns could be preserved.

The Amarasi motifs show subtle variations on the basic rhomb shape with hook elements (see

fig. 48). The patterns often bear poetic names such as *no'e riu*, which means "flowing water," or simple descriptive ones like *kai ne'e*, "six hooks." One motif called *natam koroh* shows a bird—*koroh* in the local dialect—surrounded by a complex hook-and-rhomb design (see plate 15). This motif is associated with the late King Koroh because of its name but is not necessarily reserved for royalty; there are no such restrictions on the motifs of Amarasi, although, as we noted earlier, narrow red stripes denote high status.

Both the sarong and selimut of Amarasi are laid out with repeating warpwise bands of ikat decoration that are separated by narrow solid-colored bands. The large selimut worn by men feature two panels containing these ikat-decorated bands on either side of a plain white central panel. The color white symbolizes purity, and the white center on these selimut may be embroidered with tiny lizard, human, or geometric figures. This arrangement of three panels, two outer ones of ikat-decorated bands or multicolored stripes bordering a central panel decorated with a different technique, is characteristic of selimut in Timor.

The Iban Dyaks of Borneo

Dong-Son-style patterns are prominent on the textiles of the Iban Dyaks, the only tribe of Borneo that makes warp ikat weavings. The Ibans are Ancient People who live in northern Borneo, mostly in the region of Sarawak, a state of Malaysia, but they are closely tied to the tribes of Indonesia. The similarity between the Iban motifs and those of Timor in particular is often striking. The most important warp ikat textile made by the Ibans is a large selimut called *pua kumbu* (*kumbu* refers to its red *mengkudu* color). These extraordinary weavings are not worn as clothing but are displayed at ceremonies. *Pua kumbu* may feature variations of hook-and-rhomb patterns over their entire surface. Stylized snakes, dragons, lizards, and other animals plus human figures in poses typical of Neolithic design are also used as ornaments (see fig. 49 and plate 16). Another type of warp ikat weaving is a very short sarong called *bidang*. Worn by women, it typically bears intricate designs similar to those found on some of the *pua kumbu* and also to those featured on some weavings of Timor (see fig. 50).

Fig. 48. Dong-Son-style hook-and-rhomb motif. Timor.

Fig. 49. Warp ikat *pua kumbu* with dragon motif. Cotton;
red and white using natural dyes; 220 cm. × 138 cm.
Made in the 1940s in central Rajang River area, Sarawak,
Malaysia. Authors' collection.

Fig. 50. Warp ikat *bidang* with hook-and-rhomb motif.
Cotton; deep red using natural dyes; 103 cm. × 51 cm.
From central Rajang River area, Sarawak, Malaysia.
Authors' collection.

The Bataks of North Sumatra

In North Sumatra, selimut of the Batak people
are decorated with geometric patterns that are
very similar to the ikat designs of Borneo and
Timor; but the Bataks produce these patterns in
supplementary weft technique. Batak ikat motifs
are usually simple arrowhead or diamond shapes
in white against a single background color that
may range from deep maroon to blue-black.
Animal figures and other complex motifs appear
on houses, carved staffs, and medicine boxes
rather than on textiles. Among some Batak
tribes, the colors rather than the motifs on the
weavings are symbolic: white symbolizes purity;
red denotes bravery; black represents eternity;
yellow is associated with dignity; and green
means prosperity. Among the Simulungan tribe
of Bataks, for example, the combination of colors
in a weaving chosen for a specific ceremony is
more important than the motif.

Traditional costume for both Batak men and
women is a selimut called *ulos*. This cloth is
seldom worn today except during ceremonies.

Each Batak tribe weaves a distinct type of textile, and not all the tribes use the ikat technique. The southernmost Bataks, the Mandeling tribe, make a dark cloth decorated with woven techniques, beads, and gaudy pompoms, while the northernmost Karo Bataks produce supplementary-weft-decorated weavings with gold or silver threads on red cotton. Karo Bataks also do some simple ikat work, especially on headcloths worn by married women. The Simulungan Bataks who live east of Lake Toba make cloths decorated with both ikat and woven techniques. The Bataks on Samosir Island in the middle of Lake Toba weave ikat-decorated *ulos* with wave or spearheadlike patterns in gradiated shades of blue (see fig. 51).

The weavers who are most active today are the Toba Bataks who live along the south coast of Lake Toba in the vicinity of Tarutung village. Tarutung is particularly noted for its weavings, and the best-known of all Batak *ulos*, the *ragi*

Fig. 51. This puppet is dressed in traditional Batak *ulos*. Called *si gale gale*, puppets like this are carved for childless persons so that their souls will rest in peace and not haunt the living. The arms and legs can be manipulated by strings to make the figure appear to dance. *Si gale gale* often play an important role in traditional Batak ceremonies. Tomok, Samosir Island, North Sumatra.

hidup (the name means "long life"), is woven here and in the surrounding area. The *ragi hidup* features simple ikat and complex woven motifs combined on the same cloth (see plate 32). Panels of delicate Dong-Son-style geometric patterns are woven in fiber—pineapple or agave—and then later sewn onto warp-ikat-decorated panels to complete the cloth. The ikat designs themselves are simple arrowhead shapes in white against a dark background; the contrast of color, texture, and design is this textile's most interesting feature.

Ritual Uses of Textiles

One of the most important functions of *ulos* among the Batak tribes is their role as ritual gifts. *Ulos* are formally given by certain family members to other relatives at all traditional Batak ceremonies. This presentation follows specific social or family divisions; certain kinship groups are always the givers while others are always the receivers. Among the Bataks, textiles are an important part of the exchange of goods that takes place to complete marriage arrangements. In the societies of all Ancient Peoples, the family of the groom must pay a brideprice, which usually includes livestock, jewelry, and money, while the family of the bride has obligations in return such as providing food for the wedding feast and giving textiles to the groom's family. At a Batak ceremony, one *ulos* must be given by the family of the bride to the parents of the groom, and another to the groom himself.

The brideprice and the gifts given in return by the bride's family work as a system of distributing and sharing goods among all Ancient Peoples. Wealth (that is, livestock, jewelry, and textiles, as well as money) is exchanged along designated lines so that over the years large quantities of goods can be spread out evenly in the society. Some items may have an added value over and above their obvious one—for example, livestock of a particular color may be worth many ordinary beasts or special types of textiles may be highly prized. The history of an object can also add greatly to its value.

The exchange of gifts also illustrates the polarity of male and female and the need for both to be in balance, a concept which is found throughout the Indonesian archipelago. Generally, Indonesians view everything in the universe as being either masculine or feminine. In the ritual exchange of goods for a marriage, both the male and female sides—the families of the groom and the bride—must make some contribution. The gifts themselves are also seen as either masculine in nature, like livestock, or feminine, like textiles. Ideally, there should be a balance between these two qualities, and this may be achieved in a variety of ways. A simple example is found in Sumba where a ritual gift of horses must consist of a pair, one male and one female. A more widespread example is seen in the banners that commonly appear as festival decoration in many parts of Indonesia: a piece of cloth (feminine) is attached to a spear-shaped pole (weapons are always masculine).

In Sumba and Flores there are gold or silver earrings that symbolize the female side of this polarity. These are called *mamuli* ("golden pendant") in Sumba, and their shape is said to represent the female sex organ (see fig. 52); when

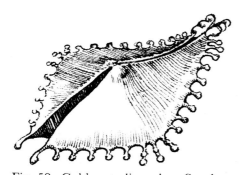

Fig. 52. Gold *mamuli* earring. Sumba.

mamuli are exchanged they are always paired with a "masculine" chain to complete the balance. In Sumba, according to traditional law, when *mamuli* are part of the brideprice the husband is said to own the body of the woman and all the children of that marriage.

In West Sumba, most weavings are decorated with stripes and simple ikat patterns like arrowheads and diamonds, quite unlike the visually exciting hinggi of East Sumba. The only ikat motif of interest is shaped like the *mamuli* earrings. The *mamuli* figure is also seen on cloth from the Lio district of Flores, sometimes hanging from the mouth of a snake or from the branches of a "tree of life." The distinct shape of the *mamuli* also appears in Savu on selimut and as far away as southern Sumatra on the woven textiles common to that area. *Mamuli*-like earrings can also be seen dangling from the ears of the central figure on the *pua kumbu* from Borneo in figure 49.

Betel nut, chewed for its mild intoxicating effect not unlike that produced by tobacco, is an important part of the brideprice and plays a role in the social life of all Ancient Peoples. It is offered to guests as a sign of respect and even if a guest does not chew it, etiquette requires him to at least put some in his pocket. In Sumba, when we visited the homes of weavers, the host would often give us a small basket of betel nut. According to Sumbanese social etiquette, this basket and its contents were a gift which we could offer in return back to our hosts.

Almost three thousand kilometers away in North Sumatra, betel nut plays an important role in the ceremonies of the Bataks. Before *ulos* cloths are exchanged at any ceremony, the Bataks make a ritual of chewing betel nut, which they believe brings the participants closer together. Bataks say that they become "of the same blood" through this sharing.

This feeling of kinship is necessary because when an *ulos* is passed from one person to another, some of the essence of the giver is passed along with the cloth to the receiver. In these gift exchanges, as in other rituals, there is a deeper significance than can be seen in the superficial act. When goods change hands, a bond is formed, ties are strengthened, or some result is sought. Bataks believe an *ulos* in itself is just cloth; it has no intrinsic power to cure illness, for example, or bring prosperity. Instead, the *ulos* functions as a means of transferring power. Thus, the most important factor when a gift of textiles is made for a particular aim is the spiritual force of the donor; an *ulos* can guard against evil spirits or sickness, but only to the extent that the person who presented it is strong.

This concept of power being transmitted through an object does not apply just to textiles, nor is it found only among the Bataks. When visiting villages in Sumba, Savu, and other places in East Nusatenggara, each of us was always served more rice than one person could possibly eat. We later learned that a guest is always served all the food that has been prepared so that whatever is left in the guest's bowl may later be consumed by the family of the host; these leftovers are said to be "blessed" with some of the spirit of the guest, and this spirit then passes onto the family as they eat the rice.

More than power may be transferred through textiles. King Manubulu of Rote Island in East Nusatenggara told us that in his kingdom a special weaving was used to pass on legends and stories. When we met King Manubulu he was in his seventies but showed the vitality of a much younger man. He is king of the Korabafu district, but for a while after World War II he was king of all Rote. He laughed as he told us about being king of the entire island, saying that all he got from the job was splitting headaches and sleepless nights. Customs have changed a lot in King Manubulu's lifetime, and he enjoyed telling stories about the old and new as much as his listeners enjoyed hearing them.

One of his family's heirlooms is a selimut called *lafa'ina*, made up of alternating black and ikat-decorated bands. This cloth was once worn to war by kings of Rote, but according to King Manubulu it had another important function. The *lafa'ina* was hung over the body of a dead king to protect the corpse from falling dust; the only other cloth that could be used for this purpose was the fabled Indian patola cloth. Designated relatives of the dead king were required to bring a *lafa'ina* and one buffalo to the burial or pay a fine of one kilogram of gold to the king's family. King Manubulu thought this enormous fine was hilarious; it would certainly ensure that the *lafa'ina* and the buffalo always arrived. Although textiles play an integral role in Rote burial ceremonies, the *lafa'ina* was not interred with the body. Instead, it was kept by the family of the dead king until they were required to bring it to another burial themselves. As the *lafa'ina* was passed from one family to another (and one kingdom to another) at the time of a death, the history connected to the cloth was learned by the new holders, and the story of the person who had just died was added to its legend.

All East Nusatenggara tribes, as well as most other Ancient Peoples, have oral cultures, and heirloom weavings, such as the *lafa'ina* with its accumulated legends, are probably one of many ways developed by the tribes to help them preserve historical information. Using such devices, events of several hundred years ago can still be described; no doubt there is a bit of embroidering on the facts, but at least the past is kept alive in the memory of the people.

Textiles in Burial Ceremonies

In Rote, the dead are buried in their tribal costume, and these weavings are quite different from the *lafa'ina*. Rote selimut are patterned with a variety of floral motifs that are formed by small squares of color, and these give a mosaic effect to the design (see plate 17). Unlike in Sumba, no animal or symbolic patterns are used. The layout and the motifs of the Rote weavings have been greatly influenced by the Indian patola cloths. According to King Manubulu, the peoples of Rote and Savu are closely related, and Rote sarong are quite similar to sarong woven in Savu, especially in the layout of the pattern and the color.

Not just in Rote but among all Ancient Peoples, the tribal weavings play established roles in the burial ceremonies, as shrouds for the deceased and as clothing for the mourners. Followers of the animistic religions as well as converts to Christianity feel they must be buried in their traditional weavings. Bataks are interred wearing an *ulos,* and designated relatives must bring other *ulos* to be placed on top of the coffin. These textile offerings are not buried but are instead taken home by the family of the deceased. When *ulos* are required for a ceremony, there is a heavy penalty if they are not provided, which indicates the significance attached to them. Failure to bring *ulos* to the burial can severely strain relations among the family members.

Burial ceremonies are a great event in the lives of the Ancient Peoples, reflecting the importance of ancestor cults and the afterlife. If a person of high stature dies, the burial can be delayed for years because of the lengthy preparations necessary for the ceremony. During this interim period, the body may temporarily be buried until the arrangements are completed; then the body is disinterred and reburied. These elaborate affairs usually involve animal sacrifices, feasting, and exchanges of gifts, and may go on for days. The building of stone monuments in memory of the deceased is a Megalithic tradition once common among Ancient Peoples. Large tombs are still features of many villages, but the custom of erecting them has almost disappeared.

A burial took place when we were visiting the Sa'dan Torajan district in South Sulawesi. The burial ceremonies of the Sa'dan tribe are notable among Ancient Peoples so we felt fortunate to be able to witness part of this event. Death chants were sung for days prior to the actual burial. On the day of the main ceremony, guests from surrounding villages came laden with gifts of

Fig. 53. At a traditional funeral ceremony, the Sa'dan Torajans use warp ikat cloths from Rongkong to decorate a pavilion for welcoming guests. Near Rantepao, South Sulawesi.

bamboo tubes filled with palm wine, pigs lashed to carrying poles, and tethered water buffalo—provisions for the big feast. Each group of guests entered the village in single file and paraded around the courtyard displaying their gifts to the hosts and to those who had arrived previously. The new arrivals were received by the hosts in a specially constructed pavilion, the sides of which were hung with textiles (see fig. 53). After being offered betel nut, the guests were given a place to sit under one of the rice-storage barns with a good view of the village common. Six water buffalo, including a white-faced bull worth ten plain buffalo because of its rarity, were sacrificed and the meat was divided among the guests. For a king or very wealthy person, sometimes more than one hundred buffalo are slaughtered, although this kind of extravagant display is being discouraged by the government. Pigs were also slaughtered to provide food for the feast. There was drinking and dancing, and on the whole, like most burial ceremonies among the Ancient Peoples, it was more of a festive affair than a time of grief.

The Sa'dan Torajans do not make warp-ikat weavings themselves. For their burials, they prize

ikat cloths woven by the Western Torajans in the districts of Rongkong and Galumpang, and they obtain these boldly patterned textiles by trade. Selimut from both regions are red, black, and white with repeating geometric designs in the Dong-Son style; the patterns of Rongkong tend to be angular while those of Galumpang are more curvilinear, but otherwise they are quite similar. It is these cloths that decorate the pavilion in figure 53. The motif most commonly seen on these textiles is called *se'kon* (see plate 18), and in some areas the cloths are referred to as *papewao* or "fabrics that serve to clothe the dead."* Thus, in addition to being used as decorations, the weavings are sometimes used as shrouds for the corpse.

After a Torajan burial ceremony, the body is usually placed into a hole carved into the side of a cliff. Carved wooden effigies with movable arms, legs, and genitalia are made for prominent people and are clothed to represent the deceased (see fig. 54). Groups of these eerie figures stare with fixed expressions from balconies in front of the tomb entrance. At one time, these effigies

* Frits A. Wagner, *Indonesia: The Art of an Island Group* (New York: Crown Publishers, 1959), pp. 53–54.

Fig. 54. Torajan ancestor figures are carved and costumed to represent persons of importance who have died. These cleverly made mannequins have movable arms, legs, and heads. Londa, South Sulawesi.

were reportedly clad in bark cloth that was changed in a ritual once a year, but nowadays they are dressed in woven cloths like those worn by the villagers. Sa'dan people prefer plain black clothing for everyday wear and occasionally woven-patterned fabrics for ceremonial dress.

Among the animistic peoples of East Nusatenggara, the body of the deceased is dressed in tribal weavings, tied into the fetal position, and placed in a bamboo chair. When the body is buried or placed in a tomb, usually with offerings such as betel nut, food, weavings, and Chinese ceramics, the bamboo chair is discarded in a special place believed to be haunted to distract any evil spirits that might want to interfere with the soul of the dead.

On Savu Island, royalty and common people alike are buried wearing weavings associated with their clan, but a special burial shroud is reserved for the shaman-priest of the native religion. Many Ancient Peoples once depended on these shamans as authorities on traditional law, and consequently they wielded great power in the society. In Savu, these shamans are still active and are called *deo rai*; they decide the times for planting and harvesting, perform rain-making ceremonies, and cure the sick. The death of a *deo rai* is kept secret while several other people in the traditional hierarchy prepare him for burial. They cut off his nails, hair, and tongue, wrap his body in the burial shroud, and bury him near sacred rocks during a secret ceremony in the middle of the night. Only afterward do they announce his death to the other villagers.

This burial cloth for a shaman is called *wai meah hi i'taba* by Savunese. It is a coarse, loosely woven homespun fabric with some crude ikat decoration, quite different from the highly refined weavings associated with Savunese. A woman must weave this shroud alone in the dead of the night. The cloth is then kept until it is needed in a taboo basket that no unauthorized person is allowed to touch; baskets like this are often used to store sacred textiles and ritual objects. Despite the primitive appearance of this burial cloth, Savunese believe it to be very powerful. Nowadays, when Savunese of the native religion convert to Christianity, they must open up the taboo baskets and throw away these cloths as proof of the strength of their new beliefs.

In a village in western Savu, accompanied by a young Savunese teacher, we visited a ceremonial house where taboo baskets are kept; inside there were many of these containers hanging from the rafters. We asked a village woman what kind of weavings were kept in the baskets. A long discussion in Savunese ensued in which, we later learned, our enthusiastic friend tried to persuade the woman to open the baskets and show us the cloths. The woman became so upset at the idea of doing so that she began to weep and our friend backed off. Only on one special day each year may the baskets be safely opened; on this day the cloths are aired and replaced until the next year or until the death of a *deo rai*.

Another example of how weavings are used in burials also comes from Savu. When an important person died, a horse was sometimes "sent" along to aid him in his journeys after death. The dead man's family provided a selimut to be placed across the horse's back and a friend of the deceased was invited to ride the horse to the gravesite, where it was sacrificed. To be chosen as the rider was a great honor and after the ceremony the friend would keep the weaving that had been on the horse as a remembrance or keepsake of the dead man.

The theme of the horse and rider can be seen again in one of the most interesting of all traditional burial ceremonies found among the Ancient Peoples, that of an East Sumbanese king. The kings of Sumba are gradually dying off, and though the modern burial ceremony is still impressive, it is not as lavish an affair as it was in the past, when months were spent preparing for it. Shortly after death, the body of the king was tied in a crouching position, wrapped in hinggi—sometimes as many as two hundred—and kept in a specially constructed house until the day of the ceremony. Guests coming from all over Sumba brought gifts of textiles and jewelry to be displayed with the body.

When all the guests had arrived and the preparations were complete, a burial procession to the gravesite began, led by a slave dressed in the king's clothing and riding the king's favorite horse. As the procession moved, this slave fell into a trance, and through him the king spoke, issuing his last orders before his spirit left for the afterlife. At the gravesite, the horse was killed, and it is said that the slave, too, was sacrificed so that he might continue to serve his master. The "horse and rider" motif often seen on

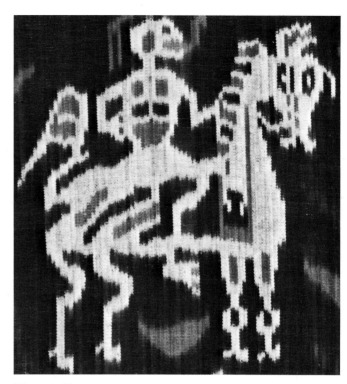

Fig. 55. "Horse and rider" motif on a warp ikat *hinggi kombu*. Red, rusty black, blue, and white. From East Sumba. Toyama Kinenkan Foundation collection.

Sumbanese hinggi is a representation of this custom (see fig. 55). A piece of Chinese ceramic ware was placed on the head of the dead king and his body, bundled in *hinggi kombu*, was put into a stone tomb along with offerings of food, betel nut, and gold jewelry. In keeping with the importance of the burial rites, Sumbanese say that the finest hinggi were always saved to place in the tomb or bury with the king.

3 Other Ikat Cloths and Tie-Dyeing

Many of the cultural developments that took place in the Indonesian archipelago were spurred by groups of people who migrated to the islands bringing with them new ideas. First a Neolithic culture (around 2500 B.C.) and later a Megalithic (1500 B.C.) culture were introduced by early immigrants. The results of these influences can still be seen in some tribal cultures today. Megalithic stone monuments, for example, continue to play a vital role in the rituals of the societies on islands such as Sumba and Nias and in the Torajan region of central Sulawesi. Other Neolithic and Megalithic characteristics that remain intact include animistic religions and craft techniques such as bark cloth.

The great wave of migrations from southern China and Annam (northern Vietnam) between the eighth and second centuries B.C. brought the Dong-Son culture that is so important in the context of warp ikat weaving. A bit later came the somewhat less influential Late Chou culture. The technique of warp ikat and distinctive motifs such as the hook-and-rhomb pattern were introduced during this period. The influence of the Dong-Son culture was so widespread in Indonesia that it may be viewed as a background against which further development took place. Ancient Peoples in the more inaccessible regions were passed over by the succeeding influences, and this explains their basically Dong-Son culture of the present day.

The Indian Legacy

The next strong influence on the islands of Indonesia came from India and left an imprint particularly on Java and Bali. It is difficult to date precisely the archipelago's earliest contacts with India, but there is evidence that small trading posts were already well established in Sumatra and Java by the second century A.D.

By the seventh century A.D. the power that would eventually become the maritime and commercial empire of Srivijaya (732–1010) and hold sway over lands as far away as northern Thailand was starting to exert its influence. The capital of the Srivijaya kingdom was in the area of Palembang, South Sumatra, a perfect location to monitor traffic in the strategic Straits of Malacca and a crossroads for cultural trends of that time. The kingdom's dominant religion was Mahayana Buddhism, an Indian contribution. This sect was dominant in India at that time, and Indian priests were making their voices heard as far away as Sumatra and Java.

Unfortunately, few physical traces of the great Srivijaya kingdom survive in Sumatra; instead, we must travel to Central Java to see its monuments. In particular, the complex of temples on the Dieng Plateau of Central Java, built by the kings of the Shailendra dynasty of the Srivijaya kingdom in the early eighth century, offer indisputable evidence of India's influence in Central Java. Parallels can be drawn between the style of architecture on the Dieng Plateau and that of some existing temples in India built at about the same time.

The greatest monument of the Shailendra dynasty and its deep involvement with Buddhism is Borobodur, an enormous stupa located near Jogjakarta in Central Java. Borobodur, with five levels of bas-reliefs depicting the life of

Buddha, is one of the largest Buddhist monuments in Southeast Asia and was used by kings and priests as a place of meditation.

By the mid-ninth century, a second great Indian religion, Hinduism, had reached the royal courts of Java; but instead of Buddhism being rejected in favor of Hinduism, the two intertwined and coexisted with the native Javanese animism inside the palaces. The temple complex at Prambanan near Jogjakarta, built in the late ninth century, is the legacy of this Hindu period.

In the tenth century the court in Central Java suddenly moved, for reasons that are still a mystery, to East Java, and the Central Java area became inactive for a few hundred years. From the vicinity of present-day Malang, the court exerted strong influence over most of the archipelago during the Singasari (1222–93) and Majapahit (1294–1520) dynasties. During these periods, Indian influence began to wane and temple architecture reverted back to a more Javanese style; animistic designs with connections harking back to the Dong-Son began to reappear as Indian elements began to fade.

Religion and architecture were not the only legacies of the period of Indian influence. The introduction of the Pallava script to Java from southern India made it possible for the first time to write down native legends and stories that until then had been transmitted orally. With the script came the *Mahabharata* and the *Ramayana*, India's two great Hindu epics that became the basis of the dance and drama of both Bali and Java.

India may have also provided an aristocracy and made less obvious contributions to some of the outer islands of Indonesia. We heard legends in remote areas of East Nusatenggara telling of how the earliest ancestors of the royal houses came from India or from over the "Western Sea." In West Sumba, the son of a clan chief related the local version of East Nusatenggara history. His people tell of a family—a mother and father, two sons, and a daughter—that left India and sailed east toward Indonesia. They reached Bali, and there the daughter remained, bringing with her a skill in music and dance that is the heritage of Balinese today. The rest of the family continued sailing eastward until they reached West Sumba, where the eldest son, a fierce warrior, stayed to teach the ways of battle to native Sumbanese. The mother and father,

who had great knowledge of the arts of magic, settled on the tiny island of Savu while their youngest son disembarked in Belu, central Timor—even today, the people of Belu and Savu claim a close kinship. And Savunese are widely reputed by East Nusatenggara tribes to have magical powers. Stories of their feats continue to be told. Around the turn of the century, Savunese warriors reputedly walked across the sea to conquer part of neighboring Sumba.

India, then, has been generous in its contributions to the religions, architecture, and literature of Indonesia. And, if the legends can be believed, it may also have been the ancestral homeland of some of Indonesia's people. In addition, India furnished innovative techniques of fabric decoration such as weft ikat, tie-dyeing, and supplementary weft weaving. As important as these techniques were the new motifs derived from imported Indian textiles.

The Patola

One of these imports in particular, a striking silk cloth called the *patola*, has had a tremendous effect on the textile motifs in many areas of the Indonesian archipelago. We have, in fact, already had occasion to refer to it several times in connection with warp ikat motifs. This influential weaving couples attractive patterns with an unusual double ikat technique; both its warp and weft threads are separately bound and dyed so that they interlock on the loosely woven cloth to create a decorative pattern (see plates 19 and 20). Generally, in Java and Sumatra the cloth is known as *cindai* or *cinde*, a word which means "ikat on silk" in the Gujurat area of India. From Bali eastward, it is most commonly referred to by the name we use here, patola, which means "variegated silk cloth" in a number of modern Indian languages.

Double ikat is an extremely difficult technique and is quite rare in the world. In India, the technique is thought to have originated in Benares, from where it spread across the country. As early as the eleventh century, the city of Pattan in Gujurat (northwestern India) was famous for its silk textiles that were called patola, and by the seventeenth century this name definitely referred to these double ikat cloths.

Unfortunately, only a few families in Pattan still weave patola fabric today; among them it is worn as a wedding *sari*—an Indian garment worn wrapped around the body—and is woven in *sari* lengths (about 5 to 7 meters by 1.2 meters). Outside India, the technique is found on the main islands of Japan and Okinawa, and in Tenganan Pegringsingan, a small village in southeastern Bali.

The first traders to bring the patola cloth to Indonesia were probably Moslem Indian merchants from Gujurat. These same traders may have also been instrumental in the spread of Islam through the archipelago. The patola was first mentioned in European records in the early sixteenth century, and by the seventeenth century the cloth was often seen on the Malay Peninsula and in Indonesia. Sometime toward the end of the seventeenth century, the Dutch East India Company gained a monopoly on the trade of this sought-after textile and carried it to the Philippines, Java, Borneo, and Sumatra. It was as trade items under this monopoly that most of the patola cloths entered the Indonesian archipelago during the seventeenth and eighteenth centuries.* In the eighteenth century, patola cloths were in such great demand that factories were set up on the Malay Peninsula and in Europe to produce cheap cotton copies for export to Indonesia.

The soft silky texture and shimmering colors of the true Indian patola, as well as its striking designs and motifs, must have captivated the Indonesians, accustomed as they were to somber-colored homespun cotton weavings. The bright colors of the patola were originally produced with natural dyes, but in the 1800s weavers in India switched to aniline dyes, dyes produced synthetically from coal-tar products. Silk was not indigenous to Indonesia and its texture was greatly admired by the wealthier upper classes.

Wherever the patola cloths went in Indonesia, they influenced local textiles and became coveted possessions and treasured heirlooms. They also assumed an important role in many local traditions, and even magical powers were attributed to them.

In Central Java, the patola cloth was so highly admired that trousers made of the fabric became part of the ceremonial dress for the sultans of Jogjakarta and Solo (see fig. 129, chapter 6).

* The historical information on patola was taken from two sources: A. N. Gulati, *The Patola of Gujurat* (Bombay: Museums Association of India, 1951), and Alfred Bühler, "Patola Influences in Southeast Asia," *Journal of Indian Textile History* 4 (1959).

Today fragments of the original double ikat cloths are sewn into belts and other accessories that are worn as part of the traditional wedding costume for common people. Wearing some of the cloth so closely associated with the sultan is intended to make the bride and groom feel like royalty on the day of their marriage.

Balinese Hindus believe that the patola provides protection against evil spirits, and they display it in many religious ceremonies. The cloths were once hung from cremation towers and also appeared as altar cloths. The patola cloths in plates 19 and 20, which probably date from the nineteenth century, were found in Bali. The patola has another unusual attribute in Bali. A woman in Klungkung, eastern Bali, told us that many islanders believe that if an insane person can be persuaded to sniff the smoke from a burnt thread of the patola, his sanity will be instantly restored.

In East Nusatenggara, too, textiles are often thought to possess the power to protect or to bring good luck, and certain weavings are reserved for ritual uses only. In some areas of this region, the patola cloths have assumed an importance in local customs, and it is here that they have also had the most influence upon local textile designs. The patola was a symbol of high rank in East Nusatenggara and was owned and used only by kings, members of the aristocracy, and priests. It was worn by the kings of Savu to their wedding feasts and hung to shelter the bodies of dead kings in Rote. The patola's great value made it a highly desirable part of the marriage gifts among the upper classes.

We found that the patola was still a source of mystery and legend when we tried to trace one in East Nusatenggara. In western Savu, we were told that there was a "fourth generation" descendant of the first patola cloth on the island, which Savunese legend says was brought from India by an early ancestor. The heirloom, whether it was a real Indian patola or a Savunese copy, was kept in one of the taboo baskets that hold sacred objects in a ceremonial house, and no outsider was permitted to see it. In Sumba, too, people said that patola cloths are still kept with other sacred objects in the topmost part of the high roofs of the traditional houses, a special storage place for sacred items, but we could not persuade anyone to take one down. In Rote, we were told that patola cloths could still be seen in eastern Flores or in Alor, while in Flores people told us to seek them in Sumba. We followed up many of the rumors of the whereabouts of the genuine patola but the cloth always remained elusive and we never saw one.

But we could see its influence. The humid, tropical climate of Indonesia is not kind to textiles, even when they are well cared for. As the imported silk patola began to disintegrate, the weavers made new cloths, more or less copying the original ones using cotton and a regular warp ikat technique so that these substitutes could assume the roles that the real patola had begun to play in local traditions. It is believed in East Nusatenggara and Bali that if one makes a reproduction of a magical cloth such as the patola, the copy will retain some of the attributes of the original. These patola copies were thus accepted in place of the Indian originals for the brideprice and for burials and other rituals.

The most obvious effect of the patola, and the one that has lasted until today, was on the motifs and layouts of the patterns on textiles of such diverse areas as Java, Bali, Sumatra, and the East Nusatenggara islands.

In India the patola cloths featured a wide variety of patterns, but only a few of these appear to have been brought to Indonesia. These new motifs, however, proved to be so attractive to Indonesian weavers that they were added to local patterns and in some cases replaced them. Patola motifs appear on many types of textiles; in fact, the influence of the patola was so pervasive that textile traditions which were not affected, such as those of the Bataks, Torajans, Dyaks, Timorese, Minangkabau (West Sumatra), and the people of Lampung (southwestern Sumatra), are notable.

A round eight-pointed floral motif, called *jilimprang* in Java, is the most popular patola motif among Indonesian textile weavers (see fig. 56). In Java, *jilimprang* appears on batik, and in East Nusatenggara, especially on Savu, Rote, and Flores, it is a very common pattern on warp ikat textiles.

57

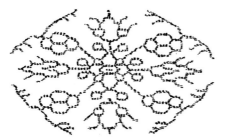

Fig. 56. *Jilimprang* motif. Savu.

58

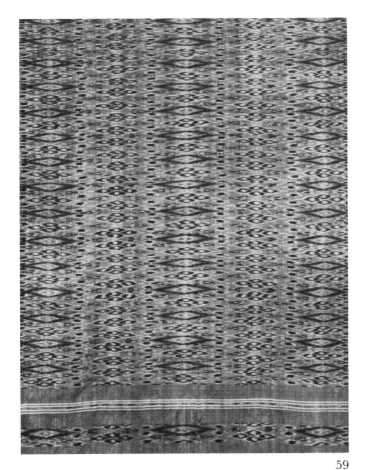

59

60

61

Figs. 57–61. These five cloths illustrate the influence of the Indian patola cloth on Indonesian textile design. Figure 57, a supplementary weft selindang from Palembang, South Sumatra, features the *tumpal* motif and striped border. Figure 58, a warp ikat selimut from Rote, displays another variation of the patola layout. Figure 59 is a northern Balinese silk weft ikat cloth with pattern and layout inspired by the patola. Figure 60, a sarong from the Lio district of Flores, uses a modified patola pattern. Figure 61 is the *selenda sinde* cloth from Lio that exactly duplicates the design of the original patola. These cloths appear in color in plates 30, 17, 27, 12, and 11, respectively.

The other patola-derived pattern most commonly seen on Indonesian textiles consists of interconnecting rhomb shapes (see plate 20). Called *patola ratu,* the name given to it by Sumbanese on whose textiles it frequently appears, it has already been discussed in chapter 2 in connection with central-band motifs on hinggi and ikat-decorated sarong (see plate 5).

A few other patola designs found on the imported patola cloths are featured on Indonesian textiles. One is a repeating pattern of heart shapes, common on textiles from Lomblen. Another type of patola features elephant figures, and may be the original source of the elephant motifs found in Flores and Sumba.

The short ends of the patola cloth bear a pattern of repeating triangles known in Indonesia as *tumpal* (see plate 19). This *tumpal* design is most often described by Indonesians as a spearhead pattern, but its true origins have been lost, as have those of many motifs. Some believe that *tumpal* is a stylization of bamboo shoots (a fertility symbol) or possibly even a human figure. Although this motif appears on the Indian patola, it is very common on a variety of Indonesian textiles and also appears on the Dong-Son bronze drums. Some scholars have suggested that the motif may have originated in Indonesia, been borrowed by Indian sources, copied, and then reexported to Indonesia. If this were true, the example of India borrowing from Indonesia would be quite a reversal of the usual trend. In any case, the patola did certainly introduce (or reintroduce) the motif to many areas of the archipelego.

The layout of the pattern on the patola is important to note, for its influence on textile design in Indonesia was as strong as that of individual motifs like the *jilimprang*. Completing the *tumpal* borders on the short ends of the patola is a row of round or heart shapes, and along the cloth's lengthwise edges (selvages) are several stripes enclosing smaller ikat figures (see plate 20). The *tumpal* border and these side motifs enclose the main pattern, which is variable and may be the round *jilimprang* motif or any one of the other patola motifs. This type of layout with the selvage stripes and tumpal borders, borrowed from the patola, can be seen on textiles from such diverse areas as Palembang on Sumatra, Bali, Rote, Flores, and other East Nusatenggara islands (see figs. 57–61).

Weavers tend to choose different aspects of the patola to incorporate into their own textiles. Some East Nusatenggara weavers concentrated on the layout of the design; the cloths, for example, of Palembang, Rote, and Bali in figures 57, 58, and 59 are designed with the *tumpal* borders and the striped edges enclosing the main pattern. Sometimes a modified patola pattern is used, like that in figure 60. The *selenda sinde* cloth in figure 61, made in the Lio district of eastern Flores, duplicates both the layout and the *jilimprang* motif of the patola, but other weavers in Flores and Rote often follow the layout while choosing their own tribal motifs for the dominant design.

In other areas, only specific motifs of the patola were borrowed for use on traditional cloths. In East Sumba, as we have seen, the *patola ratu* motif appears on the ikat sarong that bears the same name (see plate 5) and in the central band of many *hinggi kombu*. The sarong worn by women in Savu, Rote, and Flores often feature just the round *jilimprang* motif used like a local design to decorate ikat bands. Javanese batik may also feature the *jilimprang* motif. None of these cloths show any sign of the patola layout with the *tumpal* border and side stripes; the patola patterns are substituted for local motifs as design elements but there has been no change in the traditional layout of the cloth as a whole.

The patola had a particularly strong influence on the textiles of Flores and of the islands of Lomblen, Adonara, Alor, and Solor that are located directly to the east. To the north of Flores lies Ambon (South Malukus), one of the most important of the Spice Islands and, in the past, a major trading center for the patola. Flores's position made it an excellent gateway for the patola to enter the other islands nearby, and probably most of the patola cloths found in the area came through it. Tracing the influence of the patola in several regions of Flores shows more precisely the kind of influence the textile had on native motifs.

In Flores, over the years, patola-derived patterns have become associated with the snake deity, which as we saw in chapter 2 is a very important part of the animistic religion of that island. To the people of eastern Flores, the original patola motifs, such as *patola ratu* and *jilimprang*, looked like snakeskin, and once this similarity was noted the patola motifs began to become confused with traditional Flores patterns, which often depicted snakeskin themselves. In parts of Flores, the Indian patola cloths are called *sinde* (or *side*), a variation of the word *cindai* used in Java. Eventually, the word *sinde* began to refer to any pattern related to snakes. For example, a sarong with a motif that pictures a pair of entwined snakes (looking rather like the Greek letter "omega") is called *sinde*, but it is unlike any known patola motif. On the other hand, the word *sinde* appears in the name of the selimut that faithfully copies the patola layout, the *selenda sinde*.

Fig. 62. The *jilimprang* motif taken from the Indian patola cloth can be seen bound on the threads stretched on this ikat frame. Maumere, Flores.

As mentioned in chapter 2, many of the old traditions that were once adhered to in a wider area of Flores are still alive in the Lio district. Here, villagers are familiar with the Indian patola cloth, and they faithfully reproduce its motifs on some of their own weavings. Although they have borrowed the Flores name for patola, *sinde,* to refer to certain native motifs that are related to snakeskin or snakes, when they see the true patola motifs they know exactly where they came from. In Nggela village, villagers said they no longer had any Indian patola cloths, only their patola copies—the *selenda sinde* made in regular warp ikat—and they told us to look for a real patola in Sumba where they were convinced that priests of the traditional religion still owned the cloths.

In neighboring Sikka, where customs and textile motifs were very similar to those in Lio before the people's conversion to Catholicism several hundred years ago, quite another situation has developed. Here all memory of the original patola cloth has been lost while its pattern clearly remains. No one we talked with

in this district had ever heard of a patola, a *sinde,* or any other cloth from India. To help us in our search, the villagers suggested that we talk to the widow of the last ruling king because the old nobility is usually the ultimate authority on matters of tradition and folklore. This seemed a good idea, for in East Nusatenggara only a member of the nobility would have owned a real patola. The queen was a very old woman, and we felt sure that she would know something about the history of the patola in Sikka, but she too shook her head saying that she had never heard of such a cloth. As we sat on her porch, having reached another dead-end in our search for this elusive cloth, woman after woman passed by the queen's house wearing handmade sarong that were decorated with exact copies of the patola's *jilimprang* motif. Each woman, when asked, had a different name for the motif: some called it *renda* or *rempe* while others said it was *medang* or *leo,* but there was no mistake— the designs were often perfect replicas of the eight-pointed flower motif so typical of the patola (see fig. 62). In Sikka, the motif was still actively in use, but its origins had been completely forgotten.

There can be no doubt that India had a great impact on developing cultures in Indonesia, and the Indian patola cloth has left its imprint, acknowledged or not, on many of Indonesia's contemporary textiles. Its patterns and layout have been borrowed, but as far as we could determine, no one has tried to copy the patola in the double ikat technique that makes it so special.

Gringsing Double Ikat Cloth

Rare double ikat cloths are made in a single village in southeastern Bali, but there is little evidence to link the technique here to the patola of Gujurat in India. Called *gringsing*, these cloths from Tenganan village show no discernible influence of the patola in their motifs despite the effect the Indian cloth had on textiles in other parts of Bali. However, the technique used to create the motifs of the gringsing is the same as that used on the patola: both the warp and weft threads of gringsing cloth are ikat-patterned in such a way that they produce an integrated motif on the finished fabric.

Many textiles bear the name of the place where they are woven, but the gringsing cloth is so important that its village, formally known as Tenganan Pegringsingan, takes part of its name from the cloth that is made there. Gringsing and the people who make it are surrounded by an aura of mystery. Tenganan is one of several villages in Bali that are inhabited by the Bali Aga or "pure Balinese," people who trace their history back to the time before Hinduism was introduced to the island.

The walled village of Tenganan has remained aloof, by choice, from the rest of Bali and continues to adhere to its own customs. Balinese say that if a Bali Aga marries an outsider, he or she is forever banned from reentering the village. Today, the Bali Aga practice a type of Hinduism, but their beliefs do not always coincide with those of the majority of Hindu Balinese. Overtones of animism and pre-Hindu customs still survive, a reflection of the Bali Aga's relation to Ancient Peoples found elsewhere in Indonesia.

The Bali Aga fascinate other Balinese, who seem convinced that many bizarre rituals and strange customs are secretly practiced in their villages. Balinese eagerly told us how the young men of Tenganan choose their brides by tossing flowers across a curtain; whoever is hit by the flower becomes the future bride. This is a rather romantic story. Other tales border on the macabre. A Balinese friend described with horrified delight how weavers in Tenganan formerly dyed the gringsing cloth with human blood obtained by slashing the wrists of old people of the village just before they died. The color of the finished cloth does resemble dried blood. By the time we first visited Tenganan, we had heard the "dyed in blood" story from several narrators, each one adding more gory details. Our hosts in Tenganan dismissed this story with a shrug, and said "maybe, in the past."

Gringsing is treasured throughout Bali because it is believed to offer special protection against evil vibrations; the name *gringsing* is thought to have originally meant "illness averting" among the Bali Aga, and undoubtedly the strange stories about the Bali Aga and their cloth have enhanced gringsing's reputation among the other islanders. Because of its reputed powers, a double ikat gringsing cloth is required for many religious ceremonies in Bali. At some time during his or her lifetime, a Balinese must have his eyeteeth filed flat so as not to enter heaven looking like a "fanged demon," and during the tooth-filing ceremony a piece of gringsing with uncut warp threads must be placed under the participant's head. Gringsing are also wrapped around temple relics and coffins to keep away evil spirits, and they are used at the ceremony of a child's first haircut and at some marriage rites.

Gringsing are worn by dancers of the *baris tekok jago,* a ritual dance performed at cremation ceremonies. These spear-carrying dancers perform before the actual cremation in order to drive away evil and smooth the path to heaven for the soul of the deceased (see plate 23). A double ikat gringsing selindang can also be used as a *saput,* or formal waistcloth. A Balinese must wear this cloth to be properly dressed for entering a temple or participating in a formal occasion.

We found that the Bali Aga today do not believe their gringsing cloth has magical properties of the kind other Balinese attribute to it. The villagers of Tenganan wear their gringsing sarong and selindang as festive dress for special occasions. These are the very best pieces of gringsing; it takes many years to make a single double ikat cloth, and naturally the weavers

Fig. 63. A small cotton gin is used to clean raw cotton as the first step in making gringsing double ikat cloth. Tenganan, Bali.

Fig. 64. For making thread, a spinning wheel introduced by the Japanese has replaced the simple spindle in Tenganan, Bali.

want to keep their finest work for themselves and their families, selling only pieces that they consider flawed to Balinese outside the village. Of the less than two hundred families living inside the walls of Tenganan, there are only a few still actively engaged in the weaving of gringsing. But at one time, when most women wove the cloth, special ceremonies were held at night for village girls so that they could learn the complicated weaving techniques.

Many of the processes involved in making a double ikat are similar to those used in warp ikat weaving—explained in chapter 1—although there is the additional step of patterning the weft threads. All thread used to make gringsing cloth is handspun cotton made by the weavers with tools not unlike those used by many Ancient Peoples in East Nusatenggara. Briefly, a weaver cleans the seeds from raw cotton with a gin (see fig. 63) and fluffs the cotton fiber with a bow. Until World War II thread was spun on a simple spindle weighted with old Chinese coins, but now Tenganan weavers use a spinning wheel that was introduced to the village by the Japanese during their occupation of Indonesia in the early 1940s (see fig. 64). Once spun, the thread is measured and at the same time formed into a skein on a niddy noddy, or measuring frame, identical to that used in East Nusatenggara.

At this point, before the weaver can proceed with the ikat work, she pretreats the threads for the red dyeing that will come later in the process. *Mengkudu* root is the main component of the red dye in Tenganan just as it is in East Nusatenggara, and this dyestuff requires that the threads be soaked in an oily mixture before they are dyed. In Tenganan, the pretreatment bath is made of *kemiri* nut oil from the candlenut tree and lye made from wood ashes and water. The threads are alternately soaked overnight in this liquid and then aired in the sun for a period of five to twelve days before they are considered ready for the *mengkudu* dyebath.

After the cotton threads have been treated with oil, the weaver can begin to arrange them for binding; in the case of double ikat, the warp threads must be warped and the weft threads must also be specially arranged. The skeins are wound into easy-to-handle balls and then the warp is laid out on a frame that will hold the threads as they are bound. The process for the warp threads is the same as that for warp ikat textiles; as the weaver wraps the threads onto the frame, she counts them and twists a piece of fiber around each group that will make up an ikat section.

Since most gringsing cloths are quite small, the weaver can ikat several of them at one time. Each cloth is treated as a single panel; that is, it is warped separately, the ikat sections are marked, and the threads are secured with string. Then all the warp threads for one weaving may be laid on top of the threads for another so that the work

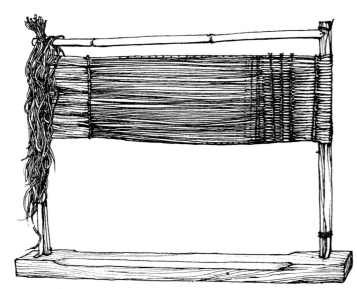

Fig. 65. Tenganan weavers use an upright frame for warping and binding the warp threads. Bali.

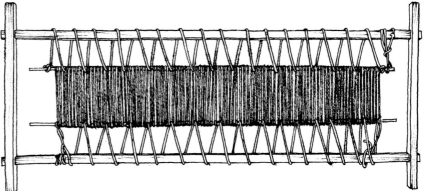

Fig. 66. Tenganan weavers bind the weft threads on this unusual frame. Bali.

on them can be combined. Henceforth, the two (or more) panels are treated as one during the ikat and dyeing processes.

In the case of double ikat, the weft threads will also be bound, so they too must be carefully measured and arranged on a frame. The design of the frame used for laying out and binding the weft threads is different from that of the frame that holds the warp threads, as can be seen by comparing figures 65 and 66—this frame is adjusted to the width of the desired weaving. Today, Tenganan weavers also employ a tool called a bobbin rack to help them lay out the weft. This device, commonly used in making weft ikat weavings, is a recent introduction to Tenganan and consists of a rack that holds up to fifty bobbins.

The weaver saves herself a lot of tedious work with a bobbin rack because she can lay out many weft threads at once. She winds enough thread on each bobbin to produce one complete motif on the woven fabric. Gathering up the weft threads from the bobbins, she wraps them as a group around the inner dowels of the frame. Each thread within the group follows the same path through the warp during weaving. On each

pass of the threads around the frame, the weaver marks the threads with a piece of fiber so that later it will be easy to identify the ikat sections for binding. By handling the weft threads together in this way, the weaver only needs to bind in the pattern once to produce as many identical motifs as there are individual weft threads. After dyeing, this group of threads will be disassembled and rewound onto bobbins for weaving.

The bindings of the warp and weft must be precisely measured so that the perpendicular threads will mesh on the finished weaving to give the proper integrated design. Part of the great skill in weaving double ikat cloth is in planning the design and in making the exact measurements necessary for binding. Some gringsing patterns are geometric, the easiest type of design to produce with this technique. But other common designs show complex curving human figures, demonstrating that technical difficulty in no way limits the weavers of Tenganan (see plate 22).

The manner of binding the warp and weft threads, each on their separate ikat frames, is identical. The weaver draws charcoal guide-

Fig. 67. Bali Aga women often use a finished weaving as a guide when binding the warp threads of a new piece. Tenganan, Bali.

lines perpendicularly across the threads to help ensure that the pattern is perfectly symmetrical. Often she keeps a finished gringsing cloth nearby as a reference, but this is her only aid in remembering the motif (see fig. 67); the designs are not drawn on paper and then transferred to the threads. The weaver glances at the model piece frequently as she wraps the threads with *agel* fiber (called *kubal* in Tenganan) and ties a secure knot.

When both the warp and weft threads are bound, they are ready to be dyed blue. Tenganan weavers no longer do their own indigo dyeing; instead, they send their bundles of thread for dyeing outside the village to the nearby town of Bugbug.

After the threads have been dyed blue (see chapter 1 for a complete explanation of the indigo dyeing process), they are put back on the ikat frames so that some of the bindings can be opened for the red dyebath. Any area that is desired a bright red has been bound during the indigo dyeing and now needs to be uncovered. It is not necessary for Tenganan weavers to bind any of the blue areas since the indigo color is not featured on their cloths. Indigo-colored areas

are always dyed over with *mengkudu* red, which produces the dark, rusty brown color that resembles dried blood.

Tenganan weavers do their own red dyeing, and it is this step that lengthens the time needed to complete one cloth to eight or more (sometimes up to fifteen) years. The *mengkudu* root needed for the red dye is scarce. Tenganan weavers do not have their own trees but must obtain the dyestuff from nearby Nusa Penida, an island that lies off the east coast of Bali. The process of making the dye in Tenganan is very similar to that found in East Nusatenggara. The *mengkudu* root that yields the red pigment is crushed to a pulp with a mortar and pestle and mixed with powdered bark from the symplocos tree, which acts as an aluminum mordant that will fix the pigment on the fiber. These ingredients, soaked in water, make up the dyebath. Lye water is not used as it is in East Nusatenggara, possibly because it is part of the oil pretreatment process.

The pretreated, bound threads are alternately soaked in this dye at night and aired in the sun for three days. After the threads are thoroughly dry, they are stored away for several months

Fig. 68. Patterned warp threads must be arranged in their proper order to prepare them for weaving. Tenganan, Bali.

while the weaver collects enough dyestuff for a new batch. Then the dyeing process is repeated. The threads must be dyed many times, and it often takes years before they have reached the desired color. Although the scarcity of the dyestuff is the main reason for the long periods between dyeings, weavers also insist that the color darkens and improves with aging; possibly this is because the dye continues to oxidize on the fibers.

When the threads have been dyed to the correct shade, the weaver removes all the fiber bindings. The warp threads are laid out on a frame to prepare them for the loom (see fig. 68), and the weaver makes sure that they are in the proper order; at this point, too, she must separate all the panels that were combined and bound together. The weaver also adds plain-colored threads (*mengkudu* red, indigo blue, or white) to border the ikat patterns on each side of a shawl. Because of its greater width, only one-half of a sarong can be woven at a time; the two halves are later sewn together.

To keep the warp threads from shifting during the actual weaving process, the weaver binds them between several split sticks. To complete the preparation of the warp, she brushes it with rice-water starch, stretches it, and transfers it to to the poles of the backstrap loom.

Special care must be taken with the weft threads for a double ikat. The threads that were bound together must now be separated and wound one by one onto bobbins. The dyed areas on each of the long weft threads represent one complete motif, and during weaving, when one of these threads runs out after a number of passes back and forth through the warp, the next thread will begin and repeat the motif.

Double ikat cloths are woven in a loose plain weave with an equal number of warp and weft threads per square centimeter. Thus, all the threads show equally on the woven fabric. (In contrast, warp ikat textiles are also woven in a plain weave, but their warp threads are set closely together and the weft is not beaten in too strongly; the result is a warp-faced fabric in which the warp threads are more visible because there are more of them per square centimeter.) Gringsing, like the patola, is so loosely woven that the fabric resembles gauze.

On the loom, as the weaver lays down each line of the weft, she must always make sure that

Fig. 69. The weaver uses a pick to align the warp and weft threads on the loom. Tenganan, Bali.

Fig. 70. *Wayang patlikur isi* motif. Bali.

the pattern is aligned before she beats the thread into place. If the motif is not clear, she uses a small pick to help straighten the threads so that the final pattern meshes as closely as possible (see fig. 69). We once watched a novice at work weaving her first gringsing, and seeing her struggle showed clearly just how difficult it is to line up the warp and weft so that the pattern interlocks perfectly.

A variety of unique patterns appear on the double ikat cloths of Tenganan, particularly on the sarong and selindang that the villagers wear themselves. However, a few motifs are predominant on the shawls that are found in Bali outside Tenganan.

The most widely seen pattern is a relatively simple geometric design called *sanan empeg*. This motif appears on narrow (about twenty-five centimeters) sashes with uncut warps; these are used by Balinese at tooth-filing ceremonies (see plate 21).

The two other patterns often seen on these "exported" gringsing cloths feature human figures that are called *wayang*. One of these motifs, *wayang patlikur isi*, shows a front-facing figure crowned with a headdress that is very similar to the headgear worn by the *baris tekok jago* dancers who perform at cremation ceremonies (see fig. 70).

The other *wayang* motif, *wayang putri isi*, shows a complex figure of a man with a woman kneeling beside him (see plate 22). These curving asymmetrical figures are a challenge to the weaver of double ikat cloth. The figures are seen in a three-quarters view, a stance which shows the head and feet in profile with the shoulders facing forward. This view of the human body is instantly recognizable and uniquely Indonesian. It is found on temple reliefs that date back to at least the fourteenth century, such as those at the Javanese Hindu temple of Candi Jago near the city of Malang.* This style of portraying the human figure is also seen today in the Javanese and Balinese puppets that are used for the traditional art of shadow plays. These puppets, known as *wayang kulit*, are made from leather and are held by a puppeteer behind a screen—light from behind the puppets throws their shadows onto the screen.

How the weavers of Tenganan Pegringsingan came to weave this unusual cloth with its singular motifs and difficult technique has sparked lively debate among textile scholars. That they developed the technique themselves from a base of warp ikat seems unlikely—so few weavers in the world can do double ikat. Yet there is no concrete evidence indicating that the double ikat

* Alfred Bühler with Urs Ramseyer and Nicole Ramseyer-Gygi, *Patola und Gringsing* (Basel: Das Museum fur Volkerkunde und Schweizerische Museum fur Volkskunde, 1975–76), p. 34.

patola cloth was the inspiration. Because of gringsing's unusual qualities—its difficult technique, unique designs, and rich colors, and the magical properties attributed to it by Balinese—the cloth ranks as one of Indonesia's most precious textiles.

Weft Ikat

The history of weft ikat textiles in Indonesia is quite different from that of warp ikat and double ikat cloths. Warp ikat was introduced into the archipelago well in the distant past and has developed among people who had little contact with outsiders. And, as we have seen, the origins of double ikat in Tenganan are still a mystery.

The technique of weft ikat, which involves the resist-patterning of the crosswise threads, was introduced by Indian and Arab Moslem traders in the fourteenth and fifteenth centuries, at about the same time that Islam was advancing through Sumatra and Java. Most contemporary weft ikat cloths are woven by people who consider themselves devout Moslems. They live in well-traveled areas, often coastal regions, and have had frequent contact with the outside world.

Noteworthy weavers of weft ikat textiles in Indonesia include the descendants of Arabs in East Java (especially in the city of Gresik, near Surabaya), the indigenous people in the area around the city of Palembang in South Sumatra, the people on the coasts of Bali and Lombok, and, particularly, the Bugis people. THE BUGIS: The Bugis are a seafaring group who have settled on many islands of the archipelago; they can be found living in South Sumatra, South Sulawesi, East Java, Lombok, Sumbawa, and the major ports of Indonesian Borneo (Kalimantan). Small groups also live in the seaports of East Nusatenggara. Bugis are not confined to Indonesia; colonies of them also live on the Malay Peninsula, on the Sulu Sea islands of the Philippines, and in Sabah, a Malaysian state in the northeastern part of Borneo.

The Bugis were once feared as pirates, but they have settled down and are now noted in Indonesia for their devotion to the Islamic faith. As a people, they are relatively recent seventeenth-century converts to Islam. They still work on the sea, however, and Bugis sailors often carry interisland trade. Their small sailboats are a familiar sight in most seaports in Indonesia.

Bugis women engage in weaving silk weft ikat cloths that are highly regarded by other Moslem Indonesians. Javanese and Sumatran men prize the Bugis weavings, particularly as garments to wear when they make the pilgrimage to Mecca. The weavings of the Bugis who now live in central South Sulawesi are the most famous, although other Bugis groups, especially those in Palembang, South Sumatra, and in the port of Samarinda in East Kalimantan, also weave fine cloth.

Besides the obvious differences of technique, one point that distinguishes weft ikat from warp ikat cloths is the material. Traditionally, most weft ikat textiles are made of silk. The few areas—notably, East Java and Bali—that today make weft ikat cloths in cotton or rayon originally produced silk fabrics. Sericulture is not indigenous to the islands of Indonesia, so the use of silk is a strong indication that the technique, like the material, was imported.

Silk weft ikat cloths were originally woven by women working at home on a backstrap loom, but recently the craft has developed to a cottage-industry level. The Bugis villagers of Tajuncu in South Sulawesi have even begun building a silk industry using modern methods of cultivation to supply thread for the colorful Bugis sarong that are woven in nearby villages.

Sericulture is virtually nonexistent in Indonesia today, so we found it very interesting to visit an area devoted to silk production. Tajuncu village has totally committed itself to this minor industry. The mulberry trees that furnish leaves to feed the silkworms are an integral part of the elaborate gardens surrounding each house. Beneath the raised floors of the villagers' homes are racks of growing silkworms, and the attics are filled with harvested white cocoons.

The silk cocoons are converted into thread in several workshops along the road that passes through the center of Tajuncu. Making silk thread is quite different from the familiar work of spinning cotton found elsewhere in Indonesia. First, the silk cocoons are placed in scalding hot water to loosen their fibers. With calloused fingers, girls pluck a cocoon from the steaming water and dexterously pick out the end of its fiber. The fiber from each cocoon is called a bave, and ten to fourteen of these fibers are needed to form a single silk thread. The group of baves is fed through a reeling apparatus that twists first in one direction and back in the other, a process that removes the moisture so that the

Fig. 71. Villagers of Tajuncu fashion ingenious devices for reeling silk thread from discarded bicycle parts. Note the silk cocoons in the basin at lower right. South Sulawesi.

fibers cling together. Outside of the government-sponsored cooperative with its semimodern equipment, villagers make their own reeling devices from old bicycle wheels and pedals (see fig. 71).

Silk that has been grown and spun in Tajuncu is sent to the nearby village of Sempange on the edge of Lake Tempe, where it will be woven into cloth. This part of South Sulawesi, known as the Sengkang district, is the center of Bugis weaving. People say that the original inspiration for the cloth came from a sarong left on the shores of Lake Tempe by the gods, and now the edge of the lake is the site of most of the silk weaving in the area.

The houses in Sempange surround the shores of the lake and sit atop tall stilts, providing a cool and shady work area underneath. We visited a small workshop in Sempange where all the looms were conveniently set up under the house while the rooms upstairs were given over to the other processes.

The method of making weft ikat that is practiced in the workshops of Sempange is virtually the same as that used in Bali, East Java, South Sumatra, and Kalimantan, where this cloth is also woven. The weft threads are first laid out on a very simple square frame of the same width as the finished fabric (see fig. 72). The process is much like that used in Tenganan to lay out the

Fig. 72. Weavers in East Java, Bali, and South Sulawesi use a simple frame for laying out and binding the weft threads. Gresik, East Java.

Fig. 73. A rack holding many bobbins saves time in laying out the threads for ikat weavings in East Java and Bali. Gresik, East Java.

weft threads for the double ikat cloth. A Sempange bobbin rack usually holds twenty to thirty bobbins (see fig. 73), and as the worker takes up the threads from all these bobbins he wraps them as a group around the frame just as the weft will later go back and forth through the warp on the loom. Weft ikat cloths usually bear small repeating patterns, and each thread from a bobbin bears the entire pattern that will appear on the finished cloth. Enough weft threads to make two or three identical sarong are bound simultaneously. As the worker lays out the weft threads on the ikat frame he marks them with fiber—the resulting ikat sections will be wrapped with binding material.

Most weft ikat sarong also have a *kepala* or "head," which is a break in the main pattern of the sarong. This section, with its contrasting design and often contrasting color, is bound on a separate frame (see plate 24). Workers usually bind enough thread for three or four *kepala* sections at one time.

In the workshops of Sulawesi, as well as Java and Bali, much of the actual ikat work

is done by young men (see fig. 74). Some charcoal lines are drawn across the weft threads as a guide, but the actual motif is bound from memory or is created on the spot as the young man works. Today, plastic string is the favorite ikat material because of its excellent resistance to the dyes (which probably makes the tightness of the binding less important). The string is wrapped around the ikat sections in the same manner as for warp ikat textiles.

In Sempange, the dyer works in a small hut set apart from the main house. There he tends open fires over which sit large iron pots containing hot dyes (see fig. 75). Manmade aniline dyes are used exclusively for contemporary weft ikat cloths, and are capable of giving a wide range of colors. As many as five distinct colors may appear on one sarong; when the only available dyes were natural ones, such as indigo and *mengkudu* red, the choice of shades was very narrow.

Dyers use a special method to create the multicolored patterns. To dye a small individual design, such as a flower, an outline is bound

Fig. 74. Young men do the intricate binding work. Gresik, East Java.

Fig. 75. Threads for weft ikat fabrics are dyed in hot synthetic dyes. Sempange, South Sulawesi.

around the desired figure, and the dyer then carefully spoons the dye inside the bound outline. The bundle of threads may or may not be removed from the ikat frame for this step. When the moisture in the dye has evaporated, this colored area is then sealed up with binding material. This process is repeated for each motif that contrasts in color to the background. After all the variously colored designs are bound and sealed, the dyer dips the entire bundle of threads into the main background color. When the threads are dry and the ikat bindings are removed, all the colors stand out distinctly. This dyeing method gives a greater possibility of color schemes since the person creating the design need not worry about how different dyes will mix, but it can also lead to some unusual color combinations.

Since the weft threads carry the pattern, preparing them for weaving is an important step. Groups of weft threads were bound simultaneously for dyeing, and the most primitive method of separating them is for the weaver to remove one individual weft thread at a time by hand and wind it onto a bobbin. In the workshops of Sulawesi, Bali, and Java, however, a hand-operated winding tool aids the worker in this step (see fig. 76). One wheel of this device holds the long bundle of threads that were

bound and dyed together previously. The weaver takes the end of each thread in the bundle and fits it into a separate groove on a second winding wheel. When this second wheel is rotated, each thread from the larger bundle will be individually wound into a small skein. The skeins can then be wound easily onto their own bobbins (see fig. 77). Each bobbin thus contains enough thread to create a single repetition of the weft ikat motif.

Usually the warp threads are a plain color, but they can also carry a random ikat pattern. These markings on the warp threads have no motif and no relation to the weft design; they appear as white lines or dashes along the warp of the fabric and add a visual accent to the weft motif. This technique is referred to as warp-weft ikat, and it is not to be confused with the precise interlocking designs of double ikat.

Sometimes, the selvage edge of a weaving may bear an actual warp ikat pattern, a common decorative device in East Java (see plate 25). This narrow border, two to three centimeters wide, is treated separately from the rest of the warp and weft; bound and dyed as for warp ikat, it is then put into its proper place at the edge of the warp threads on the loom.

Weft ikat cloths are woven in a weft-faced weave; that is, the warp is spaced rather widely

Fig. 76. After dyeing, weavers use a winding wheel to take apart the weft ikat sections so that their individual threads can be wound onto bobbins. Gianyar, Bali.

Fig. 77. Each long weft thread is wound onto a separate bobbin. Gianyar, Bali.

Fig. 78. Workshop weavers use semimechanized "flying shuttle" hand looms to produce weft ikat cloth and silk cloth with woven patterns. Sempange, South Sulawesi.

and the weft threads are beaten in very tightly. Consequently, with more weft threads per square centimeter, the weft visually dominates the fabric. The warp threads may sometimes differ in color from the weft, and since a little of the warp shows through even on most weft-faced fabrics, this contrast tends to give the cloth an iridescent effect. A patterned weft that is predominantly red may be woven into a blue warp, for example. The overall appearance of the fabric is then a violet color that, as the cloth moves in the sun, seems to shimmer. This trick is often used in Bali to produce a rayon and cotton cloth that has the luster of silk.

Once Bugis women wove at home on back-strap looms, but today village girls gather in the workshops after school to weave the Bugis-style silk sarong. They work on hand looms with "flying shuttles" that quickly and mechanically move the bobbin back and forth through the warp to create the fabric (see fig. 78). Once the warp is set up, the weaving begins. Each bobbin is passed back and forth through the warp to give a single repetition of the motif—producing six centimeters of woven fabric, for example. When one bobbin of thread has been depleted,

the weaver quickly replaces it with another. When it is time to add the sarong's contrasting *kepala* motif, the weaver takes one of the bobbins bearing that motif and weaves its thread into the warp. Then she returns to the bobbins bearing the regular patterns. As the bobbin passes automatically through the weft threads, the weaver tugs the weft to the right or left to adjust the pattern. The clarity of the pattern depends on the weaver's skill at this point. Since the fabric is weft-faced, the weaver must also be sure to beat the weft in tightly.

When weft ikat cloths were woven on back-strap looms, the width of the cloth was determined by the span through which the weaver could comfortably pass the bobbin by hand. Sarong or other large weavings had to be made in separate halves to be sewn together. Some older Balinese weft ikat textiles made of silk and contemporary Palembang cloths have a seam down the middle, indicating that they were woven on a backstrap loom. In South Sulawesi and East Java, weavers still stick to tradition by weaving only one-half of a sarong at a time even though they work on large hand looms. One selvage edge of the cloth is finished off but the weft threads on the other side are just left in loose loops because the halves will be sewn together.

Although the weft ikat technique is basically the same from one place to the next the textiles that result are regionally distinctive. The silk Bugis sarong are bright and iridescent in color; one almost imagines that they can glow in the dark. The motifs are primarily simple, bold patterns of squares, diamond shapes, or waves (see plate 24). These sarong are made to be used as clothing and are not assigned any special powers or made part of any rituals except as payment of the brideprice.

Bugis women wear these colorful sarong on special occasions but they are most commonly worn by the men. On Friday, the Moslem holy day, when men all over Indonesia put on their finest clothing for their weekly visit to the mosque, few can rival the Bugis men for sartorial splendor. In Ujung Pandang, men flock to the mosque in the local fashion of conservative white shirts and dark suit jackets incongruously topping lime green or hot pink silk sarong.

GRESIK: The people in the area of Gresik, East Java, share with the Bugis a strong Islamic background and a tradition of making weft ikat textiles. In the eighteenth and nineteenth centuries, Gresik was a major port used by the Dutch to handle the trade with the Gujurat area of India, where the patola cloth is woven. The Indian and Arab traders who played a role in introducing Islam also brought weft ikat techniques to the Indonesian archipelago.

In Gresik we visited a workshop that makes weft ikat sarong. In the section of Gresik where the workshop is located, we were amazed at how many people had sharp Arab features, something we had never seen anywhere in Indonesia. Possibly owing to the history of weft ikat, much of its production in Gresik is managed by Indonesians of Arab descent.

East Javanese ikat cloths are decorated with intricate geometric or floral patterns. The colors—rust, olive green, dark green, and maroon—are earthier than those found on textiles made by the Bugis, even though they are still produced with chemical dyes (see plate 25). The sarong are made from cotton rather than silk, and are used as all-purpose garments instead of clothing worn only for special occasions.

The cloth made in Gresik is always sewn into sarong, which are most often worn by Tenggerese men of East Java and by Balinese men—

these ikat-patterned sarong are rarely worn by women. The soft cotton texture of these sarong makes them an ideal sleeping garment as well as a shawl on cold nights and a shade against the hot midday sun. Examples from most of the Gresik workshops find their way to the market of Malang, an alluring town in the highlands of East Java. A few workshops around Malang also make weft ikat cloth, but it is unanimously acknowledged that Gresik produces the best sarong. A visit to a cloth market in Malang reveals an extraordinary variety of styles, colors, and patterns that provide evidence of a craft still very much alive but unfortunately little known outside of Java and Bali.

BALI: Hindu Balinese weave their own weft ikat textiles and they are the exception in the midst of all the Moslem producers of this cloth. In the past, women in Bali wove sarong in their spare time for themselves and their families, making a large variety of textiles from weft ikat to complex woven patterns and simple plaids and stripes. Older women that we talked to could remember when some villages even raised their own silkworms and spun their own silk thread. Before World War II, Bali must have been unrivaled for its sheer variety of textile patterns, techniques, and colors. The war, followed by the struggle for independence against the Dutch, unfortunately had a devastating effect on many Balinese textile traditions. Many types of cloth have not been made since that time, and homeweavers have practically disappeared. Today, cottage industries provide most of the weavings that Balinese purchase in the marketplace.

In southeastern Bali, especially around the towns of Gianyar and Klungkung, beautiful weft ikat sarong called *nduk* were once woven in the bright lush colors that seem so appropriate to this fabled island—magenta, purple, spring green, and royal blue (see plate 26). *Nduk* sarong made of silk are no longer woven in the home, but a facsimile is still produced in the workshops of Gianyar and Denpasar. These contemporary weft ikat cloths are woven in cotton or a mix of cotton and rayon. *Nduk* sarong almost disappeared at one point, but a revival began in the 1950s and the craft is flourishing today. When we first visited Bali in 1972, very few of these cloths were actually worn by Balinese (though they were a hot tourist item), but in later trips we have noticed both men and women choosing cotton *nduk* made on the island over either East Javanese ikat cloths or Central Javanese batik.

The patterns seen on the contemporary *nduk* weavings incorporate a mixture of traditional and non-traditional themes. In a single workshop one weaver might be working on a native Balinese motif such as a *barong* (mythical animal) head, while another might be weaving a cloth featuring a scene of palm trees on a beach. Motifs are also borrowed from other parts of Indonesia; for example, Sumbanese-style animals make an appearance in a new context on the *nduk* weavings. The *nduk* industry, if no longer strictly traditional, has shown the ability to change and try new themes, unlike other textile traditions that have died out or stagnated.

Other types of silk weft ikat cloths such as selindang (shawls) and altar cloths were previously made in Bali and, like the *nduk,* often portrayed human and animal figures. Such figures on weft ikat cloths are found only in Bali. All other weft ikat textiles feature geometric or floral motifs. Characters like Rama and his bird-mount, Garuda, from the Indian *Ramayana* epic or like Rangda the witch and the *barong* animal from Balinese folklore were often chosen as subjects. Some silk copies in weft ikat were made of the gringsing cloth of Tenganan and the patola cloth of India. Not all of these weft ikat cloths (there is no warp ikat in Bali outside of Tenganan) show animal figures. There were red silk cloths from Singaraja, northern Bali (see plate 27), and red cotton cloths from the island of Nusa Penida off the southern coast, both designed in a manner very reminiscent of the patola cloth. Some textiles are still woven on Nusa Penida today but they are crudely done compared with the older examples, and they are occasionally seen at various Balinese ceremonies (see fig. 79).

PALEMBANG: Very similar to some of the northern Balinese silks, particularly those of Singaraja, which incidentally is a predominantly Moslem part of Bali, are the traditional weft ikat textiles of Palembang, South Sumatra. Some Bugis people do live in the Palembang area, and they make a type of sarong, but it is quite unlike the ikat cloth of the true Palembang natives. The old Palembang cloths are often exquisite, and represent some of the finest weft ikat textiles found anywhere in the archipelago. Unlike the weft ikat textiles made elsewhere in

Fig. 79. Hindu priest Ida Pendande Oka Telage and a newlywed couple sit on a weft ikat cloth from Nusa Penida Island. The couple are wearing *prada* cloths. Denpasar, Bali. *(Wedding photograph courtesy of the family)*

Indonesia, the fine cloths of Palembang are still woven at home on backstrap looms, although by only a few families these days. The traditional technique they use differs a little from that found in the workshops of Sulawesi and Java. In particular, it is interesting to note that the weavers bind the threads on a circular frame that rotates on an axis—it looks rather like a winding tool. Weavers in Bali and possibly in Sulawesi as well at one time used this type of frame at home.

In general, the patterns of Palembang weft ikat cloths fall into three categories, geometric, floral, and mango-shaped, the last being derived from Indian sources. These traditional motifs can be extremely complex, and usually appear in several muted shades of gold, green, and blue on a deep scarlet background. The intricate ikat pattern may be partly overlaid or bordered with a woven pattern of gold threads. The few cloths that are being woven today do not, unfortunately, achieve the splendor of those created in the past.

These Palembang cloths are worn as the traditional costume of the area on festive occasions and also are an important part of the wedding gifts. One textile decorated with ikat and gold woven patterns is worn by boys on the day of their circumcision ceremony, a special rite among Moslem Palembang families.

Cloths decorated in weft ikat differ from warp ikat textiles in more than just materials and technique. The history of weft ikat in Indonesia is only several hundred years old, so these cloths generally have neither the deeper significance nor the intimate involvement in the culture that warp ikat textiles enjoy. There are few stories, even in Bali, regarding the attributes of weft ikat cloths; they are assigned none of gringsing's magical powers, nor do their motifs have any special meanings. Weft ikat textiles are a part of the traditional costume, and they are used in certain ceremonies and sometimes as a part of the brideprice. But in many areas where weft ikat cloths are woven, they seem less irreplaceable in the culture than warp ikat textiles.

Tie-Dyeing

Another dye-resist technique, tie-dyeing or *pelangi* as it is known in Indonesia, spread throughout the archipelago about the same time as weft ikat. Indeed, the two techniques share a similar history. Tie-dyeing was brought to many parts of Indonesia by traders, possibly the same Indian and Arab Moslems who introduced weft ikat. Tie-dyeing is an oft-used technique in India and, as with weft ikat, most of these cloths in Indonesia were originally made with silk. The areas best known for producing silk tie-dyed cloths—South Sumatra (especially Palembang), Bali, Java (Gresik in East Java, Jogjakarta, and Solo), and Lombok—also make fabrics decorated in weft ikat.

An exception to this picture is found in central Sulawesi, where the Torajans make very simply patterned tie-dyed cloths. This region is so remote and the technique used there so basic that it seems quite possible that tie-dyeing developed here independently.

Tie-dyeing is a relatively simple method of textile decoration. Pinches of cloth are wrapped and tied tightly with fiber; when the fabric is dyed, the binding will resist the dye and leave a pattern on the cloth. The most elemental design using this technique is a light circle against a dyed background. Several variations of tie-dyeing employ more complex stitching

techniques, but the principle is the same; as with ikat weavings, it is the tightness of the binding or the stitching that resists the dye. Tie-dyeing is related to both of the other dye-resist techniques of Indonesia: to batik, in that it is performed on a woven fabric, and to ikat cloth, in that it is a binding that acts as the resist rather than a substance such as wax. We have chosen to emphasize the technique's relation to ikat and have therefore included its discussion here.

The tie-dye technique is not subject to significant variations from place to place. A description of how tie-dyed cloths are made in Central Java gives a good idea of the basic method.

In Jogjakarta, tie-dyeing is a traditional folk craft used to decorate many accessories that are worn with batik cloth. The Joedodiningrat family has been involved in the making of tie-dyed fabric for more than seventy years (or as they would say, "from the time of the seventh sultan"). The name Joedodiningrat translates roughly as "to shine brightly," and was given to the family by the eighth sultan because of his fondness for their bright tie-dyed cloths. The Joedodiningrat family has provided the sultans with tie-dyed fabrics for headcloths *(plongkong)*, breastcloths *(kemben)*, sashes *(longong)*, ceremonial wraps *(dodot)*, and wallhangings for the royal bedchamber.

Today Ibu Joedodiningrat supervises the production of tie-dyed cloths from her home, following in the footsteps of her grandmother, who supplied the seventh sultan. Tie-dyed fabrics were formerly made of silk but today they are exclusively of cotton, for silk is too expensive and difficult to obtain. Ibu stencils the design on the cloth, but the actual binding and sewing work, as in her grandmother's time, is done by village women just outside Jogjakarta. Once tied and stitched, the cloths are returned to Ibu Joedodiningrat's house to be dyed under her direction.

Although Ibu herself does not bind the cloths, she knows the techniques well and can skillfully demonstrate the tying and stitching methods. Since most visitors to Central Java are mainly interested in batik and tend to ignore tie-dyeing, she was delighted to show us how her textiles are made. Three distinct but related methods are used to pattern the cloth; sometimes all three are combined on one piece. The three techniques

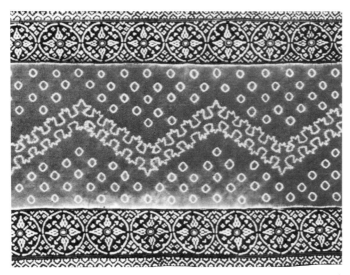

Fig. 80. Detail of a tie-dyed cloth showing the *tritik* and *pelangi* techniques in the center and the *polos* technique on the line separating the center from the batik border. *Soga* brown border and burgundy center. From Jogjakarta, Central Java. Authors' collection.

may also be used singly or together to decorate part of a textile, such as a breastcloth, that has first been given a batik border pattern (see fig. 80).

Pelangi is the general name given to tie-dyed cloths in Indonesia, but it is actually the specific term for the easiest and most common of the three methods of resist decoration. The *pelangi* technique of binding a pinch of fabric is found among all people making tie-dyed cloth. Ibu Joedodiningrat demonstrates it by tightly wrapping a pineapple-fiber thread around a pinch of cloth. She ties a secure knot in the thread and then, without breaking the thread, repeats the process again and again on other pinches of cloth until the knotted areas form an even and complete design. After the cloth is dyed and the thread removed, a pattern of small white circles appears against the colored background. Large circles, like the bull's-eye patterns found on Torajan tie-dyed cloth, are each tied separately. Objects such as stones may be tied into the cloth to give shape to the center of the circle. By carefully arranging and folding the cloth before binding it, the basic circle can be transformed into simple geometric shapes such as squares, ovals, and oblongs. The inner surface of the circle may be completely bound so that it resists the dye and is a solid white form, or it may be left open to pick up the background color, as is done in Jogjakarta. The body of the cloth may also be dyed one shade while the circle is dipped in a contrasting color.

A related technique, called *tritik* in Java, gives a wider scope of pattern possibilities and is often used in conjunction with the *pelangi* technique. The silk cloth from Palembang seen in plate 28, for example, combines both techniques. In Central Java, *tritik* alone may decorate a cloth, especially a head- or breastcloth with a batik border.

Tritik is a stitching technique that produces a linear pattern. With a needle and pineapple-fiber thread, Ibu Joedodiningrat sews a line of tiny running stitches following a design she has penciled on the cloth (see fig. 81). Pineapple fiber makes the best thread because of its strength, but several thicknesses of regular cotton thread can also be substituted. The thread must be strong, for after every few centimeters of stitching it is pulled to gather the fabric as tightly as possible. The cloth must be compressed along the entire length of the stitch to prevent the dye from seeping in and ruining or obscuring the design. While the *pelangi* technique uses thread wrapped around a section of cloth, *tritik* produces its resist line by compressing the fabric along a line of stitching.

If a cloth, usually a headcloth or a sash, has first been decorated along the edges with a batik pattern, a line of *tritik* work (called *polos*)

Fig. 81. Ibu Joedodiningrat sews a *tritik* pattern onto a sash. Jogjakarta, Central Java.

is sewn between the batik-patterned area and the inner section of the cloth to be tie-dye decorated. This line of stitching will keep the dye from bleeding into the batik.

The *tritik* technique is often used to make delicate, curving white designs against dark backgrounds, and the result is very appealing and understated. Ibu Joedodiningrat follows the traditional Central Javanese patterns, and she traces the motifs onto the cloth following old copper and leather stencils handed down from her grandmother. She takes great pride in these stencils that have helped her decorate so many fine cloths and makes sure they are well cared for.

Another stitching technique gives an all-over pattern similar to the *citcik* dots on batik. Called *cumputan,* this method is found only in Central Java. First, a grid is drawn onto the cloth to be used as a guide for spacing the stitches. With a needle and pineapple thread, Ibu makes a tiny stitch and then a second stitch over the first in a cross-stitch pattern. She pulls the thread up tightly and knots it, and repeats these two stitches along the grid until the cloth is evenly patterned. After the fabric has been dyed and the threads removed, four tiny but distinct dots appear where each cross-stitch was made.

Whether the *pelangi, tritik,* or *cumputan* technique is used, the dyeing process is the same. First, any part of the fabric that has been batik-decorated or is desired white must be covered to protect it from the dye. Ibu Joedodiningrat employs a dyer who also prepares the cloths for dyeing. All-purpose banana leaf, a common disposable wrapping for food in Indonesia, also makes a good dye-resist covering. First, the dyer heats a leaf over hot coals to strengthen it. Then he wraps it around the areas of the cloth to be protected and binds it tightly in place with fiber (see figs. 82 and 83). Since the traditional tie-dyed cloth of Central Java uses only two colors, the dyer needs to bind only a well-defined portion of the cloth—the middle for example, or the edges. For more colorful tie-dyed cloths, weavers rely on the method of dipping the center of the *pelangi* circles into a variety of colors, then binding these circles closed and dyeing a background color to achieve a variegated effect.

When the fabric is prepared, the dyer spoons hot chemical dye onto the cloth and works it into the fabric by hand (see fig. 84). Hot dyes are preferred because they penetrate the fabric bet-

ter. When the fabric has dried after the first dyeing, the dyer removes the banana leaf to reveal the undyed fabric. If the cloth is to be dyed in a second color, the dyer must protect the newly dyed section with a leaf before the second dyeing can take place.

Before the stitching and tie-dyeing thread can be removed, the dyed cloth must be aired in the the shade until it is thoroughly dry. This step is so important that during the rainy season the work must be stopped because the cloth cannot dry properly in the humid air. The threads are never cut with a knife as there is too much danger of accidently damaging the fabric; the stitching or binding is carefully pulled open by hand. The thread is broken in places, with great care being taken not to tear the cloth. If the cloth is the least bit damp, it is not strong enough to withstand this handling.

The tie-dyeing technique is somewhat limited in its range of designs compared with other methods of textile decoration such as batik or ikat. With these cloths, much of the variation instead occurs in the colors or the boldness of the patterns. The tie-dyed cloths of Central Java display subtle *pelangi* and *tritik* patterns against subdued colors like dark green, burgundy, or dark blue, colors that go well with the earthy shades and intricate patterns of batik. Other parts of Java, notably the area around Gresik, East Java (also known for its fine weft ikat fabrics), once made tie-dyed cloth, usually sashes of silk. Colors of the silks from Gresik were brighter and the designs, mostly circular, were bolder (see fig. 85). Unfortunately, the craft has died out here.

Bali is the only other place in Indonesia besides Central Java actively producing tie-dyed cloths today. Unfortunately, the contemporary Balinese cloth tends to feature coarse designs and bright colors made primarily with tourists in mind. Formerly, lovely silk shawls and sashes were created; nothing like these old fabrics is being done today. The word *pelangi* means "rainbow," and the name truly applies to the older tie-dyed cloths of Bali. The designs, simple *pelangi* motifs with a little *tritik* work, were not as striking as the blend of colors—pale orange, lime green, purple, magenta, and gold—obtained with chemical dyes. While the colors were bright and shimmery they avoided being gaudy and seemed to be very much at ease in tropical Bali.

Figs. 82, 83. Before a cloth can be dyed, the dyer wraps the areas that will remain uncolored with banana leaves. He then binds the leaves tightly around the cloth. Jogjakarta, Central Java.

Fig. 84. Dyers must heat up the chemical dye so that it penetrates the fabric better. Jogjakarta, Central Java.

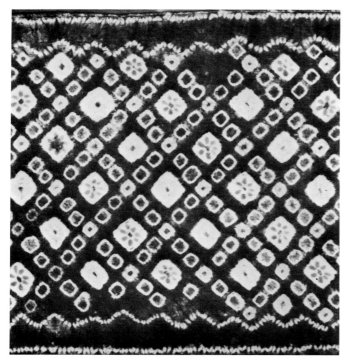

Fig. 85. Detail of a silk tie-dyed cloth. Purple with multi-colored accents. From Gresik, East Java. Authors' collection.

The silk cloths of Palembang, South Sumatra, in contrast to the cloths of Central Java, show the strongest foreign influence of all Indonesian tie-dyed fabrics. Their layout is similar to that of the patola cloth and they often feature the mango *(mangga)* or ear-shaped motif that is an Indian design (see plate 28). Predominantly red with other colors as accents, the Palembang cloths are perhaps Indonesia's most striking tie-dyed cloths. These textiles, no longer made today, were once worn as part of the ceremonial dress. The combination of fine work, good design, and attractive colors makes the Palembang tie-dyed cloths, like the weft ikat and woven textiles from the same area, truly outstanding.

4 Weaving and Woven Patterns

The sight of women working at their looms under houses or beneath overhanging thatched roofs is commonplace in the villages where weaving is an integral part of daily life. One would, however, not expect to find such a tranquil scene in one of Indonesia's crowded, fast-paced cities. Yet hidden away in the bustling South Sumatran city of Palembang, a few women still weave at home making traditional cloths called *songket*. To see this Palembang weaving, we were directed first down one street and then another, each one narrower than the one before, its houses older. Finally, we were pointed in the direction of a large teak house with a roof curved like the hull of a ship. This was the home of Ibu F. Imir. Inside a dark high-ceilinged room we could see a woman seated at her loom. Sunshine filtering in through an open window served as her only work light, and it sparkled slightly on the silver threads of the partially woven cloth. The woman lifted some threads on the loom and passed the bobbin through the crimson warp; then, leaning back against the strap that held the loom to her body, she beat in the weft. The clack echoed in the large room, making the din of traffic outside seem faraway (see plate 29).

The Backstrap Loom

No matter how specialized the technique a weaver uses to decorate the cloth, her loom remains much the same. Both ikat- and woven-patterned textiles are woven on the simple yet versatile backstrap loom (see fig. 86). Basically, a backstrap loom consists of two poles that are joined by the warp threads; there is no frame. The pole closest to the weaver, the breast or cloth beam, moves with the weaver's body, enabling her to control the tension of the warp during weaving. The breast beam is fastened

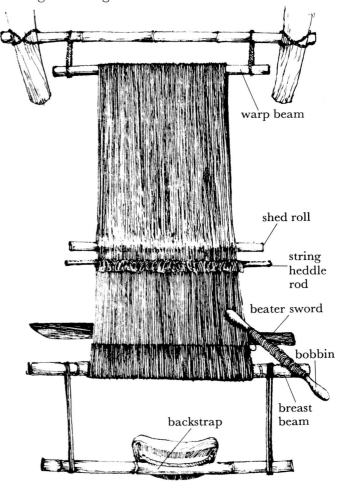

Fig. 86. Backstrap looms are common throughout Indonesia. The loom shown here is of a type found in East Nusatenggara.

127

with rope to a backstrap or support made of animal hide or wood that encircles the weaver's waist. Figure 86 shows a carved wooden support that fits together with a bamboo pole tied to the breast beam. The warp beam, the pole farthest away from the weaver, is attached to something stationary like a couple of house posts; sometimes, as in Palembang, it fits into a specially made stand.

Between the breast beam and the warp beam are devices for lifting particular combinations of warp threads. As several warp threads are lifted, an opening—called a shed—is formed for the bobbin carrying the weft thread so that it can pass from one side of the cloth to the other. For a plain-weave cloth, like an ikat-decorated textile, only two such sheds are necessary, and ikat weavers use the simplest method to open them. They attach a device called a heddle rod to every other warp thread with loops made from a continuous length of string. By lifting this rod one shed is opened. The second shed may be made in the same manner, using a string heddle rod to lift the alternate threads, or it may more simply be marked by a shed roll, a stick inserted in the second shed. The shed roll is placed behind the string heddle rod toward the warp beam; by pulling it up and toward herself, the weaver opens the second shed. Sometimes, a couple of flat sticks are inserted, one in each shed, very close to the warp beam. These are known as lease sticks and they help keep the warp threads in order.

As a woman weaves, each time she opens a shed she inserts a smooth, polished flat stick called a beater sword into the shed and turns it on its side to keep the opening clear so that the bobbin can pass through easily. When she starts a new weaving, for the first four or five sheds, she may "weave" thin sticks into the warp instead of the regular weft threads. These sticks will help keep the warp threads the proper distance apart. Then the real weaving begins. The bobbin, which is sometimes encased in a shuttle of bamboo, is first passed through one shed and then returned through the other. After each pass the weft thread is beaten in with the beater sword. The beater sword is the most personalized part of the loom; if two women happen to be weaving on the same cloth, often each one will use her own beater sword. As the cloth is woven, the pointed ends of a thin slat are inserted into both sides of the just-completed fabric close to the selvage

edges to help maintain straight sides and a uniform width. This stick is always kept close to that part of the cloth being woven.

There are two types of warp. One is called a straight warp; the other is the circular warp that is found in warp ikat weavings. A straight warp may be set up in two ways: the warp threads may be measured, cut, and tied to both the breast and warp beams, or more commonly, the warp is laid out as a continuous thread that encircles the two beams so that no tying is necessary (see fig. 87). In this case, the threads may appear to be in the form of a loose circle; the circle's upper threads form the top of one shed, and the lower threads, when lifted by the string heddle rod, form the top of the other shed. As the weaving progresses, the "top" and "bottom" threads are woven together into a single piece of fabric stretching from one beam of the loom to the other.

On a circular warp, the actual weaving takes place only on the top of the circle by alternately raising and lowering adjacent threads (see fig. 88). As the work progresses, the newly woven cloth is simply shifted around and under the breast beam as unwoven threads come up from the bottom around the warp beam. By the end of

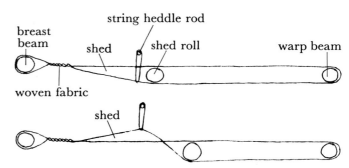

Fig. 87. How the sheds for inserting the weft are formed on a straight warp. The top and bottom threads of the warp are woven together. When the weaving is finished the fabric stretches between the breast and warp beams in a single piece. This kind of warp is used for supplementary weft cloth.

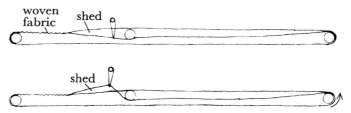

Fig. 88. How the sheds are formed on a circular warp. Adjacent threads on the top of the circle are woven together. As the work proceeds, the finished fabric gradually shifts around the breast beam. This kind of warp is used for warp ikat cloth.

the weaving, there is almost an entire circle of woven cloth. The remaining narrow section of the warp, where there was not enough room to insert the bobbin and properly batten in the weft, becomes the fringe of the cloth.

Any extra length that would make a straight warp unwieldy on the loom can be rolled up on the warp beam and then let out as weaving progresses; at the same time, woven fabric is rolled up on the breast beam. An additional pole is placed on top of the cloth just in front of the breast beam to keep the fabric from slipping, and the woven part of the cloth is then rolled around both of these beams. As the fabric nears completion, the weaver can keep rolling up the finished cloth and move closer to the warp beam to weave as much of the warp as possible.

As a woman weaves, she regulates the tension of the warp threads by the pressure of her weight against the backstrap. When lifting the string heddle rod or the shed roll to form a shed, she leans forward a bit so that there is some give in the warp. Then, as she beats in the threads, she increases the tension by leaning back. The pressure of the strap on the weaver's back is widely believed to be harmful to growing girls and this is one reason why weaving skills are learned only after a girl is fully grown. Weaving requires a surprising amount of physical strength, and one common characteristic of women who do a lot of it is their erect posture, which they maintain even in old age. In backstrap weaving, the body of the weaver acts as a part of the loom; the graceful flowing motion of a weaver at work, body and loom working together as one, is a pleasure to watch.

Supplementary Weft Textiles

The basic loom and the parts just described are sufficient for the plain weaves used in ikat fabrics, but woven patterns demand additional devices. The most common decorative weaving technique used in Indonesia is supplementary weft weaving, in which extra weft threads of a material or color different from that of the threads of the regular warp and weft float over and under the basic fabric. These extra threads are passed through varying combinations of warp threads to form a particular design whose contrasting color and texture make it stand out against the plainly woven background cloth.

The best known supplementary weft weavings in Indonesia are the *songket* cloths that are patterned with metallic threads—often of real gold or silver. The songket technique was introduced by traders visiting Indonesia and is practiced today in the same areas where silk weft ikat textiles are made. These areas were relatively accessible to trade routes and their people were wealthy enough to be able to afford the imported silk and the gold and silver threads. Songket are woven by the Acehnese and the Karo Bataks (both northern Sumatra), the Minangkabau (West Sumatra), the Balinese, the Sumbawanese, and some Bugis people, but the songket of Palembang, South Sumatra, is considered to be the finest in Indonesia.

PALEMBANG SONGKET: As the center of the Srivijaya Empire (A.D. 732–1010), Palembang once dominated a large part of the Indonesian archipelago and Southeast Asia. Today, Palembang is still a large city, an active port sprawling on both banks of the Musi River, and is supported by trade and oil. The river is choked with sampans piled high with fruit and large cargo vessels carrying manufactured goods. Many villagers from surrounding areas have been drawn to Palembang, and the crowded city seems to be in constant motion, its glorious past almost forgotten in the present-day commercial rush and the new influx of people.

Some of old Palembang still remains, although it is well hidden, and a few Palembang families who can trace their ancestry back to the Srivijaya kingdom keep its customs alive. In several large houses by the river, native Palembang women like Ibu Imir weave songket cloth in the traditional way and display an old-fashioned hospitality. Only after serving plates of local treats and glasses of sweet hot milk set in delicate silver holders would Ibu Imir begin to talk about her weavings. Sitting on a mat spread out on a polished teak floor, she was surrounded by several of her daughters and as she spoke she occasionally directed them to demonstrate for us the various processes of making songket.

The preparation of the threads is the first step in songket as it is in all weavings. The warp threads must be carefully measured and warped in the usual way. Formerly, the threads were probably dyed using natural dyestuffs, but nowadays both cotton and silk thread are often already colored (usually red) when they are

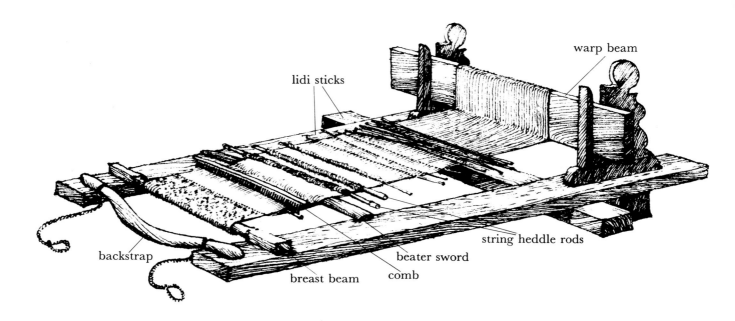

lidi sticks

warp beam

string heddle rods

backstrap

beater sword

breast beam   comb

Fig. 89. A Palembang backstrap loom for making songket
cloth. Extra length in the warp has been wrapped around
the warp beam. Small *lidi* sticks mark the pattern sheds for
the supplementary weft threads.

purchased. If a supplementary woven pattern is
to appear over a silk weft ikat motif (see chapter
3), then of course the weaver must also bind and
dye the background weft threads. Generally, on
a songket, Ibu Imir prefers to use a cotton warp
with the silk weft. This combination forms a
stronger base for the supplementary threads than
an all-silk base would. As she attaches the
straight cotton warp to the breast and warp
beams, she threads it through a wooden comb
that will help maintain the proper width and
separation of the warp threads. The warp beam
of the Palembang loom is shaped like a flat
board rather than being round like bamboo,
and it sits in a special stand (see fig. 89).

In order to lift the warp to form the two sheds
for the plainly woven background cloth, the
weaver attaches two string heddle rods to their
corresponding warp threads. A couple of lease
sticks, which like the comb help maintain the
even spacing of the warp threads, are usually
inserted in the warp near the warp beam.

Once the threads for the background warp
are set up on the loom, the weaver can begin the
counting work for the supplementary weft pattern. Instead of going over one warp thread and
under the next, as in plain weave, the pattern weft
may skip over or under several warp threads at a
time. These gold (or silver) pattern-weft threads
will thus appear to float over and under the

surface of background cloth. For each "line"
or pass of a pattern-weft thread, the weaver must
choose the particular combination of warp
threads that will be lifted to form a single pattern shed. Counting the warp threads for each
pattern shed is a time-consuming part of making
songket. We watched Ibu Imir count out the
warp threads for a line, quickly flicking through
them with a wooden pick and then inserting a
thin stick to mark the pattern shed. The pattern
is produced from memory or by looking at a
finished selimut, a sarong, or a small woven pattern square. For a single pattern, up to two
hundred of these sticks, called *lidi*, may be used,
each one marking a different combination of
warp threads.

Rather than use the *lidi* sticks themselves to lift
the warp threads to form the pattern shed, Ibu
transforms each one into a smaller version of a
string heddle rod. With a continuous length of
white string, she connects the warp threads to
be lifted by each *lidi* stick to another stick placed
on top of the warp. Once the "*lidi* rod" is attached
to the warp threads, the stick marking the pattern shed is removed. The *lidi* rod works in the
same way as the primary string heddle rods. In
between each pass of the regular weft thread,
Ibu lifts one of the *lidi* rods to form a pattern
shed and carefully passes the gold weft thread
through the warp by hand. After the return pass

of the regular silk weft, the next *lidi* rod is raised and another gold thread is carefully moved through the shed.

The pattern on a single line of songket can be carried by a continuous weft thread, that is, one that travels from one edge of the cloth across to the other, or by many discontinuous threads. In the latter case, the metallic threads are held on small bobbins that are passed by hand through their proper sections of the warp and then left dangling on the finished line until it is time for the next pass. Discontinuous wefts are used for widely spaced patterns or designs in which several types or colors of pattern threads appear. As each *lidi* rod is used in order, usually beginning with the one farthest from the weaver, it is pushed toward the warp beam and stored with the unwoven warp; when all the sticks have been used, they can be reused in reverse order to repeat the pattern as a mirror image.

The thread used in the old Palembang songket textiles contributed a great deal to their rich, lustrous beauty. Imported from India, this special thread *(benang emas cantung)* was covered with real gold or silver. Unfortunately, it is no longer available to Palembang weavers. The metallic thread commonly used today is flat, shiny, and tinsellike in comparison. Even a contemporary songket made with the highest quality of craftsmanship tends to look gaudy when compared with the older examples, which are rich and quietly elegant. Ibu Imir bemoans the unavailability of the *emas cantung* thread today and resorts to taking apart old cloths, thread by thread, to recover some of it to save for special pieces.

Ibu Imir makes several distinctions among the kinds of traditional Palembang textiles that she and her daughters still weave. The simplest type is a sarong with a white cotton motif in supplementary weft technique on a silk background *(bunga pacih)*. This sarong is not a true songket because it does not utilize silver or gold threads, but it is one of the first types of supplementary weft cloths attempted by young Palembang women as they begin weaving. A sarong with this type of ornamentation is usually worn by a married woman.

There are a variety of songket sarong, selimut, and smaller selindang (shawls) woven in Palembang. The two favorite motifs of weavers in the city are an eight-pointed star and a rose design. One type of sarong featuring these motifs, called *bunga tawar,* sometimes combines both gold and silver threads on the same piece: silver for the star-and-rose patterned body of the sarong, and gold for the *kepala* or break in the motif, which is a *tumpal* (spearhead) design. If the main body of the sarong is decorated with silver or gold and accents of brightly colored silk thread are added to the motif (either by supplementary weft technique or by embroidery), the style is called *bunga cina* ("Chinese flower"). Selimut or selindang can also be decorated in either style, using only metallic threads, as for *bunga tawar,* or with the addition of silk embellishments, as for *bunga cina.* Most Palembang selimut feature a row of triangular *tumpal* motifs along the fringed edges and stripes containing patterns along the selvages, and this layout clearly resembles the basic design of the Indian patola (compare plate 19 with plate 30).

Ibu Imir feels that a type of weaving called *bunga lepos* requires the most skill. This lightweight, all-silk cloth is cut and sewn into a long blouse worn with a sarong. It is decorated with delicate, widely spaced motifs of gold thread, sometimes with additional work done in colored silk threads. Each small motif requires a separate bobbin to hold the pattern weft.

Palembang women wear sarong for ceremonial occasions such as weddings and circumcisions. At a traditional wedding, four girls clad in Palembang weavings slowly dance before the bride as she is presented. The effect is dazzling; all the women are wearing red cloth with gold or silver patterns and elaborate headdresses of gold in the shape of fluttering leaves.

Songket cloths have a material value due to the real gold or silver that was once incorporated into them. In fact, we heard that although songket is part of the exchange of gifts necessary for a marriage, it is given by the groom's family to the bride's. This is contrary to the normal custom, for textiles are generally regarded as feminine throughout Indonesia and are usually a gift of the bride's family. So in this case, songket seems to be valued in the same way as money or livestock—the usual masculine gifts. Songket cloths are a kind of wealth and a part of the traditional dress, but like other relatively newer types of textiles such as weft ikat cloths, they do not seem to have any ritual uses or deeper levels of meaning.

Technically and visually, the textiles of Palembang are superb, the finest songket found anywhere in Indonesia. It would be a pity if Ibu Imir and the few others weaving in Palembang were the last to make these traditional cloths. When we were in Palembang, women were discussing the possibility of forming a cooperative to continue the art, but organization usually means the use of large hand looms and the division of labor. Sometimes good weavings from a technical standpoint are produced, but inevitably the personal touch, the care that makes each weaving distinct, is lost.

MINANGKABAU SONGKET: The Minangkabau people of West Sumatra have already gone a long way toward making this move from the home to a cottage-industry level. Many weavers in the area have given up their backstrap looms in favor of large hand looms that are set up and owned by cooperatives.

Even on these large looms much of the technique of supplementary weft weaving remains the same. The warp threads must be counted for each line of the motif and thin *lidi* rods are used to mark each pattern shed (see fig. 90). As on a backstrap loom, the *lidi* rods are stored close to the warp beam and can be used first in one order and then in the opposite order to produce the pattern in reverse. The two string heddle rods for the plainly woven background cloth are lifted by foot pedals and the bobbin holding the background weft is shuttled across automatically, but each *lidi* rod must be lifted individually and the silver and gold supplementary weft threads must be passed through the warp by hand. On Minangkabau textiles, the pattern weft is often not a single thread across the warp but is set in by several small bobbins. A lot of work goes into a songket even when it is woven on a large loom, but the hurried atmosphere and the fact that the cloth is made for someone else does not bring out the best from the weavers. The new Minangkabau songket simply cannot compare to the older pieces that women wove for themselves.

These West Sumatran weavers also share one problem facing weavers in Palembang: the quality of the silver and gold thread available today is inferior to that of the thread they formerly used. Old Minangkabau songket had a light and delicate character quite different from that of the heavier Palembang weavings, and part of their shimmering effect came from the thin gold or silver thread that the older women said came from Europe. Almost the

Fig. 90. Even though Minangkabau weavers work on large hand looms, they must still count out the warp threads for each pass of the bobbin containing a supplementary weft thread. Padang Panjang, West Sumatra.

entire front surface of some of the older weavings, especially the long rectangular selindang and narrow sashes, is covered with this metallic thread in fine repeating geometric patterns. The supplementary weft threads on these pieces float mostly on the face of the cloth, while the silk background cloth shows mainly on the reverse side. Today, Minangkabau weavers must make do with the same poorer quality metallic thread that is used in Palembang. This flat, shiny thread not only lessens the beauty of a piece but it also blurs regional differences—weavings made with the same material tend to look alike.

Minangkabau women wear a selindang draped over one shoulder in the style found all over Indonesia, and they also fold it into a distinctive headdress. This traditional Minangkabau headcovering is shaped into two cones that are supposed to resemble the horns of a water buffalo. The West Sumatrans closely associate themselves with this animal, and a well-known legend relates how they once settled a dispute with a neighboring kingdom by staging a buffalo fight. The other kingdom reputedly had the strongest buffalo in the area, but the Minangkabau won the match by using their wits. They tied horns onto a nursing calf; the calf approached the large buffalo and began nudging its belly in search of milk, goring it with the attached horns. Minangkabau say that after this victory the people of West Sumatra combined the words *minang* ("victorious") and *kabau* ("buffalo") into a name for themselves. Buffalo fights are still a widely attended local sport and the roofs of Minangkabau houses, as well as the women's headdresses, are shaped like buffalo horns to commemorate the triumph of the little buffalo. Among other people in Indonesia, too, the water buffalo is more than just a field animal; widely recognized as a symbol of prosperity and fertility, it is a form of wealth and the most important animal of sacrifice among the Ancient Peoples.

Despite its importance to the Minangkabau, the buffalo does not appear in any of their woven motifs. The most commonly seen patterns are strictly geometric, though some of them are said to have originally been inspired by or named for such natural objects as flowers *(melayang)*, crabs *(sirangka bugis)*, and fish drying on sticks *(atue bada)*. Contemporary Minangkabau weavings usually feature border patterns with widely spaced small designs scattered across the body of the cloth (see fig. 91). The ends of selindang and the *kepala* of the sarong are decorated with the ubiquitous *tumpal* (spearhead) motif. The true traditional patterns of West Sumatrans do not show any influence of the patola, but many of the designs that appear on their cloths follow a layout similar to that of the Indian cloth. This style is relatively new and may have been derived from Palembang weavings. Many textiles made in West Sumatra today are more similar to Palembang weavings than to the older Minangkabau songket, a resemblance that is heightened by the fact that weavers in both places today use the same materials to make their cloths.

BALINESE SONGKET: Among other Indonesian songket cloths, Balinese supplementary weft weavings deserve a special mention. Some of these cloths portray human and animal characters taken from the Hindu *Ramayana* epic and

Fig. 91. Detail of a Minangkabau supplementary weft selindang. Silver threads against a wine-colored silk warp. From West Sumatra. Authors' collection.

from Balinese folklore; patterns of this type are unique to Balinese songket, just as similar figures are found only on Balinese weft ikat textiles. Most supplementary weft cloths made in Bali, however, feature more simple designs. Red sarong (either of silk or cotton), which were once commonly used for festive dress, feature small geometric motifs of silver or gold. There are many types of woven-patterned cloth in Bali; sometimes the supplementary weft motif is executed with both metallic and silk threads, or the cloth may be wholly decorated with colorful silk threads. The striking combinations of the colors that Balinese favor, such as yellow, orange, purple, magenta, and green, are bright yet they harmonize on the older weavings. These cloths may have woven patterns of a single color running from one edge of the fabric to the other, or a discontinuous motif may be woven in using so many different colors that the cloth looks as though it had been embroidered (see plate 31). Supplementary weft weavings, like weft ikat cloths, were once woven by Balinese women at home, and even now they are still made one by one in the same way, although today cotton is the most commonly used material. There is as yet no large-scale cottage industry for the production of woven-decorated textiles. A wide variety of past and contemporary Balinese fabrics including sarong, waist sashes *(saput)*, breastcloths *(kemben)*, and altar cloths are decorated with woven weft patterns.

THE RAGI HIDUP: A few people in Indonesia have traditionally made supplementary weft weavings entirely in cotton. These textiles differ in their materials, patterns, and usage from the songket and from cloths decorated in silk weft, both of which are used only for festival wear and are a tangible form of wealth. In contrast, the woven-decorated cotton cloths, like warp ikat textiles, have a ritual role in the societies that make them. These are the Ancient Peoples or closely related cultures, and it is probable that they were weaving such textiles before the technique was learned in the more accessible areas that were influenced by Indian and Arab traders.

One notable cotton cloth decorated by the supplementary weft technique is made by the Toba Bataks of North Sumatra. Called *ragi hidup*, this cloth is worn as part of the traditional costume among the Toba Bataks, but it is particularly associated with burials. Like other Batak weavings, the *ragi hidup* is used in the ritual gift-exchange system described in chapter 2. The *ragi hidup* is actually a composite of several panels bearing simple warp ikat motifs that are sewn to two supplementary weft woven sections to form a large rectangular cloth (see plate 32). Batak woven patterns are more complex than their dye-resist ikat ones, and the *ragi hidup* is particularly interesting for its Dong-Son style hook-and-rhomb motifs executed in the supplementary weft technique (see detail, plate 32). These patterns as they appear on the *ragi hidup* are almost unchanged from the original Dong-Son designs that came into Indonesia more than two thousand years ago, and they are amazingly similar to the motifs found thousands of kilometers away on Timor Island. This is a good indication that the technique of supplementary weft weaving in cotton has quite a long history in the Batak region. It is unlikely that a new technique would be used to reproduce these traditional patterns, for, generally speaking, new patterns are introduced at the same time as a new technique.

SHIP CLOTHS: Cotton cloths patterned by supplementary weft threads are woven by a few other Ancient Peoples, for example, the Sa'dan Torajans of South Sulawesi, the Manggarai of western Flores, and the people of Lampung at the southern end of Sumatra.

The people of Lampung are closely related to the other Ancient Peoples found in Indonesia, but over the years they have become so mixed with Javanese that only a few of their traditional customs remain. One of the most extraordinary textiles of Indonesia, known as the "ship cloth," was made in the Lampung district, but the last of these cloths was woven several decades ago. Another Lampung cloth, a sarong decorated in warp ikat and embroidery, is also an unusual and important weaving, but it too is unfortunately no longer made (this sarong is described in the section on embroidery, below). Throughout this book we emphasize the Indonesian textiles that are still made today, but the textiles of Lampung were such a unique and superb technical accomplishment that they cannot be omitted. Although a few types of cloth are still made in Lampung, most notably a sarong decorated with gold embroidery, it is a pity that an area with so rich a weaving history makes no textiles today that come close to its previous achievements.

The large ship cloths usually measure about three meters in length by one meter in width and were made only in the Kröe area of Sumatra near Lake Ranau. These weavings are characteristically patterned with the "ship of the dead" motif, hence their nickname, but they are called *palepai* in their native Kröe. The most striking of the cloths bear a single large ship as their pattern, but others may show two or even four ships (see plate 33). Another type of ship cloth has rows of strangely stylized human figures (see fig. 92). The "ship of the dead" theme dates back at least to the Dong-Son bronze drums. The idea that the dead are carried away to the afterlife in a ship was once common in Indonesia, Southeast Asia, and the Pacific region, and many people in these areas are believed to have buried their dead by sending them out to sea in boats. Later, extending this theme, tombs were often made in the shape of a ship; such tombs can still be seen among Ancient Peoples like the Iban Dyaks. In Savu, people told us that palm boats are still made for the dead and launched westward, toward the home of the ancestors, from a special point on the island.

Fig. 92. Stylized human figure from a Sumatran ship cloth.

plementary weft cloths, using *lidi* to mark the pattern sheds. The counting of the warp threads for each line of the pattern must have been a formidable task, since the pattern of the ship cloth does not repeat as the geometric patterns of most songket weavings do. The two halves of the cloth (the front and the back of a large ship, for example) may not even be exactly symmetrical; thus, the pattern *lidi* could not be re-used in reverse order for the second half of the design without at least some adjustments. For over three meters of cloth, the weaver had to keep this constantly changing pattern in mind. The cotton pattern-weft threads are often discontinuous, too, so that several colors may appear in one line of the weaving. Natural dyes were used for the blue, rusty red, black, and golden yellow colors most often seen on the ship cloths. On some pieces a few threads of silver or gold may have been woven into the border pattern, but generally the ship cloths are all cotton. Finally, aside from the complexities of the design, the size and weight of the cloth must have been difficult to handle on a backstrap loom even when the extra length was rolled up on the warp and breast beams.

The manner in which these textiles were used is as unusual as their design and the technical skill needed to weave them. Only the nobles of the Kröe area could own the ship cloths, and they used them as wallhangings at marriage, burial, circumcision, and other ceremonies. At a marriage ceremony, for example, the bride would sit before her husband's family's *palepai*; the ship on the cloth represented the change or transition in her life, in this case, her move from one household to another. The symbolism of the ship, originally meaning the transition from the world of the living to that of the afterlife, seems to have taken on a broader meaning encompassing any great change in the stages of a person's life.

The ritual use of the ship cloth continues among those few aristocratic families who still own one, but most of the cloths are now in the hands of museums or private collectors. Only a few thousand ship cloths were made in all, and by the 1930s they were already highly prized and much sought after by European collectors.

Smaller cloths of the same type of work as the large ship cloths were made in a wider area of southern Sumatra, and ownership of these weavings was not restricted to a certain class.

The ship motif with its powerful symbolism of death and the afterlife is combined on the *palepai* with another expressive figure, the "tree of life." This motif, which represents fertility and life-force, is also found throughout the archipelago. On ship cloths the tree appears as a branching mast growing from the center of the ship.

Kröe weavers worked an incredible display of animals, birds, and stylized human figures around these two primary themes. Human figures may appear in the form of those in figure 92 wearing strange, horned headdresses, or as Javanese-style *wayang* as in figure 138 in chapter 6. These ships and human figures are set off by ornate background decoration that, in its use of hook figures, shows Dong-Son influence. The ship cloths were woven on a backstrap loom, probably in much the same way as other sup-

Fig. 93. Supplementary weft *tampan* cloth. Cotton on cotton; white and brown using natural dyes; 40 cm. × 36 cm. Made in the early twentieth century in southwestern Sumatra. Authors' collection.

These *tampan,* as they are called, display a wide range of designs that include small ships, "tree of life" motifs, birds, and animals, as well as all-over geometric patterns (see fig. 93). Like the large hangings, these cloths also played a ceremonial role in Lampung culture. At feasts, *tampan* were used as coverings for gifts that circulated among different families in a system similar to that in which warp ikat cloths play a part. This exchange of gifts, such as the *tampan* cloths, helps strengthen family ties. But even these small cloths are no longer woven today.*

Supplementary Warp Textiles

Supplementary weft decoration is found in many areas of Indonesia, but a more difficult technique in which supplementary warp threads form a woven pattern against a cloth is found only in East Sumba and Bali. In this method, extra warp threads contrasting in material and color to the regular warp and weft threads

float over and under the surface of the plain background cloth.

EAST SUMBA: In East Sumba, this technique is used by noblewomen to make a sarong worn for such ceremonies as burials and ritual dances. Called *lau pahekung* in Sumba, this sarong is plain colored or striped except for a broad band of woven decoration near the bottom (see plate 34). Sumbanese weavers say that the *lau pahekung* is a very old type of weaving and that its motifs have not changed since ancient times. The simple yet forceful designs on these sarong differ in style from the patterns found on the ikat-decorated textiles of East Sumba, perhaps because they have been so carefully guarded. The designs are preserved on models made from thin sticks and heavy string that duplicate the pattern of the supplementary warp threads as it will appear on the weaving (see fig. 94). Each generation of weavers copies the figures on the model exactly, adding none of the individual variations that enliven Sumbanese ikat cloths.

The supplementary warp sarong often feature Neolithic-style human figures that are no longer

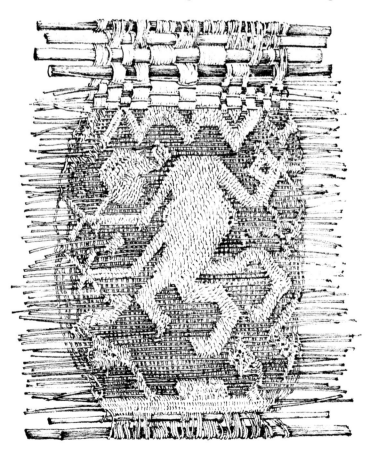

Fig. 94. In East Sumba, the traditional designs used in supplementary warp weavings are preserved on models like this one from Waingapu.

* Much of the preceding discussion is based on the important work of Dr. Mattiebelle S. Gittinger, as reported in "South Sumatran Ship Cloths," *Bulletin of the Needle and Bobbin Club* 57 (1974).

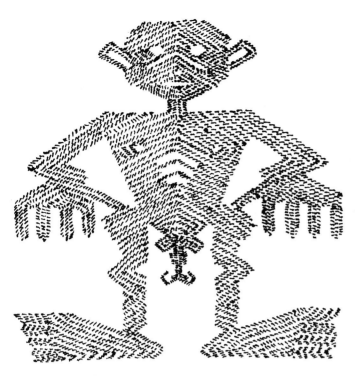

Fig. 95. *Tukakihu* motif. East Sumba.

Fig. 96. Many thin *lidi* sticks are used to mark the supplementary warp pattern for a *lau pahekung* sarong. Waingapu, East Sumba.

a common sight on contemporary Sumbanese warp ikat hinggi. *Tukakihu*, a standing man with both arms pointing downward (see fig. 95), *pahudu kalatahu*, a dancing man holding one hand up and one down, and *anatolomili*, a dancing man with both arms raised, are examples of the variety of front-facing figures. Skull trees, Chinese dragons (taken from the Chinese ceramic ware that was once abundant on the island), and birds, horses, and other animals also appear.

To produce this woven pattern, two types of warp are needed. The weaver takes the regular dyed warp threads and the threads for the pattern warp, which are usually a heavy, light-colored yarn, and arranges them on the poles of a backstrap loom. Both of these warps are circular just like the warp of a Sumbanese ikat weaving, and the pattern yarn overlaps the regular warp in the area where the woven design will appear. The weaver then inserts a piece of bamboo between the dyed warp and the pattern warp at a point on the top of the loom near the warp beam so that the two warps can be kept from tangling. She inserts other sticks in the warp to help regulate the tension and keep the threads straight. She attaches two string heddle rods to the regular warp threads to form sheds for the plainly woven background cloth, and then, following her stick-and-string pattern model, she threads

thin *lidi* sticks into the supplementary warp yarns to mark the pattern.

As she works on the loom, the weaver inserts a thicker and stronger stick in with the desired *lidi* stick and lifts the two together to raise a certain combination of the pattern-warp threads (see fig. 96). Each of the *lidi* sticks marking the pattern is raised in sequence together with one or the other of the string heddle rods to form a shed for a pass of the bobbin. The supplementary pattern appears in a twill weave (that is, the extra warp threads pass over two or more of the weft threads in diagonal steps) against a plainly woven background. Sumbanese weavers say that this type of weaving requires the greatest skill not only because of the complexity of the patterns, but because regulating the tension of the threads, always difficult with a circular warp, requires particular care with the addition of the heavy pattern yarn.

Because learning to weave *lau pahekung* demands long hours of practice, many noblewomen nowadays find it hard to interest their daughters in learning this old art. Only certain noblewomen of East Sumba are entitled to own the pattern models and perform the technique of supplementary warp weaving, and they in turn teach it only to their daughters. A young girl begins her training by making her own pattern model of sticks and string, copied from a simple geometric motif found on an old model. As she grows older, she learns to make models that have progressively more complicated motifs. But learning the actual weaving itself comes much later. Not until a girl is about eighteen years old and has already mastered the art of making an ikat weaving does she attempt to weave a sarong patterned in supplementary warp.

Several years ago, we arrived in the small East Sumbanese village of Kaliuda (famed for its ikat weavings) and upon inquiring about the supplementary warp sarong, we were told that no one knew how to weave them anymore. Just a short time before our visit, the last woman in the village with the right to use the pattern models had died. Since no daughter of hers had learned the technique, all of her models were buried with her. No woman is allowed to weave these sarong unless she owns the pattern models, so not only were the motifs of this woman's family lost but the technique itself disappeared, ending a tradition in Kaliuda stretching back many generations.

BALI: Using the same supplementary warp method, the Balinese once made cotton hangings called *lemak*, altar decorations for their New Year celebrations. The motifs and style of *lemak* are today created by handweaving palm fiber; cotton loom weaving has disappeared. The main motif on this special cloth was a stylized figure called *cili*, a symbol widely used in Bali to represent Devi Sri, the goddess of rice and other aspects of daily life, including weaving (see fig. 97).

Fig. 97. *Cili* figure. Bali.

Other Weaving Techniques

A variety of woven-ornament techniques in addition to supplementary weft and warp weaving are found in Indonesia. One simple technique, warp pick-up weaving, is used mainly for decorative accents rather than for the main motif (see plate 35). A warp pick-up pattern is created by using *lidi* to hold certain warp threads above the shed for more than one pass of the weft. Small bands of warp pick-up weave add interest to ikat and plain cloths from West Sumba, Savu (where it is known as *raja* and decorates the *raja* sarong; see chapter 2), and other East Nusatenggara islands; the technique is also used in Bali to decorate sashes.

In Sumba, a simple warp-patterned border called *kabakil* is woven along the bottom edges of warp ikat and plain weavings using a small loom set up with warp threads of several colors. The fringe of a finished Sumbanese cloth is made up of its unwoven warp threads, and these become the weft threads of the woven *kabakil* border. The Lamboya district of West Sumba is noted for a plain white weaving that is decorated only with a multicolored *kabakil* border about six to ten centimeters wide (see fig. 98).

A few other special weaving methods are used to create the main motif on textiles in Indonesia. One of these techniques is called *pilih*, a word which means "to choose." It is an unusual variation of supplementary weft weaving. On most supplementary weft cloths, such as songket, the supplementary threads produce the pattern. With the *pilih* technique as well, extra weft threads are woven in, but instead of these threads forming the motif they become part of the background fabric. The main motif itself is carried by the regular warp threads as they float over the background in a complicated version of warp pick-up weave. The Iban Dyaks of Borneo use this technique to make cloths decorated with animals such as lizards, human figures, and geometric patterns (see plate 36). An example of *pilih* work from central Timor can be seen in the woven motif in plate 39.

Another weaving technique, called *sungkit*, is used by the Iban Dyaks and the Timorese to make delicate and detailed patterns that look very much like fine embroidery. *Sungkit* is a type of embroidered warp or wrapped warp technique, and work on it progresses very slowly, even by the standards of people who are general-

Fig. 98. *Kabakil* border on a man's cloth. Blue, white, and red threads are woven into the fringe of the finished weaving to create a decorative border. From Lamboya, West Sumba. Authors' collection.

ly unconcerned with the pressures of time. As the cloth is woven, each pattern thread is wrapped around one or two warp threads at a time. Many short pattern threads may be used across one line of the weaving, depending on the pattern and how many colors are desired, and each one is laid in separately with a needle or by hand. Motifs range from simple lizard figures to the complex multicolored hook-and-rhomb patterns that are found in central Timor and in the Iban Dyak region of Borneo (see plates 37 and 38).

Central Timor boasts a variety of complex weaving techniques, and the Iban Dyaks of Borneo share many of the same methods of decoration. The people in these two areas, along with the Bataks of North Sumatra and the Torajans of central Sulawesi, had relatively little contact with outsiders after they were influenced by the Dong-Son culture. Their traditional motifs are very similar, as are many of the methods they employ. Perhaps these weaving techniques, like the motifs, were once more widespread and have persisted only in the most remote areas.

One more of these unusual techniques shared by only a few Ancient Peoples is a type of tapestry weave called *kelim*. Tapestry weaving in general means that the weft threads only travel part way across the warp in one shed and then move in the opposite direction in the next shed. By using different colors of weft, weavers can achieve a complex pattern. In *kelim* weaving, two weft threads traveling toward each other in the same shed do not wrap around a common warp thread, so when they reverse directions in the next shed, a slit is left in the cloth. Since many different weft threads are usually used between one selvage and the other to give a colorful pattern, there are many such open spaces on each line of fabric. So that these slits do not greatly weaken the cloth, they are often staggered on adjacent lines, leaving gaps between different sets of warp threads. The geometric pattern that appears on the cloth may also incorporate the openings in the fabric as part of the decoration. *Kelim* was used to decorate such weavings as war headdresses in Timor and weavings that were worn to battle in Sumba (*rohubanggi*; see chapter 2), but we never met a weaver in East Nusatenggara who was still skilled at this technique (see plate 39).

Embroidery, Prada Cloth, and Beaded Textiles

Some methods of decorating textiles, such as embroidery, beading, application of gold dust, and appliqués, are neither weaving nor dyeing techniques. Of these methods, embroidery is the most widespread in Indonesia, and Sumatra, Timor, Sumba, Sulawesi, Borneo, and other areas present a variety of embroidered fabrics. These cloths range from the gold-patterned gift

Fig. 99. Iban Dyak embroidered cloth with motif of helicopters and human figures. Chemically dyed cotton thread on a naturally dyed red cotton background; 128 cm. × 76 cm. From upper Rajang River area, Sarawak, Malaysia. Tomoyuki Yamanobe collection.

coverings of West Sumatra and the everyday black sarong of East Sumba, enlivened with colorful chain-stitched animals, to cloths that portray the impact of the modern world on the tribes of Borneo. Figure 99, an Iban Dyak cloth from Sarawak (Malaysian Borneo), depicts a real twentieth-century motif—the government helicopters that rescue long-house dwellers in times of emergency.

The most outstanding of the embroidered textiles found in Indonesia are the sarong woven in the vicinity of the Kröe area in southern Sumatra, the same area where the large ship cloths and smaller *tampan* cloths were made. These *tapis* sarong, as they are called, served as ceremonial dress for Lampung women, and like the ship cloths they are no longer produced (see fig. 100).

The cotton *tapis* sarong are decorated with bands of brownish colored warp ikat in hooked patterns much like those found on East Nusatenggara ikat textiles. These ikat bands alternate with plain bands that are embroidered with white or yellow silk thread. Like the woven ship cloths (see plate 33) the main motif is the

"ship of the dead," peopled with strange human figures that seem to be wearing headdresses (see fig. 101). These peculiar appendages resemble buffalo horns and are sometimes similar to the stylized human forms that appear on the ship cloths. The styling of the ships and figures on the sarong and their eerie nightmarish quality are quite different from those on the ship cloths, however, and the silk-embroidered ships contrast sharply with the symmetrical ikat motifs on the other bands of the same sarong. The *tapis* ships are unlike any other Indonesian textile motifs but they are very similar to the painted ships found among the Dyaks of Borneo. This is a rare example of Late Chou influence on textile motifs in Indonesia. Such curving asymmetrical figures are characteristic of the Late Chou culture, and this style of design is generally found in Borneo in crafts other than textiles. Its appearance in southern Sumatra is just another link connecting the Ancient Peoples over kilometers of water and years of time.

In part of the Lampung district another type of embroidered sarong (unlike the *tapis*) is still made today. These sarong rarely feature any

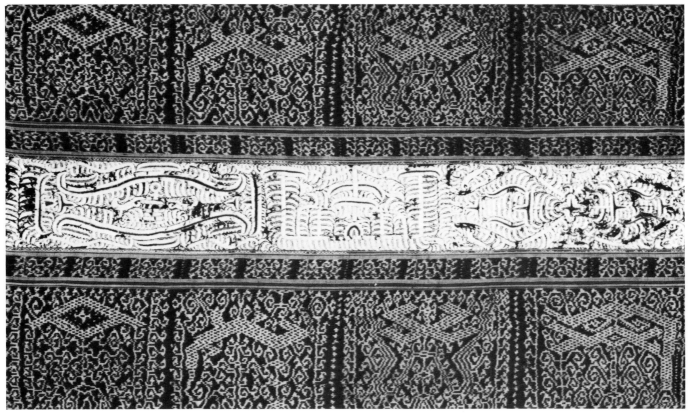

Fig. 100. Detail of silk embroidered *tapis* sarong showing "ship of the dead" motif in the central band. Naturally dyed brown cotton background. From Kröe area, Sumatra. Toyama Kinenkan Foundation collection.

Fig. 101. "Ship of the dead" motif. Kröe area, Sumatra.

ikat decoration and the material used for the embroidery is gold thread. The gold thread is laid on the surface of the cloth and tacked into place at intervals with plain thread using a couching stitch. Other shiny materials like bits of mica and sequins are also sewn onto the cloth, sometimes resulting in a rather gaudy effect. The gold motifs tend to be simple, geometric forms that lack the powerful imagery of the *tapis* sarong embroideries or the woven ship cloths. The sarong in plate 40 shows a simple ship, a realistic one, not the crescent-shaped, high-prowed ship of the afterlife.

The urge to apply precious materials to cloth was widespread during early times and is still found among some Ancient Peoples today. Gold and silver thread, coins, seeds, and beads were added to increase the value as well as the beauty of many cloths.

One way to decorate a cloth with gold is to apply a glue over the colored cloth in the form of the desired pattern and sprinkle the fabric with gold dust that will then adhere to the sticky areas. This technique is used on batik cloths to outline or emphasize the motifs and also to make *prada* cloth, a Balinese textile worn at weddings and by temple dancers (see fig. 79, chapter 3). *Prada* cloth is plain colored, usually green or purple, except for the gold pattern, which is almost always the same stylized lotus-flower design with a swastika-patterned border.

Beads were once very precious and they still retain a surprisingly high value in some societies, sometimes being worth more than their weight in gold. Attaching seeds, shells, and, later, beads to cloth is probably one of the oldest methods of textile decoration found in Indonesia. Beadwork was a common technique of textile decoration until recently on the islands of Sumba and Flores and among the Torajans, Bataks, and Dyaks.

The beaded textiles that still exist, such as a beaded sarong in Sumba that depicts Neolithic-style human figures, are often saved for rituals and are believed to have magical powers. In Nggela village in the Lio district of Flores, only one beaded textile remains, a sarong called *lawo butu,* which one of the village elders reluctantly brought out to show us. This sarong is worn for ceremonial rainmaking dances held during times of drought. With the consent of the villagers, we set about making a few photographs of the plainly striped sarong. A large band near one end of the cloth was decorated with beaded geometric figures that were literally disintegrating—it was not really a very impressive textile visually. By chance, or perhaps not, the film in the camera did not wind properly for the photos of the beaded sarong, a fact we discovered shortly after the sarong had been put away. The villagers insisted this happened because the sarong did not want to be photographed and had the power to stop the camera from working.

5 Batik: Craft of Java

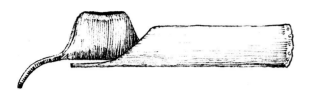

Batik is a technique of textile decoration in which a dye-resist, usually wax, is applied to the cloth; the resist prevents the dye from penetrating the covered areas of the fabric, thus creating a pattern in negative. Because batik is a dye-resist technique, it is related to ikat and tie-dyeing, but the method of applying the resist for batik is quite different from the tying processes characteristic of either of these techniques. Batik offers the opportunity to use the dye-resist to draw complete patterns directly on the cloth. In ikat, the patterns are bound onto sections of thread in a fragmented manner, and in tie-dyeing the patterns are formed by tying or stitching areas of fabric to resist the dye. Batik makers thus have more freedom in the layout of the design and can produce more intricate patterns.

The root word, *tik,* is derived from Malay, and originally in a narrow sense meant "dots" or "drops," while in a broader context it came to mean "write" or "draw." The most simple batik were made with drops of resist applied to the cloth with a stick. *Nitik,* an early type of pattern that is still popular today, incorporates the same root word, *tik,* in its name and has a fragmented dotted-line appearance, as if wax had been dropped on the cloth (see fig. 126, chapter 6). Later on, as new tools were invented, complex, highly developed patterns evolved and brought Javanese batik to a level of great sophistication.

The technique of applying wax or other resists such as rice paste to cloth to create a design is found in many parts of the world, although nowhere else does it assume the importance that it does in Java. India, Japan, Sri Lanka, China,

Turkestan, western Africa, and Indochina all produce types of batik cloth. How the technique of batik came to be found in these particular areas is not known. Did batik begin in one area and spread from there to other places, carried perhaps by traders and migrants, or was the technique born independently in several different places? In the last one hundred years, scholars have tried to piece together the puzzle, but still very little is known with certainty about the origins and spread of batik technique.

Batik Past and Present

The earliest known examples of batiklike cloth are some fragments dating from the first century A.D. that have been found in Egyptian tombs. Based on the motifs decorating those pieces, textile scholars believe that they may have been made in India.* Other examples of early batik-decorated textiles include fragments, possibly of Chinese origin, dating from the eighth century that are kept in the Imperial Storehouse (Shoso-in) collection at the Todai-ji temple in Nara, Japan.

Batik making has also had a long history in Java, although the influences on its development are very difficult to trace. The earliest certain surviving reference to batik, according to the scholar G. P. Rouffaer, is in a *lontar* palm-leaf scroll from southwestern Java that is dated A.D. 1520. The batik workers at that time were called *lukis,* or "painters," and the work they did was called *tulis,* or "writing." An even

* Alfred Steinmann, "Batik Work: Its Origin and Spread," *Ciba Review* 58 (1947), p. 2103.

earlier inscription dates from the twelfth century; it was found in East Java and refers to a unique batik motif that is still in use today, called *grinsing*. Rouffaer draws the conclusion that the craft of batik was already being practiced during this early period.* Other than the odd inscription or reference in literature, there are few surviving historical records that offer a solution to the perplexing riddle of how batik originated in Java.

Since there are so few written references to batik, there has been a lively debate as to whether batik developed independently in Java or was introduced from overseas, that is, India. Some researchers argue that because several of the other textile techniques found in Indonesia, such as weft ikat or supplementary weft weaving, were originally brought to the archipelago by traders, batik, too, must have been introduced in a like manner. The earliest known batik is thought to be from India, and it is well known that in the seventeenth and eighteenth centuries southern India had a thriving batik industry that exported cloths all over Southeast Asia and the islands of Indonesia; these cloths, therefore, could have had some influence on the development of batik in Java.

Conversely, other researchers support the theory that batik developed in Java with a minimum of outside influences. They point to the fact that early Javanese batik used dyestuffs and materials that are indigenous to Indonesia and did not rely on imported stocks. *Mengkudu* red dye and the *soga* plants used to produce the distinctive browns characteristic of Javanese batik are native to the islands of the area. Also, cotton is the basic fabric for batik while the techniques such as weft ikat and supplementary weft weaving that were introduced by traders often use imported materials such as silk or metallic threads.

Further evidence for batik being an indigenous Javanese art is that many of the motifs which appear on traditional Central Javanese batik are derived from local sources and are often stylizations of native birds and plants. An example is the *ganggong* motif, derived from the flower of a marsh plant belonging to the nightshade family (probably *Solanum denticulatum* L.);

found in Java, the plant is the source for a variety of Javanese motifs.*

If batik did develop independently in Java, its antecedents may have been primitive batik techniques that existed in pre-Hindu Java. Simple batik techniques were still found in parts of Java and among the Torajans of South Sulawesi until recent times. The lack of any tangible evidence makes it difficult to say for sure, but it is certainly a possibility that these primitive methods found in South Sulawesi and West Java were the precursors of the highly developed batik techniques of Central Java today.

One of these simpler resist-decorated cloths was made at least up until the 1950s in remote areas of the South Bantam district of West Java. Called *simbut,* it was decorated by applying a paste resist to coarse homespun cotton. A red dye made from the *mengkudu* root was brushed onto the cloth, and then the rice paste was removed by soaking the cloth in cold water. The motifs consisted of simple, unsophisticated outlines of animal forms, human figures, and magical-looking geometric symbols appearing in white against a red background. Today, *simbut* are rarely seen, and those that survive are prized as heirlooms by the people that own them.

Another rudimentary type of batik is found approximately eight hundred kilometers away from Java in the high mountains of South Sulawesi. The Torajan people of the Rantepao Valley made an indigo and white ceremonial cloth that was decorated using dye-resist techniques. This cloth is no longer made, at least in the accessible areas. Called *sarita* by the Torajans, these long, narrow textiles are still used as decorative banners at certain ceremonies. Although no one today in the area can remember how to make the cloth, earlier reports describe it as being patterned by applying melted beeswax to the fabric with a bamboo stick.†

Because Torajans were relatively isolated until the end of the nineteenth century, any connection between the *sarita* cloths once made by the Torajans and Javanese batik would have

* G. P. Rouffaer and Dr. H. H. Juinboll, *De Batikkunst in Ned. India en Haare Geschiendenis* [The art of batik in the Netherland Indies and its development] (Utrecht: Rijks Ethnographisch Museum, 1914).

* Tassilo Adam, "The Art of Batik in Java," *Bulletin of the Needle and Bobbin Club* 18 (1934), p. 37.
† Laurens Langewis and Frits A. Wagner, *Decorative Art in Indonesian Textiles* (Amsterdam: N. V. Boekhandel en Vitgeverij C. P. J. van der Peet, 1964), p. 16.

been in the distant past. Interestingly, written references suggest that similar cloths were made by other Ancient Peoples in Flores and Halmahera,* but it seems that no examples have survived up to the present.

If these reports of the existence of other such cloths are accurate, there is the possibility that the technique of batik was once more widespread among the Ancient Peoples. Outside of Indonesia, the Meo hill tribe of Burma, Laos, and Thailand still makes batik in practically the same manner as that supposed to have been used by the Torajans, applying wax and dyeing the cloth in indigo. The similarity between Meo batik and that of the Torajans may be just a coincidence, or it may mean that the craft was once practiced by many of the Ancient Peoples.

Whether the seeds of the technique originated in Java or were brought from India, it is in the royal courts of Central Java that the art of batik flourished, reaching unsurpassed technical sophistication and creating motifs of stunning beauty. By the sixteenth century, the tradition of batik making was well established among the ladies of the Central Javanese courts.

Often the impression one gets from Javanese literature and the writings of early European visitors to the courts is that making batik was an exclusive prerogative of aristocratic ladies. Whether or not this was true in the art's early days is debatable. After all, batik making among the common people may simply not be mentioned in early Javanese writings, for the literature of that period was oriented exclusively toward life in the courts and reported little of what went on outside the confines of the palace.†

Indeed, by looking at batik in the light of what we know about other textiles in Indonesia, we can imagine that although the most intricate cloths were made in the courts, peasant women probably made rougher, less sophisticated versions for themselves. This would be analogous to the making of warp ikat in Sumba, where the finest hinggi were always made by the king's weavers while the commoners made a similar form of the textile, often borrowing the royal motifs for themselves. In Java, the aristocratic women of the courts would have had the wealth needed to obtain the best materials for making fine batik,

and enough leisure time to create the elaborate traditional motifs; consequently, they would have turned out the very best pieces. While the life of the peasants has never been easy in Java, the island's land has been fruitful, and it is not hard to imagine women outside the courts making batik for themselves or their families in their free time away from their daily chores.

Over the last two centuries, batik has grown from an art associated primarily with the great courts of Central Java into an important industry. Java's most famous art form has been especially responsive to technical and social changes. By the mid-nineteenth century, the cities of the north coast between Semarang and Surabaya that include Rembang and Juana (an area known as the Pasisir Plain), were a thriving center of batik production, specializing in silk batik that were exported to Bali and Sumatra. The waxing of these cloths was done by itinerant peasant women, called *pengobeng*, who traveled around the various batik-making cities on the north coast to earn their livings. A labor study in 1930 showed that thousands of *pengobeng* were working in the Pasisir Plain area.* Today, however, the once important batik industry along the Pasisir Plain has declined to the point of nonexistence.

Other large towns along the north coast such as Pekalongan, Indramayu, Jakarta, Lasem, Tegal, and Cirebon produce distinctive cotton batik. Over the years, Pekalongan has emerged as the largest producer of batik in Java, and this city exports its products throughout Indonesia and Southeast Asia as well as to Europe, Japan, and the United States.

Batik is also made in limited quantities in southwestern Java in the towns of Tasikmalaya, Garut, Banyumas, and Ciamis. Likewise, small batik industries can be found in various towns in East Java including Sidoarjo, Mojokerto, Gresik, Kudus, Talungagung, and Ponorogo. Most of these towns produce batik whose techniques and motifs closely follow those found in the two major batik-producing areas of Central Java, Jogjakarta and Surakarta (or Solo as it is called in Java). And most of the batik produced in the aforementioned towns eventually finds its way into the markets of these two cities.

Outside of Java, Madura Island and Sumatra, mainly Palembang and Jambi, once

* Yazir Marzuki, N. Tirtaamidjaja, and Benedict R. O'G. Anderson, *Batik: Pola dan Tjorak—Pattern and Design* (Jakarta: Jambatan, 1966), p. 17.
† Ibid.

* Ibid., p. 18.

Fig. 102. Shops selling waxes, dyes, white cloth, tools, and other materials for making batik can be found along Secoyudan Street in Solo, Central Java.

produced beautiful batik utilizing techniques and variations of motifs adopted from Central Java. However, batik has not been produced in southern Sumatra, Jambi, or Madura for many years and examples from these areas are rarely seen outside of museums.

Over the last twenty years, the east coast of Malaysia has become known as a batik-producing area. The Malay batik industry is centered in the cities of Kota Bharu and Trengganu. But batik is not a traditional craft in Malaysia; the technique and some of the motifs were borrowed from Java in the 1950s. Generally, Malaysian batik is produced by using stamps to apply the wax to the cloth, a quicker method than drawing the pattern in by hand.

The ancient court capitals of Central Java, Solo and Jogjakarta, are where batik developed to its highest degree of excellence, and these two cities along with Pekalongan are still the major sources of batik. The importance of batik in Java today can be seen in Solo, the center of production for traditional Javanese-style batik. A

major landmark in the center of the city is the Sultan's Palace, and the nearby area is almost completely dominated by the production and sale of batik cloths. Secoyudan Street is the main thoroughfare, and in its shops can be found everything from basic batik supplies to the finished product. Even the air smells of hot melted wax, for behind many of the storefronts and down the numerous small sidestreets are hidden the workshops where Solo's batik is made. Pedicabs filled with bolts of cloth, slabs of wax, and partially finished pieces of batik rush busily up and down Secoyudan Street. Lining the sidewalks are merchants selling materials for all stages of the batik process.

There are shops along Secoyudan Street filled with nothing but blocks of wax ranging in color from pale yellow to deep brown (see fig. 102). Other merchants stock large selections of European and Japanese synthetic dyes as well as drums of indigo paste and the woods and barks that are used as natural dyes. In the fabric shops, bolts of graded white cotton cloth await the purchaser who will transform them with wax and dye into beautiful batik. And spread out on the sidewalk in front of other shops are hand-beaten copper pans and other batik tools. Nowhere else in Java can so many different supplies be purchased on one street, and local batik makers, factory buyers from nearby towns, and curious tourists swarm to the area in search of bargains.

At one end of Secoyudan Street is Pasar Klewar, a huge three-story market filled with hundreds of thousands of finished batik cloths that become the object of intense trading among dealers as well as casual buyers. Interspersed among the wax stores and the dye shops, the cloth merchants and the tool makers, are numerous gold shops, serving as a reminder to all who pass that batik is a big business in Solo, one that provides a livelihood for thousands of the city's residents.

Hand-drawn and Stamped Batik

The development of the modern batik industry was set in motion by the invention over a hundred years ago of a copper stamp, called a *tjap* (*cap* in modern Indonesian spelling), that applies wax over a small area of the cloth in a fixed pattern. The tjap greatly reduced the time needed to finish a piece of batik, and without it, the batik industry as it is today would not exist. Before the tjap came into use, all batik were laboriously waxed line by line using a small drawing tool called a *tjanting (canting)*. Batik is generally labeled stamped *(tjap)* or hand-drawn *(tulis)*, a classification based on the type of tool used to wax the cloth. Identifying batik by the tool used to apply the wax is apt because the craft itself has been greatly affected by innovations in tools.

THE TJANTING: The origin of the tjanting, which replaced the crude stick and led to the growth of batik as an art in Java, is a mystery. It is generally considered to be a Javanese invention. G. P. Rouffaer deduced that it may have been in use as early as the twelfth century, basing his opinion on a reference from that time to the batik pattern *grinsing*, a design requiring such control in applying the wax that it could have only been made with the aid of such a tool.

The tjanting consists of a small copper cup with a spout through which melted wax can flow out onto the cloth. The cup is mounted on a

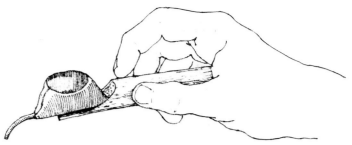

Fig. 103. A single-spout tjanting is used for drawing lines.

Fig. 104. A multi-spout tjanting is used for fill-in decorations.

wooden or rattan handle (see fig. 103). The size of the spout and the number of spouts may be varied for different functions. Small-spouted tjanting are used to draw fine lines, and those with larger cups and wider spouts are used to cover large open spaces of the cloth with wax. A tjanting may also have from two to seven spouts arranged so that parallel lines of wax can be laid down simultaneously. Other types of tjanting may have several spouts arranged in the shape of a star, triangle, or other figure so that these decorative dots may be placed uniformly on the cloth (see fig. 104).

The capability of the tjanting to draw a narrow, even, and continuous line of wax directly onto the fabric opened up tremendous possibilities in the field of design. The earliest batik in Java was probably made in the manner of the *sarita* cloth of Sulawesi, by applying the resist with a stick. This early method of waxing the fabric would have limited batik makers to simple motifs, but with the invention of the tjanting it became possible for waxers to create the complex patterns now associated with traditional Javanese batik.

Hand-drawn batik has always been based on a cooperative division of labor; therefore, the creation of a piece of batik is not usually the work of only one woman, in contrast to some of the other textile arts found in Indonesia. Even in the courts, women waxed the design and sent their cloths to professional dyers. They did not, for example, make their own dyes as ikat weavers in East Nusatenggara do. In most of Java today, the hand-waxing is done by women and the dyeing by men. A single exception can be found in Trusmi and Kalitengah villages near Cirebon on the northwestern coast of Java, where a few men also join the women in doing fine hand-waxing with a tjanting.

More men have recently taken up the tjanting to work in the new field of batik paintings, cloth pictures produced by the wax-resist technique. Although some of the male artists do all the waxing and dyeing themselves, others just draw the basic outline and leave the tedious fill-in work to women. This use of waxers to help make paintings is related, some say, to a decline in the quality of traditional batik in Jogjakarta. The demand for these dyed-cloth pictures, whose subject matter ranges from traditional Indonesian scenes to modern abstract designs, has increased dramatically in recent years, especially among visitors to Jogjakarta. The newly prosperous batik painters have hired some of the best female artisans to help them with their paintings, taking them away from the creation of traditional batik.

Today a few women still wax cloths at home in their spare time and send them out to be dyed much as was done in the old courts in Central Java. But more and more hand-drawn batik is being made in small workshops by women who wax as a means of livelihood. In the large workshops, the hand-drawn batik is made as a sideline to stamped batik, but there are still some family-run enterprises that create only the traditional *tulis* cloth. These small concerns lie somewhere between the large factories and the women working independently at home.

One such operation is managed by the family of Ibu Atmosuwanindo, a lady in her mid-seventies who has been making batik since she was a young girl. Most of her immediate family is involved in this enterprise. Her son, Pak Hadiwasita, helps her oversee the small work-shop in their home. Along with his son, Pak Hadiwasita makes batik paintings, mixes his own wax, and does much of the dyeing for the workshop. About twenty village girls work at waxing traditional Central Javanese and Cire-bon patterns. These young women come from the countryside around Jogjakarta to work with Ibu Atmosuwanindo during periods when they are not needed in the rice fields. Ibu Atmo-suwanindo herself, despite her age, puts in long days and nights waxing batik. We would

sometimes visit her in the afternoon and find her asleep beside her work, resting her head on an empty tin can because "it is cool." She would awaken, work three or four hours, and then lie back down and rest.

For many years, Ibu Atmosuwanindo waxed batik at the Batik Research Center, a govern-ment-operated center in Jogjakarta whose aim is to study and preserve old batik techniques and motifs while experimenting with new ones. Ibu Atmosuwanindo was particularly interested in preserving the traditional cloud patterns of Cirebon, and her work at the Batik Research Center was aimed in that direction.

Today Ibu Atmosuwanindo purchases old batik and recreates their motifs. Each old pattern that she finds is carefully sketched on paper, and she views these pattern models as something of an heirloom to be handed down to her children. Occasionally, ladies will visit Ibu Atmosuwanindo to commission a favorite motif or will bring batik to be copied. In this way, many old patterns are given new life. Preserving these traditional motifs is important work to Ibu Atmosuwanindo since batik is to her more than just a way to earn a living.

The open-sided shed that serves as the waxing area of Ibu Atmosuwanindo's workshop is typical of Javanese batik making. Groups of three or four young women are seated on mats or low stools around each pan of melted wax atop a kerosene stove. The fabric being waxed is draped over a rack called a *gawangan*. Talk is sporadic even for the usually loquacious Javanese as the girls focus on their work.

Hand-waxing is slow work that demands concentration and a serene frame of mind. A waxer's hand must be steady in order to draw smooth lines and lay down the evenly spaced dots of wax called *citcik*. To apply wax to the fabric, a batik maker first fills the cup of the tjanting by dipping it into the hot wax and blows lightly on the spout to unclog any solid wax. Holding the cloth over her left palm, she tilts the tjanting spout slightly upward and lets the wax flow from the spout onto the cloth. Usual-ly, she moves the tjanting from left to right or from bottom to top to draw a given design el-ement. The tjanting spout does not actually touch the fabric as it glides over the surface (see fig. 105).

In Pekalongan, where waxing reaches a high level of technical virtuosity in extremely fine

Fig. 105. Ibu Atmosuwanindo applies wax with a tjanting. Jogjakarta, Central Java.

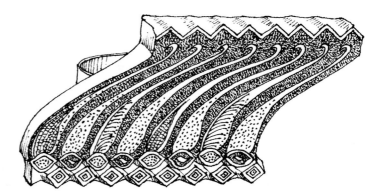

Fig. 106. A tjap is used to apply a wax pattern to a large area of cloth.

detail work—hundreds of dots may decorate a single leaf—some workshops instruct their waxers in deep-breathing exercises to help steady the hand. The act of waxing is looked upon by some women as a sort of spiritual exercise, almost a type of meditation. A saying in Javanese, *mbatik manah,* literally translates as "to make batik designs on the heart" but actually means to meditate.* Batik was once, and in many cases still is, part of the proper education for upper-class Javanese girls. The discipline and concentration required to wax complex batik motifs for hours at a time is considered valuable training. A single batik cloth can take anywhere from one to six months or even longer to finish depending on the complexity of the motif, so it is a good teacher of patience, a trait esteemed in Javanese society.

THE TJAP: In the mid-nineteenth century the art of hand-waxing was almost eclipsed by the new method of waxing the cloth with a copper stamp or tjap. Each time the stamp is pressed to the cloth, it applies an even coating of wax

in a fixed design to approximately two hundred square centimeters of cloth. The stamp revolutionized the production of batik; it took a small cottage industry, a fine art, an expression of Javanese sensibilities, and a hobby for aristocratic women, and turned it into a real commercial enterprise. The stamp was the single most important factor in creating the batik industry since it enabled batik cloth to be made quicker and more economically (see fig. 106).

The making of the copper tjap, like many of the other individual crafts that play a role in batik, is a skill passed from father to son. Pak Budisuwarno is one of the few remaining full-time stampmakers in Jogjakarta, and he learned the trade from his father. He makes copper stamps to order for workshops in his area and has trouble keeping up with the demand. In these times of change, he says, young men have become reluctant to apprentice themselves to the craft. Stampmaking still flourishes in Solo and Pekalongan, however, and Pak Budisuwarno blames its decline in Jogjakarta on the fact that each year less and less traditional batik is being produced there.

Pak Budisuwarno, like most stampmakers, does not create the pattern of the stamp himself. He works from an actual-size sketch brought to him by whoever ordered the stamp. Working with rolls of sheet copper, pliers, and cutting tools, Pak Budisuwarno first constructs a gridlike frame to which the pattern pieces can be attached (see fig. 107). Then he cuts pieces of sheet copper and bends them to the shape of the pattern, matching them carefully to the drawing. The edge of the copper sheeting will touch the cloth, applying the wax in a line. The tiny dots common on many batik patterns are made by

* Clifford Geertz, *The Religion of Java* (Chicago and London: University of Chicago Press, 1960), p. 287.

Fig. 107. Working from a sketch, Pak Budisuwarno fashions copper sheeting and wire into a new tjap. Jogjakarta, Central Java.

small pieces of copper wire or sheeting, each one attached singly to the frame so that only the tip will touch the cloth and leave a dot of wax. By setting many small pieces very close together, enough wax will be carried to the cloth to block out an entire area with wax.

After all the different sections of the motif are cut and shaped, Pak Budisuwarno notches and fits the pieces together. Then he solders the sections onto the frame. He attaches a handle to the frame and then immerses the entire tjap in melted pine resin. Once the resin hardens he files the surface of the stamp flat so that it will touch the cloth evenly. After he melts the resin off, the stamp is ready to use.

Making a tjap can take from one to three months depending, of course, on the complexity of the motif. But once it is finished, if it is well cared for, a stamp has a long life. Pak Budisuwarno claims that a tjap may be used for over one hundred years. To repair a stamp, the stampmaker readjusts any parts of the motif that have been bent through use. The stamp is once more encased in pine resin, the surfaces filed

flat, and when the resin is melted off the stamp can be used again; it is like new. The resin, in addition to making the filing easier, also acts as a cleaning agent that dissolves dirt and old wax.

Using the stamp to apply the wax takes the creative drawing out of batik—the wax pattern is put on the cloth in sections whose overall design is invariable. Some of the earliest references to batik makers call them *lukis,* or painters, because they drew with the tjanting the way an artist would use a brush. But this creative element disappears when the tjap is used.

Javanese are very aware of this difference between hand-drawn and stamped batik. The first question a Javanese will ask about a piece of batik—a friend's new purchase, for example— is "Is it *tulis* or *tjap?*" The next question is invariably, "How much did you pay?"—Javanese enjoy checking up on each other's bargaining skill.

At any gathering, such as a wedding or festival, the type of batik worn is an important sign of status (and taste). The women surreptitiously inspect each other's batik. Most Javanese ladies, many of whom have often made batik themselves, know at a glance the quality of a particular cloth. The interest is not only in status; there is a widespread appreciation and respect among Javanese of all social and economic classes for the skill needed to create hand-drawn batik.

The geometric patterns of Central Java lend themselves very well to the tjap method; in fact, it is sometimes difficult to distinguish a hand-drawn batik from a stamped one. The object of stamped batik, besides producing a cloth quickly and cheaply, is to make a piece complex enough to look as if it were hand-drawn, while that of hand-drawn batik is to make the work as flawless as possible. Paradoxically, the more perfect the hand-drawn motif appears, to a certain degree the more it may look like stamped batik. The visual differences can be slight and it may be difficult for even a Javanese to distinguish a stamped piece from a hand-drawn one.

In determining whether a batik is hand-drawn or stamped, practice and experience are the best guide, but there are several signs to watch for. Hand-drawn batik patterns are noticeably or slightly irregular; the lines waver a bit and the motifs lack the rigidity of stamped work. If repeating pattern elements, such as a flower, are compared on various sections of the cloth, they appear slightly different. On a stamped piece these elements will be exactly the same all over the cloth because they were created by the same stamp. Occasionally, an indistinct break may appear in the pattern of a stamped piece where two applications of the stamp have failed to meet perfectly; this break is considered poor work even on low-quality stamped batik.

Another difference between stamped and hand-drawn batik is the cloth. Hand-drawn batik is generally made on a finer grade of cotton cambric (known as *mori*) than stamped batik. Batik was originally made with handwoven, homespun cotton until cambric was introduced to Indonesia from India in the early nineteenth century, and then later from Europe. Batik makers quickly came to prefer the imported cambric. They discovered that the smoother surface of the manufactured cotton was easier to work on than the rough surface of the homespun cloth they had been using. The fine texture of imported cambric made highly detailed work possible because it did not snag the tjanting,

and the fabric tended to absorb the natural dyes well. The imported cloth also helped spur the development of the stamped-batik industry because it was available in large quantities.

The principal grades of cambric today are *primissima* (the highest quality), *prima*, *biru*, and *blaco* (the coarsest and cheapest cloth). Since independence in 1949, Chinese and Japanese cloth has been used, but in an effort to expand its own cambric capacity, Java is now producing all four grades of cloth.

It should be noted that cloth waxed by the tjap method is true batik; it is made with a wax dye-resist and both it and hand-drawn pieces go through the same processes after the wax has been applied. Stamped batik *(batik tjap)* should not be confused with printed cloth that bears traditional Javanese patterns and is often passed off as batik to the unknowledgeable buyer. A printed fabric has clear color only on one surface; real batik, whether it is hand-drawn or stamped, should have the same color intensity and clarity of pattern on both sides of the cloth.

Stamped batik is produced on a scale that ranges from cottage industries to large corporations employing hundreds of workers. An important factor behind the growth of batik into an industry is Chinese entrepreneurial skills. Chinese immigrants set up many of the early factories when the tjap came into use, and up to the present day they have been operating most of the major batik companies and many of the smaller ones as well.

A Chinese family owns and operates a Solo workshop called Tiga Sriti ("Three Swallows") that is located on the far end of Secoyudan Street away from the market of Pasar Klewar. Most of their batik is the classic brown, black, and blue style of Central Java and eventually comes into the hands of small stall holders in Pasar Klewar.

Very few people passing by Tiga Sriti's storefront with its few glass cases of faded pieces of batik would guess that behind it lay a bustling batik operation. Through the back of the storefront and down a corridor are the working areas, one room opening onto another. Like most batik workshops, the windows are either nonexistent or inexplicably shuttered, and people often work under the pale light of an electric bulb. The air is sultry and the fetid odor of indigo dye mingles with steam and the smell of wax.

Compared with the relative calm of Ibu Atmosuwanindo's *tulis* workshop, Tiga Sriti hums with activity. Many people are involved in each step of batik production. About sixty people are employed there, making it (by Javanese standards) a medium-sized workshop.

Principles of Batik Making

There are quite a few steps involved in making batik, and there are various methods that can be used, depending on the type of batik and the region. However, the principles of batik remain the same.

Wax resist is used to protect areas of the cloth from the dye, and it is applied first to the parts of the cloth that will remain white or require protection from the initial dyebath. The simplest batik design is a white outline or shape against a dark background, precisely the type of motif that is found on such simple batik as the *sarita* cloth of Sulawesi and the *simbut* of Bantam in West Java. Central Javanese batik motifs are often much more complex. For example, the motif or outline of the figure may be dark against a lighter colored background.

While the waxer works, she must always have a mental picture of how the batik will appear once the wax is removed—the waxed cloth is similar to a photo negative in which the light areas will print dark and vice versa. After the first dyeing, parts of the design can be freed of resist and new areas covered with wax before the second dyeing; the final combination of colors is another thing that the waxer must keep in mind as she works.

The type of batik made in Central Java is called *kain soga*, *kain* referring to a length of cloth worn wrapped around the waist, and *soga* being the brown dyestuff that is used to color the fabric. Several different traditional methods are used to make this cloth. The best known and most widely used method—and the one used at the Tiga Sriti workshop—is called *soga kerokan*. Very briefly, it involves the following steps: washing and preparing the cloth; applying two types of wax; dyeing with indigo; removing wax from the areas that are to be dyed brown; rewaxing the areas that will remain blue; dyeing with *soga* brown; and finally, boiling out the wax.

The other methods of creating *kain soga* differ from *soga kerokan* mainly in the order of the steps. For example, a quick method called *be-*

desan is used for stamped batik only. Wax is first applied to parts of the white fabric, the cloth is dyed brown, and more wax is applied. Then the cloth is dipped into indigo dye; the unprotected brown areas, when dyed over with blue, become black. Finally, the wax is removed to reveal the white and brown parts of the pattern. The result is a white, brown, and black batik with no blue.

In the *radion* method, the entire cloth is dyed *soga* brown before it is waxed. Some wax is then applied over the brown and the color is bleached out to the desired shade of white. Some of the newly lightened areas are covered with wax and the cloth is then dyed blue. The finished piece of batik is blue, brown, and white.

One more method, called *banyumasin*, is named after Banyumas, a town in the western part of Central Java that still makes a lot of stamped batik. In this method, the white cloth is waxed and dyed blue and then all the wax is removed. The parts of the motif that will remain white are waxed again and the fabric is dyed brown. The result is a black, brown, and white batik usually without any blue.

As mentioned above, *soga kerokan* is the most widely used of all these methods. For that reason, and because it shows the steps and illustrates the principles involved in batik making more clearly than the other methods, it is explained here in detail. The Javanese terms for each step in the process are heard throughout the island and because of their importance are included in the discussion.

Preparing the Cloth

Before the actual batik process can begin, the cloth is cut into the standard size of a traditional batik *kain*, 2.5 meters by 1.05 meters, or a slightly shorter piece, 2 meters by 1.05 meters, which will be sewn into a sarong. Today some long bolts of fabric are patterned with a stamp, but this is a relatively recent development.

The first step in creating batik on the white cotton begins at the well, which is a hub of activity at Tiga Sriti as it is in any batik workshop. Workers prepare the cotton cloth by rinsing it in plain water to remove any starch or sizing that was added when the cloth was woven. To make their work easier, they knead the cloth in water with their feet. Making batik takes a great deal of water; the cloth will return to the well again and again to be rinsed and washed, and there one can see unfinished batik at all different stages of production.

The factory sizing must be removed so that the cloth can be restarched with rice or cassava starch to the special thickness that is ideal for waxing (*nganji* process). If the starch is too thin, wax will penetrate the cotton fibers too deeply, and the wax will be difficult to remove when the batik is completed. But if the fabric is too heavily starched, the wax may not adhere well to its surface and may crack or fall off during dyeing. The starching has special benefits for both stamped and hand-drawn batik. It keeps the threads from being stretched and distorted when the wax is applied with a stamp, and it makes the surface of the cloth extra smooth so that it is easier to apply the wax with a tjanting.

Some additional steps may be taken before starching to make the surface texture of the cloth even smoother if the piece is to be used for intricate hand-drawn work. In this case, only cotton of the finest quality is used, and after the workman removes the factory sizing, he soaks the cloth in peanut or castor oil (*mengetel* process). Following this oil bath, the workman rinses the fabric in a lye solution made by leaching rice-stalk ashes in water. This solution removes any excess oil.

Then the cloth is folded and beaten; a workman actually pounds on it with a large wooden mallet (*nlemplong* process). This step, in combination with the oil bath, helps make the face of the fabric supple and fine so that applying wax with a tjanting will be easier. If the fabric is rough or uneven, the tjanting has a tendency to snag, making fine detailed work difficult. For stamped batik, the oil-bath and beating are unnecessary.

Waxing

The cloth is now ready to be waxed. Many women who hand-wax batik draw a few guidelines on the cloth with charcoal or a pencil before they begin to wax. Then, as they work, they fill in the details from memory or create them from imagination. If a waxer wants to learn a particular pattern, she often copies it directly from an old batik. In Central Java, there are also some paper patterns available bearing sketches of classical motifs that can be consulted as references. The pattern may be traced onto the white cloth when a waxer wants to reproduce the design, but once the motif is learned, most waxers work from memory.

A certain amount of confidence and forethought is obviously required before putting the resist on the cloth since it is not easy to correct a mistake in the waxing. A small error, such as a drop of wax that falls from the bottom of the tjanting, can be removed, but big mistakes are impossible to change short of boiling all the wax off the cloth and beginning again. To correct a minor error, the waxer first heats a metal screwdriver or large nail in the fire beneath the wax pot and floods the area around the error with water. When she touches the hot tip of the nail to the wax mistake (taking care not to burn a hole in the cloth), the water around the error becomes hot enough to melt the wax. Then the waxer rubs the area with a little cold water and off comes the wax. Correcting mistakes is time-consuming and potentially harmful to the cloth, so waxers are careful not to make too many.

Because hand-drawn batik takes so long to complete, most batik today is waxed by the quicker (and more economical) tjap method. It can take a week or less for a piece of cloth to travel through the various processes in a factory workshop if the wax is applied with a stamp and synthetic dyes are used. In comparison, hand-drawn batik can easily take as long as several months to complete.

Sometimes a combination of stamp work and hand work may decorate a cloth; then the batik is called *combinasi*. Usually the tjap lays out the outline of the figures and the fine fill-in work is done by hand. In most workshops, there are some women hand-waxing batik, but the scene is dominated by rows of men sweating over padded tables, stamping wax onto the cloth.

Behind each stamp waxer, there is a small stove and a round, flat-bottomed pan called a *loyang* that holds the wax. The stamp rests in the *loyang* on top of a filter that sits in the melted wax. The filter consists of a perforated copper plate (*angsung kawat*) and a mat (*ender*) of fibrous material (see fig. 108). The copper plate and mat are covered with an absorbent folded cloth on which the stamp is placed to pick up wax or to rest when not in use. Any impurities in the melted wax are filtered out by this arrangement so that they are not transferred to the cloth.

Stampers are paid by the piece and they work with surprising speed. Each man has his

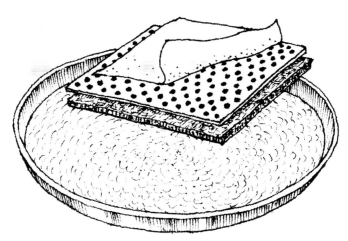

Fig. 108. Melted wax for stamping is kept in a heated flat-bottomed pan. A simple filter arrangement prevents impurities in the wax from being transferred to the cloth.

own style of wielding the stamp and his own working rhythm. He first touches the stamp to the wax-soaked filter in the pan behind him, lets the excess wax drip off, and then presses the tjap to the cloth. Every time he places the stamp on the cloth he must carefully match the stamp to that part of the pattern that has already been waxed. No guidelines are drawn on the cloth for stamped batik so a good eye is essential, and a great deal of skill is required to align each press of the stamp. When a cloth has a continuous geometric pattern, the slightest error in placing the stamp makes a noticeable break in the continuity of the motif. We rarely saw a stamper make a mistake, and the men seemed to be able to carry on good-natured banter with their co-workers while working quickly and accurately.

The repeating geometric patterns of Central Javanese batik lend themselves easily to the tjap method, but pictorial motifs are more complicated to reproduce in this manner. Some complex designs are created by using a variety of stamps of birds, butterflies, flowers, vines, and leaves, and by arranging these elements skillfully on the cloth the stampers can create elaborate floral bouquets and other scenes. Some of these stamped batik can be difficult to distinguish from hand-drawn ones because of the complexity of the designs.

Stamp work is hazardous as well as difficult. The fumes from the open pans of hot wax can cause lung damage, which stampers believe can be counteracted by drinking lots of milk. They wryly refer to their pensions as "milk money."

The stamper constantly keeps an eye on the temperature of the wax since it must be kept just right. The proper temperature is about seventy degrees centigrade whether a tjap or a tjanting is used to apply the wax. If the wax is too cold, it tends to sit on the surface of the cloth and will not penetrate enough so as to be visible on the other side. If the wax is too hot, it becomes thin and soaks into the fabric too deeply, making it hard to remove. Stampers judge the wax temperature by watching how it drips from the stamp. Hand-waxers know that the wax is too cold if it flows slowly from the spout of the tjanting and produces thin lines on the cloth. If the wax is too hot, it runs out of the tjanting quickly, spreading uncontrollably into wide lines. If the wax is the correct temperature, the lines will be just the right size and visible on the other side of the cloth.

KLOWONG AND TEMBOK WAX: In the *soga kerokan* process, two types of wax are applied to the cloth before the first dyeing, whether the cloth is waxed with a tjanting or with a stamp. First a light, brittle wax called *klowong* is applied to the areas that will be *soga* brown on the finished cloth (*nglowong* process; see fig. 109). *Klowong* wax is formulated to come off easily since it will be removed from the cloth after the first dyeing. This wax is applied (by tjap or tjanting) first to the face of the fabric and then to the reverse side. On hand-drawn batik, each line (and ideally each dot) of the motif is rewaxed on the second side of the cloth. If the wax was at the proper temperature, the original lines can be seen through the cloth and followed easily with the tjanting. The stamper must also match his first application of the stamp exactly on the reverse side. Waxing both sides of the cloth completely protects areas of the pattern from the dye so that the color will be clear on the finished batik.

The second type of wax, *tembok*, is stickier and darker in color than *klowong* wax and covers those parts of the batik that will be white on the finished cloth (*nembok* process). The word *tembok* means "wall" in Java, and this flexible wax acts as a barrier (or "wall") between the cloth and the dyes until the end of the batik process. Because the cloth will be repeatedly washed, dipped into dyes, rewaxed, and handled roughly, the *tembok* wax must be extremely durable. If it cracks or chips off, these open spots will absorb dye. The marbled effect that this creates and that people associate with batik is usually considered inferior work in Java. *Tembok* wax, like *klowong* wax, must be applied to both sides

Fig. 109. *Klowong* wax is light and brittle and is applied to the areas that will be brown on the finished cloth. Solo, Central Java.

Fig. 110. *Tembok* wax is stronger than *klowong* wax. It is applied to areas that will be white on the finished cloth. Solo, Central Java.

Fig. 111. Workshops must stock a wide variety of pattern stamps. Jogjakarta, Central Java.

of the cloth, and in special cases—such as when a pure white is desired—even a third layer of *tembok* wax may be applied on top of the first (see fig. 110).

For stamped batik, since the parts of the motif covered with *tembok* wax are different from those covered with *klowong* wax, a tjap with a different configuration is needed to apply each type of wax. Thus most stamped batik requires sets of stamps, each stamp bearing a different but related part of the same motif. *Klowong* wax is put on with a *klowongan* stamp and *tembok* wax with a *tembokkan* stamp. A simple, symmetrical batik design like *kawung* (see fig. 125, chapter 6) requires only two stamps, one *klowongan* and one *tembokkan*. But an asymmetrical motif such as a bird, for example, will need one *klowongan* stamp for the top side of the cloth and another one with a mirror image of the motif for the reverse side. To apply the *tembok* wax, a pair of stamps will be needed as well, one for each side of the cloth. Very large patterns may require two (or even more) stamps to make the complete pattern; a prawn motif, for example, may be divided with the head of the animal on one stamp and the tail on another. In a case like this, two *klowongan* and two *tem-*

bokkan are needed for each side of the cloth, making a total of eight stamps. Patterns needing as many as sixteen stamps are not uncommon, although most Central Javanese patterns require only two to eight stamps (see fig. 111).

WAX INGREDIENTS: Batik waxes such as *klowong* and *tembok* are specially formulated for the jobs they are meant to do. In general, batik resist is composed of beeswax, paraffin, resins, and fats mixed together in varying proportions. Each one of these components has individual characteristics that it contributes to the qualities of the batik resist, and by varying the ingredients and their proportions a skilled wax mixer gives his batik waxes specific properties such as flexibility or easy removal.

Beeswax from Sumatra, Sumbawa, or Timor is one of the main components of a high-quality dye-resist because it is flexible and easy to remove, adheres well to the cloth surface, has a low melting point, and is not generally affected by weather conditions such as heat and high humidity.

Paraffin, both yellow and white, is also an important addition to the basic wax formula. Its outstanding characteristics are its brittleness and its tendency to crackle. Pure paraffin can be brushed on the fabric when a crackled effect is desired. The more paraffin that is added to a batik wax, the more easily the wax will break and permit dye to penetrate to the fabric, giving a marbled appearance.

Microwax (microcrystalline wax, a type of highly refined paraffin) is added to a batik resist because it is pliant and adheres well to the cloth, yet it also helps make the wax easier to remove at the end of the process. Microwax is a relatively expensive ingredient so it is mostly found only in high-quality formulas for hand-drawn batik.

Resins help the batik wax adhere to the cloth and bind the other ingredients together. Pine resin (called *gondorukum* in Java) sticks to the fabric well, has a high melting point, and takes a long time to solidify. Another resin, eucalyptus gum *(Anisotera costatal)*, known as *mata kucing* or "cat's eye" in Java, is also a valuable addition to the batik resist because of its high melting point and good adhesion. It also adds some color to the mixture so that the wax lines will be clear and distinct on the cloth.

Another important ingredient is fat, preferably from cattle or water buffalo. Coconut oil is sometimes substituted because it is less expensive than animal fat, but its qualities are inferior. Fat has a low melting point, is easy to remove, and gives the wax greater flexibility.

To make a batik wax, the mixer melts each ingredient separately and mixes them one by one. Generally, he begins with the pine resin, then adds the eucalyptus gum. Afterward, paraffin, beeswax, and used wax may be added to the resins; the last addition is fat. When all the ingredients have been mixed together, the liquid is strained through a cloth and poured into a mold that has been coated with tapioca flour. The tapioca coating ensures that the solid wax will be easy to remove. After twenty-four hours the cooled block of wax can be slipped out of the mold.

The quality of the wax affects the appearance of the finished batik because it directly influences such characteristics as the clarity of the lines and the amount of marbling. The character of the resist is also very important in hand-drawn batik, for each type of wax flows from the tjanting in a slightly different manner, some being easier to work with than others.

Preparing the waxes so that they will have the specific qualities needed for each application requires considerable skill. Wax shops and batik factories employ their own wax mixers and many batik painters mix their own wax to ensure that the wax will have the special properties they require. Each mixer combines ingredients according to his own formula and he is often reluctant to share his secrets.

A few generalizations can be made about the composition of batik waxes. The brittle *klowong* wax usually has more paraffin, less eucalyptus gum, and less fat, while *tembok* wax has a higher proportion of beeswax, resins, and fat that make it darker and more flexible than *klowong*.

Waxes for stamped batik tend to be made of less expensive materials than those for hand-drawn batik, for obvious economic reasons. Expensive beeswax, for example, may be omitted from tjap resists, but it will be included in waxes for hand-drawn batik. Conversely, used wax often makes up a higher proportion of a typical tjap formula.

Little is wasted in Java, and part of the wax maker's job is to recycle wax. At the end of the batik process, the cloth is plunged into boiling water to melt the resist. As the wax floats to the top of the water, it is skimmed off with a large sieve. After straining the retrieved wax through several thicknesses of cloth to remove impurities, the wax maker can recombine it with other ingredients to make new resist.

The following formulas are examples of actual resists used in both hand-drawn and stamped batik. The ingredients are listed here in the order they are added.*

For hand-drawn batik:

Klowong tulis	*Tembok tulis*
1 part paraffin	10 parts pine resin
1 part pine resin	3 parts paraffin
1 part beeswax	1 part eucalyptus gum
0.1 part fat	2 parts microwax
	3 parts fat
	16 parts used wax

For stamped batik:

Klowong tjap	*Tembok tjap*
5 parts pine resin	10 parts pine resin
10 parts paraffin	1 part eucalyptus gum
1.5 parts eucalyptus gum	15 parts used wax
0.5 parts microwax	2 parts microwax
0.5 parts fat	1 part paraffin
	1 part fat

* Sewan S. K Susanto, *Seni Keradjinan Batik Indonesia* [The art of batik craft in Indonesia] (Jogjakarta: Balai Penelitian Batik dan Keradjinan, 1973), p. 63.

Fig. 112. The batik pattern appears "in negative" before the cloth is dyed. The light-colored *klowong* wax will be scraped off after the indigo dyebath; the more resistant dark-colored *tembok* wax will remain on the cloth and protect the white areas throughout the dyeings. Solo, Central Java.

Indigo Dyeing

After the *klowong* and *tembok* waxes have been applied (see fig. 112), the cloth is taken to the dyeing room, where the indigo dyers of the workshop can easily be recognized by their blue-stained hands and clothing. Indigo dyeing, like stampmaking, is a craft that has traditionally been passed down from father to son. Even the early batik, which was monochrome blue and white, was waxed by the court women and sent out to professional indigo dyers. These dyers competed with each other to produce a superior shade of blue, and they were superstitious about the making of the dye. They believed that evil spirits could affect the dyeing and that even such incidents as a dyer having an argument with his wife could cause the dye to fail.*

To propitiate evil spirits, these dyers made offerings of such ingredients as chicken's blood, banana pulp, and fermented cassavas to the dyebath. Whether they realized it or not, these offerings may have improved the dye's color by aiding the fermentation process. As described in chapter 1, indigo needs to ferment to change its

* Adam, "The Art of Batik," p. 13.

insoluble component, indigo blue, into soluble indigo white. The most common aid to this process is some form of sugar, but some of the dyers' more imaginative additives may have served as well.

Today in Central Java indigo dye is generally made from indigo paste, lime, and iron vitriol (ferrous sulfate) mixed with water. The proportions of these ingredients vary from one dyer to the next. At the Tiga Sriti workshop, the dyer uses two parts indigo paste, one part lime, and one part iron vitriol to sixty parts water.

At the workshop, the dyer mixes the indigo in a large water-filled sunken vat. First, he adds half the total amount of iron vitriol and half that of lime, after each ingredient has been diluted separately in water. Approximately ten hours later, he dissolves the remaining iron vitriol and lime and pours these solutions into the vat. At this time the dyer mixes the indigo paste with hot water and slowly stirs it into the other ingredients. By carefully watching the color of the liquid in the vat change first from yellow to green and finally to dark blue as the indigo ferments, the dyer decides when the solution is ready.

Most workshops are equipped with a rack that can hold approximately twenty pieces of waxed cloth at one time. The dyer can crank this device up and down into the dye vat (*medel* process; see fig. 113). Each time the rack is lowered the cloth is left in the dyebath for about fifteen minutes; it is then raised and exposed to the air for the same length of time. This airing is necessary for the oxidation that will turn the indigo white on the cotton back into indigo blue to produce the color on the fibers. The dipping and exposure process is repeated from twenty to sixty times (usually ten times a day) depending on the shade of blue that is desired. When the exact color is obtained, the dyer sends the cloth back to the well to be rinsed of any excess dye that has not been fixed into the fibers.

The dye solution will become weak with repeated use, and the dyer can revitalize the mixture by adding one quarter of the original amounts of indigo paste, iron vitriol, and lime. The dye bath is allowed to rest overnight and is ready to use again the next day.

A mistake in the dyeing is, of course, even more difficult to correct than one in the waxing. But an experienced dyer will say that he can make a few adjustments to the blue dyebath if

Fig. 113. Indigo dyeing is done in large vats where many cloths can be dyed at one time. Jogjakarta, Central Java.

Fig. 114. After the blue dyeing, the *klowong* wax is carefully scraped off the areas to be dyed *soga* brown. Jogjakarta, Central Java.

he is not entirely satisfied with a particular batch. Dyers say the ingredient that gives them the most problems is the lime, which is added to make the solution alkaline and improve the solubility of the dyestuff. The wrong amount of lime can have a marked effect on the color.

When the blue dyeing has been completed, the next step in the *soga kerokan* process is removing the brittle *klowong* wax so that the brown dye of the next dyebath can penetrate those areas of the pattern; the thick *tembok* wax will remain on the fabric throughout this process. First the cloth is briefly soaked in cold water to harden the wax so that it will be easier to scrape off. Young workers then carefully scrape the lighter colored *klowong* wax off both sides of the cloth with a dull knife or a bent piece of tin from an old can (*ngerok* process; see fig. 114). When the scraping is finished, the cloth is sent back to the well and rinsed in cold water to help remove any small clinging particles of *klowong* wax. The cloth is then washed once more in water to which some caustic soda or bicarbonate of soda has been added, and finally it is rinsed thoroughly.

The parts of the cloth that have been uncovered during the scraping process are white and ready to be dyed brown, but before this is done any parts of the cloth that are to remain indigo blue on the finished cloth must be protected with wax. Wherever the brown dye meets the blue on the fabric, the result will be black. This third waxing (*mbironi* process) is done by women; even on stamped batik this step is always done by hand.

Small areas are waxed with a tjanting, but to cover wide patches of the cloth the waxer wraps the wide spout of a large tjanting with a narrow strip of cotton cloth so that it applies wax over a wide area of the cloth. She may also wrap a small stick with cloth and use it as a brush.

This waxing process requires a different type of wax, called *biron*, which is composed primarily of used wax. A typical formula for *biron* wax is three parts pine resin, two parts paraffin, and one part fat to sixteen parts used wax.* *Biron* wax need not have such qualities as the easy removability of *klowong* or the flexibility of *tembok* since it only has to protect the cloth through the brown dyeing; it can therefore be made from less costly ingredients.

At the same time the waxers apply the *biron* wax, they touch up any areas where the *tembok* wax has been damaged. If the *tembok* wax has cracked due to rough handling, repairs can be made by heating a large nail and using it to "solder" the breaks. This extra step ensures that the white areas will not be spoiled by dye seeping in through cracks in the wax. But a good *tembok* wax should not need too much touching up at this point.

After the third waxing, the cloth goes back to the well to be washed once more, this time with detergent, which will help the fabric absorb the brown dye. After careful washing, it will be returned to the dyers to be colored the rich brown that is so distinctive of Central Javanese batik.

Soga Brown Dyeing

The dye which gives the brown color is known as *soga* in Java. This mordant dye is made of a

combination of several barks and woods that are harvested in Java, especially around the area of Solo, Jogjakarta, and Ponorogo (southeast of Solo). Some materials are also brought in from Kalimantan and Sulawesi. Each ingredient has its own color, and by varying the proportions, dyers can obtain a wide range of earthy hues.

The three main ingredients of the dye used today are: the bark from the shrub *soga tinggi* (*Ceriops candolleana* Arn.), which gives a reddish brown or chocolate color and has the properties of a mordant; the bark from the *soga jambal* tree *(Ceasalpinia sappan)*, which produces shades ranging from chocolate to yellow brown; and the wood of the *soga tegeran* tree *(Cudrania javanenesis)*, which produces yellow if used alone. Several other ingredients that may be added include *soga java* (sappanwood), which gives a reddish color, and the bark from the *soga kenet* tree, which produces a reddish brown color, but these are less common. In former times, *mengkudu, loba* (from the symplocos tree), safflower, turmeric, cochineal (a red dye derived from insects), annatto (*sari kuning;* a yellowish red dye derived from pulp around the seeds of the *Bixa orellana* tree), and pine resin may also have been added to the dye.

Since the colors can be varied depending on how each dyemaker combines the ingredients, each batik-making area developed characteristic shades of *soga*. Jogjakarta, for example, was noted for clear white, crackle-free backgrounds, and deep, earthy browns. In nearby Solo, dyers produced creamy yellow backgrounds by initially tinting the cloth with annatto and mixing browns that had a slight yellow tint. Today, however, the distinction between colors and even patterns in the Jogjakarta-Solo area has virtually disappeared so that it is almost impossible to identify the city in which a particular piece of batik was made.

Tiga Sriti in Solo is one of the few workshops producing stamped batik that have continued to use natural *soga* dyes. Dyers there make a *soga* dye by mixing four parts *soga jambal* bark, two parts *soga tinggi* bark, and one part *soga tegeran* wood. To make the dye, workers first chop the wood and bark into small pieces and add the wood chips to water. The liquid is then boiled down to one-half of its original volume and set aside until the *soga* chips settle to the bottom. The clean top water is the dye solution. When the liquid is used for dyeing, it is warmed slight-

---

* Susanto, *Seni Keradjinan Batik Indonesia*, p. 61.

Fig. 115. Vats for the *soga* brown dyebath are small, and the cloths are dyed one at a time. Solo, Central Java.

ly, but never enough to melt the wax. This contemporary dye is fairly simple but the old formulas were often quite complex. A classic Solo dye, for example, included:

50 parts *soga jambal*
12 parts *soga tegeran*
25 parts cochineal
10 parts *soga tinggi*
2.5 parts pine resin
6 parts safflower

These ingredients were soaked overnight in water or boiled to obtain the extract for the dye. Years ago, when natural dyes were used for all Central Javanese batik, natural *soga* extracts were sold in powder form.*

A *soga* vat is much smaller than that used for indigo and the dyer hand-dips each piece into the dye (*menyoga* process; see fig. 115). The pieces must be immersed and aired until dry from fifteen to thirty times. Since each cloth can only

be dipped a few times each day, this can be quite a lengthy process.

After numerous immersions in the *soga* solution, the dye must be fixed onto the fabric. In the easiest fixing method, the dyer soaks the cloth in a solution of lime and water for fifteen to thirty minutes and then lets the cloth dry in a windy place. Or the dyer may boil a mixture of annatto, alum, and *soga tegeran* wood in water and then steep the cloth in this liquid. In the past, the fixing baths were often as complex as the dyes and contained ingredients such as safflower, borax, alum, lemon juice, and saltpeter. One classic fixing solution in Solo included the following:*

6 parts borax
7 parts annatto
1 part lemon juice
6 parts alum
37 parts palm sugar

* Ibid., p. 75.

* Ibid.

Fig. 116. After all the dyeing is finished, the wax is boiled out in a large cauldron. Solo, Central Java.

Fig. 117. The finished batik with the pattern known as *sidomukti solo*. Compare figure 112. Solo, Central Java.

Finishing the Batik

Once the cloth has been dyed in *soga* and the color has been fixed, the only step that remains before the batik is complete is to remove the wax. In the Tiga Sriti workshop the wax is boiled off the cloth in a large cauldron that sits atop a wood-stoked furnace (see fig. 116). The boiling water usually contains a little soda ash or caustic soda that facilitates removal of the wax. A workman plunges several pieces of cloth into the water, stirring and lifting them with a long pole. The intense heat and weight of the cloths make this job the most physically exhausting in the workshop. As the melted wax floats to the top of the water, the worker skims it off and saves it. This recovered wax will be mixed with other ingredients to make new resist.

Once all the wax has been removed, the cloth is washed thoroughly and the batik is finished (see fig. 117). Batik cloth is often washed in a solution obtained by soaking a sticky fruit called *larak* in water. When the fruit is put in water it releases a soapy, slippery substance. Before com-

mercial soaps and detergents were available in Java, *larak* solution was used for washing clothes. Today, women still wash their hand-drawn *soga* batik in *larak* because they say it improves the color over the years.

Other Dyes and Dyeing Techniques

Although natural dyes are still preferred by a few factories in Jogjakarta and Solo, in the past few years their use has declined drastically. Some of the best hand-drawn Central Javanese batik is still dyed with *soga* and indigo, and a small number of workshops like Tiga Sriti produce naturally dyed stamped batik. A few dyers still work at home accepting small orders for natural dyeing, but they are becoming rare. Partly due to the time involved in using natural dyes and mainly to their rising cost, most workshops and dyers have turned to synthetic dyes. Until recently, it was common to find natural indigo used with synthetic brown dyes, a kind of intermediate step, but in the past few years Javanese-grown indigo paste has virtually disappeared from the dyestores. This decline is unfortunate, for during the nineteenth century Java was one of the largest indigo exporters in the world.

As the population of the island grows, much of the land once used for indigo has been turned into ricefields. Similarly, the trees yielding the *soga* dyestuffs are becoming rare, and consequently supplies are scarce and expensive. The owners of Tiga Sriti lament that soon the only way they will be able to keep their prices competitive will be to make the switch to synthetic dyes.

On the north coast of Java, traditional batik featured other natural colors besides indigo blue and *soga* brown. Batik from Lasem, for example, was famous for a natural green (made by combining indigo and natural yellow) and red (using *mengkudu* and annatto). Some older Cirebon batik used *mengkudu* red and indigo blue as well as black (which was made from indigo and *soga* fixed on the fibers with ferrous mud, young coconut meat, and coconut tree leaves). Pekalongan batik was the most colorful, featuring shades of blue, red, purple, green, and yellow, all created by natural dyes. Dyestuffs included turmeric (yellow), indigo, *soga tegeran* (yellow), cochineal (red), and mangrove bark (purple).

Multicolored batik such as that made in Pekalongan requires special care when waxing to protect areas and when combining colors to achieve a third color. When natural dyes were used, parts of the white cloth were waxed, the cloth was then dyed, and afterward all the wax was removed for each new color. The cloth could be rewaxed and redyed several times to produce many color combinations. For example, white cloth would be partially waxed, then dyed light blue. Some of the light areas would be covered with wax and the cloth redyed in blue to get a darker shade. All the wax would then be removed. By waxing over parts of the white, the light blue, and the dark blue, and then redyeing the cloth in yellow, the uncovered white areas would become yellow, the uncovered light blue parts would turn light green, and the dark blue sections exposed to the yellow dye would become dark green. Thus, the cloth would be colored light and dark blue, yellow, light and dark green. Even more colors could be added in the same manner. Before a waxer and dyer attempted to work with so many colors on one cloth, they obviously had to have a very clear idea of how they wanted the finished cloth to look and how the colors had to be combined to get the desired result.

Today the multicolored batik found in Java, as well as much of the *soga*-colored batik, is made using cold-water synthetic dyes. Synthetic dyes were introduced into Java by the Dutch in the late nineteenth century, and today they are still imported from Europe and Japan. Most dyers use either indigosol, a vat dye, or naphthol, an azoic dye derived from coal tar.

The color ranges of indigosol and naphthol dyes are quite different; indigosol dyes are preferred for pastel shades while naphthols are commonly used for brighter and darker colors, including *soga* browns. The method of dyeing is also different for these dyes. Naphthol dyes require that the cloth first be immersed in a naphthol solution and then in a color salt solution that raises the color on the fabric. There are many types of naphthol, each of which will produce a different shade when combined with a particular color salt. Indigosol dyes require only one immersion in a dyebath, but the colors require oxidation in the form of exposure to sunlight or the air to bring out the color. After oxidation, the indigosol colors are fixed in an acid bath.

The introduction of synthetic dyes greatly expanded the color choices for batik. But using the synthetic dyes to try to match the natural colors has not been entirely successful. A great deal of research has been done in Java and dyers can approximate many brown shades of *soga* with synthetic dyes (usually naphthol), but they have yet to duplicate the richness and depth of the natural colors.

A new technique has helped exploit the possibilities offered by the synthetic dyes. The multicolored contemporary batik from Pekalongan are now created with the help of a dyeing technique that was introduced from India about the turn of the century. This method, called *coletan*, involves painting the dye directly onto the cloth rather than dipping the cloth into the dye. *Coletan* greatly speeds up the batik process since contrasting colors can be applied without laboriously removing wax, drawing on new wax, and redyeing as was done in the past (see fig. 118).

A motif, a flower for example, is first outlined in wax either by tjap or by tjanting. Then indigosol dye is carefully brushed onto the figure with a frayed stick of rattan. The wax outline

Fig. 118. In Pekalongan in northern Central Java, indigosol dyes are brushed directly onto the cloth.

will prevent the dye from bleeding outside of the design. With this method it is possible to make a bouquet of pink, yellow, and turquoise flowers with green leaves without waxing, dip-dyeing, and rewaxing. The dyer can even shade individual leaves or petals from light to dark, thus adding interest and depth to the overall visual effect. The colored motifs can be entirely sealed off with wax on both the top and reverse sides, and then the cloth can be dip-dyed in a contrasting background color.

If a batik is to show a colorful design against a pure white background, *coletan* makes the task of covering the entire background with wax unnecessary. There is always the danger of a large waxed background being spoiled by the wax cracking during the dyeing, so *coletan* dyeing offers a safer alternative.

Over the years, the scope of batik has grown steadily wider. If in the beginning the technique was not exclusively an accomplishment of the royal courts, at least it was closely associated with the upper classes in Central Java. The advent of the tjap, the importation of cambric in large quantities, and more recently the use of synthetic dyes have made possible the production of batik on a large scale; batik has thus become available to a wider range of people. Of all Indonesia's textile arts, batik has made the most successful transition from an art and folk craft to an industry. Although some natural creativity has been lost in this transition, there is still a place for hand-drawn batik, and most important, the art of batik is still alive.

6 Batik:
Patterns Old and New

Pasar Klewar, the large batik market in the center of Solo (Surakarta) is one of the best places in Java to view the extensive range of batik motifs. Many of the workshops in Solo, and other batik-producing areas as well, sell their batik in Pasar Klewar, and inside the market, subdued brown and black batik from Central Java contrasts with brightly colored cloth from the north coast. But even the seemingly endless choice of motifs available in Pasar Klewar represents only a fraction of the traditional patterns found in Java.

The three stories of Pasar Klewar contain row after row of tiny, dimly lit stalls, each one packed from floor to ceiling with stacks of folded batik. Most of these stalls, like the one owned by Pak Harri Sastromulyono, are designed with a raised wooden platform where the vendor can unfold pieces of batik for display (see fig. 119). Pak Sastromulyono, like the other vendors, will

Fig. 119. Pak Sastromulyono and his wife operate a stall in the large batik market, Pasar Klewar, in Solo, Central Java.

Fig. 120. Motifs similar to those on *sarita* cloth appear on many traditional Torajan village houses. Palawa, central Sulawesi.

Fig. 121. Carvings that will decorate the sides of traditional Torajan houses are still made by hand using ochre for the red color, ordinary soot for the black, and lime for the white. Sa'dan, South Sulawesi.

patiently open one batik after another, each with a different design, until the buyer has found the one pattern that pleases him. After the customer makes his choice, the polite yet serious ritual of bargaining can begin.

According to Pak Sastromulyono, each stall is an outlet for one or more workshops. The bulk of the trade in Pasar Klewar comes from merchants who have their own shops or stalls in the smaller towns of Java, like Magelang and Temanggung. Each stallholder has a small clientele of regular buyers, and despite the throngs of people strolling through the market, only a little of the business actually comes from casual visitors.

The Tradition of Batik

From Pasar Klewar and other city markets, batik is distributed throughout Java, eventually finding its way into all levels of the society from rich to poor. Batik is worn by poor peasant women working in the ricefields, by the wives of high-ranking officials, and by performers of the traditional Javanese arts such as shadow play and dance.

The traditions concerning batik have become, over the years, more secular and sophisticated compared with those of other textiles. Batik is primarily used as a garment, and it lacks the ritual attachments of warp ikat textiles and many other Indonesian cloths. The motifs, although not without meaning, do not have the magical intent sometimes found in textile traditions around the archipelago.

In chapter 5 we mentioned the primitive batik called *sarita* that was made by the Torajans of South Sulawesi. It is an example of a cloth that functioned as a ritual object, and the motifs that appear on it are often similar to those that adorn the Torajan ricebarns, coffins, and houses (see figs. 120 and 121). The bold geometric designs are symbols that are meant to bring fertility, to protect against danger or illness, or to denote wealth and status. For example, many motifs are inspired by the water buffalo, an animal which is very important in Torajan culture. Torajans measure their wealth in buffalo and sacrifice them at funeral ceremonies as a demonstration of the wealth and status of the deceased. Motifs connected with the buffalo are thus used with the idea that they have the power to bring wealth. Javanese batik motifs are not used with this naive intent to gain something.

Sarita cloths were used as headcloths by successful Torajan warriors in ritual headhunting ceremonies until the Dutch abolished the custom of taking heads early in this century (see plates 42 and 43). The art of making *sarita* then declined, although some *sarita* cloths are still displayed today at special ceremonies. The celebration upon the completion of a new house, for example, is an important event because Torajan houses are richly decorated with carvings and their construction is a major undertaking. Guests from neighboring villages bring a variety of gifts such as palm wine, chickens, and other foods for a feast. Pigs are the prized gifts and are carried into the village compound in gaily festooned litters. Banners made of many types of textiles such as Javanese batik, Indian woodblock prints, and weavings from East Nusatenggara, but most notably the *sarita*, are hung from each litter.

The primitive batik of West Java, the *simbut* cloth, is more closely related to the *sarita* in its usage than to classical Javanese batik. The *simbut* features simple outlined figures of animals and symbols against a red background. Like the *sarita*, the *simbut* is taken out only for ceremonies, especially weddings, where it is displayed as a hanging. For those who own one, it is a *pusaka*, or sacred heirloom.

Central Javanese batik may also be considered a *pusaka*. A friend of ours obtained an old batik that was made inside the palace walls in Jogjakarta. When she gave it to us, she insisted that we keep it safe in a cupboard, and that we never use or display it; if we followed her advice the batik would then be our *pusaka* and bring us good luck. But cases like this are rare. On the whole, the batik cloths of Java, whether of the Central Javanese courts or the north coast, are not magical or ritual objects like the *sarita*, the *simbut*, or the textiles of the Ancient Peoples. Nor are they used as wall displays or as part of a gift exchange as many other textiles are.

The main use of batik is as a garment for ceremonial or festive dress, although nowadays many people can afford to wear it daily (see plate 41). There are several types of batik

garments. The wrap-around *kain panjang* ("long cloth") measures 2.5 by 1.05 meters and is the most common of batik cloths. It is the traditional dress of women in Central Java and is also worn by men acting as palace guards, musicians, and dancers and by other performers of classical arts. A woman puts it on by holding one end of the cloth stationary and wrapping the rest of it around her waist. To hold the *kain* firmly in place, she binds it with a 6-meter-long sash from her rib cage to the top of her hips. A tight-fitting long-sleeved blouse called a *kebaya* completes the outfit.

Another traditional garment is the sarong; slightly shorter than the *kain panjang*, it is sewn into a tube. Today the sarong is worn mostly by men although it was originally worn by women in Central Java and may still be seen on women along the north coast. A man steps into the sarong and, holding each side of the tube, folds one side over the other until the cloth is snug about the body; he then rolls the cloth at the waist to secure it. The design of a sarong differs from that of a *kain panjang* in that it features a *kepala*, or "head," an area with a contrasting motif that is worn down the front by women and in the back by men. The most common *kepala* motif, especially along the north coast, is the spearheadlike *tumpal* (see fig. 122), while diagonal *parang* motifs and other designs distinguish the break in Central Java.

A third type of batik garment, the *dodot*, was reserved for the sultans, their families, and court officials. It is a huge piece of cloth, four times the size of a regular *kain panjang*. A diamond-shaped area in the center of the cloth, the *tengahan*, is left undecorated or may be tie-dyed. The sultan wears a *dodot* over trousers made of patola cloth while noblewomen wear it over a *kain panjang*. There are many ways of arranging the *dodot*, and it is often folded up in the back, thus giving the effect of a bustle; this shape may be seen in the *wayang* leather shadow-puppet figures. In former years, an ordinary bride and groom were allowed to wear a *dodot* on their wedding day so that they would feel like royalty for that day.

Smaller pieces of batik are used as accessories to the *kain panjang* and sarong. A selindang measures about 2.05 by 0.5 meters and is folded lengthwise and draped over one shoulder for festive dress. It is a practical cloth, and a woman can use it to haul a burden or carry her baby. A narrow rectangle of cloth also served as

Fig. 122. *Tumpal* motif on a batik sarong. Red, green, yellow, and cream. From Lasem, northern Central Java. Tama Art University collection.

a *kemben,* or breastcloth, which was worn before women adopted the tight-fitting *kebaya* blouse. Squares of cloth with a plain diamond-shaped *tengahan* center are folded into the elaborate traditional headcloths, *ikat kepala,* worn by men in Java. There are many different ways of folding the headcloth, and it was once possible to distinguish which region a man came from by looking at how his *ikat kepala* was arranged.

Even the Dutch in Indonesia wore batik, and at least in their homes, many Dutch women dressed in *kain panjang* and *kebaya.* Men wore loose-fitting trousers of batik cloth that were called *slapbroek.* Similar pants are still worn by the Minangkabau men of West Sumatra.

Motifs of Central Java

The true distinction of batik in Central Java lies not in its uses but in the beauty and variety of its motifs. The number of motifs alone is impressive. The scholar G. P. Rouffaer counted three thousand patterns by name in the early twentieth century, and that survey was admittedly incomplete. The profusion of motifs is partly due to the freedom of design made possible by the versatile tjanting; if a pattern can be

drawn it can be duplicated on cloth with the tjanting.

In Central Java, batik has a long history of close connection with the traditional culture. Javanese believe that batik appeared at about the same time as the *wayang* shadow plays and *gamelan* music, which would be around the eighth century, although according to Rouffaer the earliest mention of batik was probably not until the twelfth century. Inspiration was drawn from many sources, including India, Islamic culture, China, Japan, and Europe, but the result of this blend is distinctively Javanese.

One of the most important early influences on batik design is related to the conversion of Javanese to Islam. The first sign of Islam is an inscription dated 1102 in Leran. By 1582, when the great Mataram Empire (which eventually split into the courts of Jogjakarta and Solo) was founded, Islam was pervasive in Java.

The introduction of Islam is generally believed to have had a modifying effect on batik motifs. Islamic tradition discourages the portrayal of living things in a realistic manner. The Koran does not actually forbid the representation of living things, but artists who did so were denounced by Mohammed because by creating something with potential life, they were seen as competing with God. This prohibition is a social custom that varies widely in strictness throughout the Islamic world, but its results are most clearly seen in mosques. In the Middle East they are decorated with calligraphy and arabesque patterns that symbolize a heavenly view of the world and offer the faithful a tranquil atmosphere for prayer.

This Islamic reluctance to use human and animal figures as decoration was a contributing factor to the stylization that is such an important characteristic of Central Javanese batik motifs. The subjects of many Central Javanese patterns are derived from local flora and fauna, and these have been abstracted until they are unrecognizable. The manner of portraying the figures thus shows an Islamic influence while the subject matter itself is Javanese.

Batik has a close connection with Javanese court life and the *priyayi*, a class of gentry. *Priyayi* are sometimes landowners and usually work in white-collar jobs (which are highly respected in Java) but not in trade. The superior education of the *priyayi* has given them a leading role in Indonesian cultural life. There are six *priyayi* "high arts." Batik is one of them, along with *tembang* (poetry), *lakon* (dramatization of Javanese myths), *joged* (court dance), *wayang* (shadow play), and *gamelan* (music using an almost entirely percussive orchestra). The practice of batik, like that of music and dance, is viewed as a way to develop spiritual discipline, and it reflects the value that the *priyayi* place upon mystical achievement, art, refinement, and etiquette.

Two important *priyayi* concepts are *alus*, which means sensitive and cultured, and its opposite, *kasar*, which means coarse, rough, and rude. *Alus* is the highest praise that can be given a fine piece of batik. Non-*priyayi* Javanese regard *wayang*, *gamelan*, and batik as reflections of the refined, or *alus*, *priyayi* way of life and respect these arts accordingly.*

The six high arts are related, and it is not unusual to find *priyayi* who have mastered more than one. An acquaintance of ours, an accomplished batik painter, is also a storyteller for shadow plays and a musician; his wife is a court-dance teacher who also makes batik at home in the classical way for her family.

* Clifford Geertz, *The Religion of Java* (Chicago and London: University of Chicago Press, 1960), pp. 287–88.

A contemporary maker of shadow-play puppets in Jogjakarta also designs batik motifs. The association between these two arts is a traditional one, and batik motifs are closely connected with several types of *wayang*. The flat leather puppets *(wayang kulit)* for the shadow plays are usually decorated with batik patterns. Another type of *wayang*, *wayang beber*, is an early type of play in which the story is told with a painted scroll. These scrolls, one of the first forms of painting in Java, often feature designs similar to batik motifs.

In the nineteenth century, many *priyayi* women not only made batik for themselves but also supported their families by selling some of their work while their husbands spent time at the courts in activity for which they received no pay. Although today many non-*priyayi* women in Central Java work at hand-drawn batik, the early close connection with the *priyayi* culture remains and the motifs still retain an aura of aristocratic refinement.

In the eighteenth and nineteenth centuries, particular motifs were exclusively reserved for the use of the sultans of Central Java and certain members of their courts. In the late eighteenth century, the third and fourth sultans of Solo issued edicts proclaiming specific patterns *larangan*, or "restricted"; that is, they could only be worn by appointed people. The *larangan* motifs included *parang rusak* and the *garuda* mythological bird which, according to the Solo edicts, were to be used by the crown prince and his consort; the *semen* designs with *mirong* or *sawat* wing figures and the diagonal *udan liris* pattern were for sons, daughters, brothers, and uncles of the ruler; the *sawat* crest and classic *kawung* patterns were worn by secondary sons of the sultan, that is, sons of wives other than the first. Ordinary Javanese in the region of Solo and Jogjakarta were forbidden to dress in batik with these motifs. But as the power of the sultans and the courts declined, these restrictions gradually lost their force, and today motifs are freely worn by all classes of people.

All Central Javanese batik motifs share some general characteristics, such as an avoidance of straight lines and open space. Batik artists feel that straight lines are still and rigid, and whenever possible they soften them with decoration. They also dislike large empty areas and attempt to break up any such spaces by filling them in with ornamentation. Generally speaking, the surface of most Central Javanese batik is covered with repeating patterns; even many of the free-form motifs repeat themselves over the cloth with only small variations.

Batik makers use an array of patterns called *isen-isen* to decorate areas that seem too empty. *Isen* motifs consist of dots, lines, and small repeating figures that bear a variety of imaginative names. *Citcik* dots are the most common of *isen* patterns and may be used in a line, singly, or in groups of two, three, or more. Special tjanting have been designed to lay down clusters of *citcik*, and up to seven dots at a time may be applied on the cloth using a tjanting with as many spouts. Close parallel lines called *sawut* are another method of decorating leaves, feathers, and other figures. When the entire background for a motif is covered with such lines, the decoration is called *rawon*. Curving parallel lines are called *andan-andan*, or "wavy hair." Other *isen* motifs depict coconut buds *(manggaran)*, pigeon footprints *(tapak dara)*, grooves of the nangka tree *(catcah)*, birds' eyes *(mata deruk)*, and rice stalks *(ada-ada)* to mention a few. *Isen* motifs used as border patterns are called *cemukirran*. A group of ornaments called *modang* are conventionalized leaf-and-flower motifs that are used to border the diamond-shaped *tengahan* centers of headcloths and breastcloths.

Beyond the most general division of geometric and free form, traditional batik patterns of Central Java can be broken into several categories. One broad category known as *ceplokkan* consists of geometric patterns made up of interlocking squares, diamonds, circles, and other figures. Another sizable group of motifs is the *garis miring* type; these designs run diagonally across the cloth. A large number of the free-form patterns of Central Java can be termed *semen*, which are motifs with meandering vine and tendril patterns; these can be either the main design or a backdrop for other figures. Of course, many patterns do not fit neatly into any single classification, but these three basic categories help impose some order on the multiplicity of batik designs.

CEPLOKKAN: The first group, *ceplokkan*, includes patterns that are inspired by nature. These motifs are loosely based on plants, flowers, insects, or animals, these last being extremely stylized and schematized. The subjects may appear as if they are being viewed through a kaleidoscope, for *ceplokkan* patterns are often based

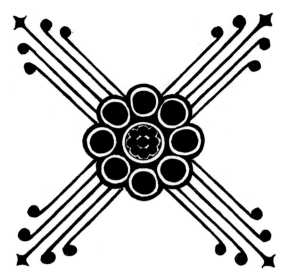

Fig. 123. *Ganggong* motif. Central Java.

on a circle split into four segments. But other shapes such as triangles, squares, and octagons are also worked into the designs.

Flowers such as the hibiscus *(bunga sepatu)*, orange blossom *(kembang jeruk)*, clove flower *(kembang cenkeh)*, pepper flower *(kembang lombok)*, banana blossom *(kembang pisang)*, and coconut flower *(kembang kelapa)* generally appear viewed frontally. Conventionalized images of fruits and seeds like cloves, coffee beans, nutmeg, and *salat* fruit may be incorporated into the design.

An unusual aspect of *ceplokkan* designs is that many subjects are viewed in cross-section. Sugar cane, mangosteen fruit, and various other plants and fruits look as if they were sliced in half. A large group of *ceplokkan* patterns features an element called *ganggong*, which is based on a stylized cross-section of a marsh plant (probably *Solanum denticulatum* L.; see fig. 123).

Animals, as well as plants, find their way into the *ceplokkan* patterns, but in such a way that their forms are often unrecognizable. Sometimes only a single detail of the anatomy is incorporated into the design. Most *ceplokkan* animal forms are made to conform to a circular shape, and a variety of insects such as butterflies and beetles, for example, are easily adapted for use in this way. Other animals furnish only a design element; crab claws, fish scales, and bird wings are examples of parts that are taken for their ornamental value. Some *ceplokkan*, such as those that feature medallions and squares, are purely abstract, or at least if they were taken from a natural source it has been long forgotten. Within this framework there is ample room for indi-

Fig. 124. *Ceplokkan* motif on a batik *kain*. *Soga* brown, black, and cream. From Central Java. Tama Art University collection.

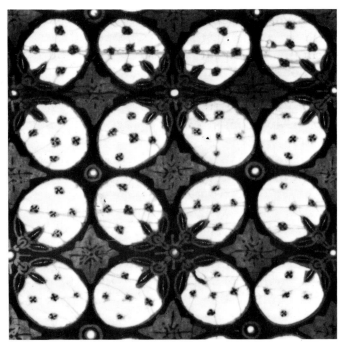

Fig. 125. *Kawung* motif on a batik *kain*. *Soga* brown, black, and cream. From Central Java. Tama Art University collection.

vidual expression, and batik makers and artists throughout Central Java are creating new *ceplokkan* patterns all the time (see fig. 124).

The *ceplokkan* group encompasses several of the oldest known batik patterns. One of these is the *kawung* motif, which can be traced as far back as the Hindu-Javanese period in Java when it was carved on reliefs of temples such as the late-ninth-century Prambanan Temple near Jogjakarta (see fig. 125).

Batik is thought to have reached a creative peak in the seventeenth and eighteenth centuries, but during this time little was written concerning its motifs. The origins of many classic batik motifs such as *kawung* have thus become obscured in time, and today several different explanations are often heard for each pattern. Since a *kawung*-like pattern appears on Hindu-Javanese temple reliefs, some say that it must have originated in India and was imported to Java. Other sources claim that the motif was inspired by the round fruit of the *arenga* palm or even by a round insect. *Kawung* is based on groups of circles, and since Central Javanese believe that the circle symbolizes the world or universe, the motif was once one of the restricted patterns reserved for the ruler and his immediate family.

Another ancient motif, *nitik,* also fits into the *ceplokkan* category. *Nitik* patterns are formed of connecting geometric figures but are distinguishable from "classic" *ceplokkan* patterns by their abstract character. *Nitik* patterns are composed basically of white bars and dots arranged into complex geometric forms against a dark, usually black, background.

Several explanations are given for the unique configurations of the *nitik* motifs. First, it is often said that the broken-line effect is an attempt to copy woven patterns using batik technique; the fragmented, broken lines are supposed to give the effect of threads going over and under the background fabric. Another theory is that *nitik* patterns are descended from the early batik cloths that were made by applying wax with a stick, for when a wax pattern is created in this way the lines take on a broken appearance. The name *nitik* also has the same root, *tik,* as *batik,* a word which means to draw or to drop something (such as wax) onto fabric. A third, but tenuous, explanation connects *nitik* patterns and the patola cloth of India. The lines of the patola, like those of the *nitik* patterns, also have a fragmented look, and one of the most popular of all *nitik* motifs features the *jilimprang* figure found on the double ikat patola.

Nitik-style motifs are still very popular today. There are many patterns with such names as *sekar cenkeh* (clove flower), *sekar kentang* (potato flower), *sri gunung* (holy mountain), *cakar ayam* (chicken's claw), *rambutan* (a fruit), and *matahari* (the sun; see fig. 126).

A style of *ceplokkan* that was popular thirty to fifty years ago features patterns that are larger in scale than those commonly made today. These designs are said to resemble, and were perhaps inspired by, the tile floors common in many older Dutch houses in Java (see plate 44). In these designs, a large geometric framework of squares, circles, hexagons, and other forms contain traditional motifs such as *parang, kawung, grinsing* (resembling fish scales), and *truntum* (a small teardrop-and-circle pattern).

Some motifs, although based on geometric figures, are not usually categorized as *ceplokkan*. One such pattern, *banji*, is derived from the swastika, a mystical symbol to such diverse peoples as Peruvian Indians, the Vikings (to whom it was the symbol of Thor), and many Asians. In India, it is the symbol of the Hindu gods Vishnu and Shiva, while in Japan and China it is closely connected with Buddhism. *Banji*, the name commonly given to this pattern in Indonesia, comes from the Chinese *ban* ("ten") and *ji* ("thousand"). Thus, *banji* becomes "the motif of the ten thousand," and is believed by Chinese to have come directly from heaven. Despite the fact that the Chinese name *banji* is used in Indonesia, the motif may well have originally been imported from India during the period of Hindu influence; in any case, *banji* is acknowledged to be a very old batik motif.

A simple *banji* motif is often used as a border, the same way the Chinese employ it, on Balinese weavings including the gold-covered *prada* cloth, and on the silk batik of Rembang and Juana on Java's north coast. The *banji* motif is modified and treated as an all-over pattern in Central Java (see fig. 127). Each arm of the swastika is extended into a rectangle that encompasses secondary designs such as flowers, *parang*, or *isen* patterns. The town of Banyumas in western Central Java is especially famous for *banji*-patterned batik in brown and black.

Another motif, *sidomukti solo*, is sometimes classed as a *ceplokkan*. This is the motif shown in the photos of the batik process in the previous chapter. Diamond shapes frame figures such as plants, butterflies, and bird wings against a design of tendrils. *Sidomukti* means "brown background," and corresponding motifs are *sidomulio solo*, with a white background, and *sidoluhur solo*, with a black background for the same figures.

The *sidomukti solo* motif is associated with weddings, especially in Jogjakarta. Shops sell and rent special wedding dress, usually batik decorated with the *sidomukti solo* pattern, for use by both the bride and the groom. These wedding cloths are decorated in *prada* fashion: the motif is outlined with glue made from fish scales and then dusted with powdered bronze. Formerly gold dust was used to highlight the motif. Wedding shops also provide other regalia, like velvet jackets with silver and gold decoration, fezlike hats, and belts made of patola cloth fragments.

GARIS MIRING: Motifs that run diagonally across the cloth are very distinctive of batik and form a second major category of Central Javanese patterns called *garis miring* (see plate 45). The best known of *garis miring* and perhaps of all batik motifs are the *parang* designs, especially *parang rusak*. *Parang rusak* was, like the *kawung* motif, once worn only in the royal courts of Central Java (see fig. 128). *Parang rusak* can be literally translated as "broken knife," and the motif may have been derived from the wavy-bladed kris knife of Java. The light or undyed part of the *parang*, however, resembles the broad, flat blade of the Indonesian machete that is itself called *parang*. Another explanation for this unusual motif relates it to the lotus plant. The dark triangular element of the pattern is said to picture a conventionalized lotus leaf.

Another story heard in Jogjakarta connects the *parang* motif with the waves of the southern sea. Long ago, a sultan went to Parangtritis, a beach south of Jogjakarta, to make an offering to Lara Kidul, the goddess of the southern sea. The sultan, it is said, was so impressed by the waves breaking over the rocks that he fashioned their image into the motif.

Parang rusak, whatever its origins, is a visually powerful motif and was once considered sacred. In fact, batik cloths using the motif were presented as offerings to ancestral spirits. This use of batik is the closest parallel to the ritual uses of textiles among the Ancient Peoples; there are no common references to any other batik patterns being used in this manner.

Parang rusak has three variations based on size: the small *parang rusak klitik*, the medium-sized *parang rusak gendreh*, and the large *parang rusak barong*. The *parang rusak barong* motif decorates ceremonial batik worn by the sultans of Jogjakarta and Solo (see fig. 129). It is also seen on the cloths of court dancers, and in the shadow

Fig. 126. *Nitik*-style *matahari* motif on a batik *kain*. *Soga* brown and black on a yellow background. From Central Java. Tama Art University collection.

Fig. 128. *Parang rusak* motif on a batik *kain*. *Soga* brown, black, and cream. Central Java. Tama Art University collection.

Fig. 127. *Banji* motif on a batik *kain*. *Soga* brown, black, and cream. From Central Java. Tama Art University collection.

Fig. 129. G. P. H. Poeroeboyo (Sultan VIII) of Jogjakarta wearing a batik *dodot* decorated with a motif called *parang rusak barong ceplok garuda*. *(Photograph courtesy of the Kraton Tourist Office, Jogjakarta, Central Java)*

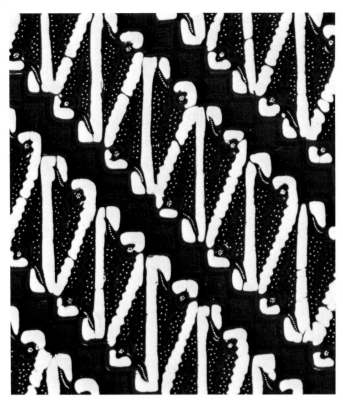

Fig. 130. *Parang cumpring* motif on a batik *kain*. *Soga* brown, black, and cream. From Central Java. Tama Art University collection.

Fig. 131. *Udan liris* motif on a batik *kain*. *Soga* brown, black, and cream. From Central Java. Tama Art University collection.

plays, *wayang kulit* puppets such as Arjuna, the hero of the Indian *Mahabharata* epic, are depicted wearing *dodot* cloths with *parang* patterns to indicate their high status.

Most of the diagonal motifs that make up the *garis miring* category are variations on *parang* types. The bold lines of *parang rusak* may be varied into more delicate forms such as, to mention only a few, *parang panjang*, said to resemble fish hooks, *parang centang*, named for curls of hair, *parang pakis*, inspired by ferns, and *parang cumpring* (see fig. 130). *Garis miring* may be designed with diagonal bands of other traditional Central Javanese patterns such as the teardrop-and-circle *truntum* (see plate 45). *Parang* motifs may also serve as a backdrop for floral designs, a style that is common in Tasikmalaya and Banyumas in West Java.

Udan liris is a diagonal motif that falls into the *garis miring* category (see fig. 131). *Udan liris* means "light rain." There is a *gamelan* tune of the same name, one of several examples that show the connection between batik and this traditional Javanese music. In the *udan liris* pattern, narrow diagonal bands enclose a variety of delicate motifs, usually *isen* designs, sometimes including *parang* patterns. The fine dark lines of *udan liris*, which stand out against a cream-colored background, are very difficult to wax. *Udan liris* batik was once worn only by the sultan's immediate family.

SEMEN: The third major group of batik motifs, generally known as *semen*, comprises vine, leaf, and flower patterns. The name *semen* is derived from *semi*, which means "bud." Buds and tendrils, rather than flowers and leaves, are the more important components of *semen* motifs (see fig. 132). The foliage varies from naturalistic to highly conventionalized. A *semen* motif may by itself be the sole decoration on a batik. A form of *semen* featuring thick vines with only a few hairlike tendrils is known as *lung*, a style that has many variations. *Pisang bali*, a very popular motif, is a conventionalized representation of a banana plant. *Semen sidomulya* is a variation consisting mostly of leaves, while leaves and buds are most prominent in *semen ragas*.

The leaves and curling tendrils of *semen* motifs often form the background for birds, animals, and other figures. The *garuda* bird is one figure that often appears against a *semen* background. It may be depicted as a bird with the head of a *naga*, or snake. *Garuda* is, in Hindu mythology, the king of birds and the mount of the god

Fig. 132. *Parang ngreni,* an example of a *semen* motif, on a batik *kain. Soga* brown, black, blue, and cream. From Central Java. Tama Art University collection.

Fig. 133. *Sawat* figure on a batik *kain. Soga* brown, black, blue, and cream. From Central Java. Tama Art University collection.

Vishnu, and it appears as a character in the *Ramayana* epic. In India *garuda* is an emblem used as a royal insignia by followers of Vishnu. Today the *garuda* is more venerated in Indonesia, where it is the emblem of the republic, than it is in India.

The *sawat* figure, one of the most recognizable of batik patterns, is a more common motif than the *garuda* bird. It is a stylized form of *garuda,* consisting of a bird's tail in the shape of a fan flanked on either side by spread wings (see fig. 133). *Sawat,* like *parang* and *kawung,* was one of the *larangan* restricted motifs. In the seventeenth century it served as a crest for Sultan Agung, who resisted the Dutch and tried to unite Java. The stylization of *garuda* into *sawat* may well have been the result of Islam's disapproval of the portrayal of living things; in this way did a Hindu symbol became the crest of a sultan and an important batik motif.

Sawat frequently appears against a variety of *semen* backgrounds. The figure may be pared down even further: often just two wings will appear without the tail in a popular motif called *mirong.* Or a single disembodied wing may be used alone in the motif called *lar* (see fig. 134). These *mirong* and *lar* wings are described as ei-

Fig. 134. *Lar* motif on a *semen* background. Central Java.

ther living wings, which are decorated with *isen* lines, or as dead wings, which are only outlined (see fig. 135).

Another figure often seen in *semen* motifs is *pohon hayat,* the "tree of life" that is found all over Indonesia. It is portrayed in a conventionalized way with prominent roots, stems, and stylized leaves (see fig. 136). Mountains *(meru)* are shown in cloudlike formations, while flames *(lidah api)* are presented in a highly abstract manner. Stylized buildings often appear on batik, most often drawn like pavilions.

Semen patterns often form a background for naturalistic depictions of birds and animals. Cockatoos, peacocks (originally from India), as well as the *garuda* and a host of other less easily identifiable birds are common figures. To Javanese, birds, which are referred to as *peksi,* represent the heavens or upper worlds. Chinese-style phoenixes may sometimes appear on batik in Central Java, and some of these bird-and-flower patterns are drawn in a more natural style than most *semen* motifs.

Animal life may be drawn against a *semen* background, although in general, mammals are not common patterns in Central Java. A variety of different sea creatures, however, such as lobsters, shrimp, and fish, and insects such as butterflies and beetles are frequently seen on batik.

The *naga,* or serpent, motif found on textiles throughout Indonesia is also a popular batik pattern. Although of Hindu origin, the *naga* serpent is sacred in Javanese beliefs and is thought to possess great strength. Snakes, in general, represent the lower world as birds do the heavens. In batik the *naga* is portrayed with a crowned head and sometimes with wings *(naga peksi)*. Occasionally, two *naga* may appear entwined so that they resemble a *garuda* or *sawat* figure (see fig. 137).

Wayang figures styled after the *wayang kulit* leather shadow puppets are the only representation of humanlike figures in traditional batik. The unusual stance of these figures, head in profile and shoulders straight ahead with the feet pointing to one side, is uniquely Javanese (see fig. 138). *Wayang* are used as solid dark forms against a figured background on batik, imitating the appearance of the leather puppets at a shadow play.

These *wayang* figures are occasionally drawn against a *grinsing* backdrop. *Grinsing* is a very

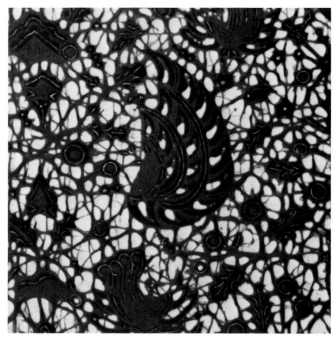

Fig. 135. *Semensriasih* motif on a batik *kain. Lar* (wing) and *peksi* (bird) motifs appear against a *semen* background. *Soga* brown, black, and cream. From Central Java. Tama Art University collection.

Fig. 136. "Tree of life" motif. Central Java.

old motif that has been discussed in relation to the earliest historical references to batik. The pattern resembles tiny fish scales, each with a black dot in its center. The *grinsing* figure is very difficult to draw, because wax must be applied around the fine dark lines and the black dot. The *sisik* pattern, which is similar to *grinsing* but lacks the black dot, is often used for *isen* decoration. *Grinsing* may also be worked into motifs as an *isen* pattern, or it may be used alone as an all-over pattern with a figure such as *sawat,* a *wayang,* or a medallion (see fig. 139).

Two unusual types of batik incorporate a

Fig. 137. *Naga* motif on a batik *kain*. Blue, brown, and cream. From Cirebon, West Java. Authors' collection.

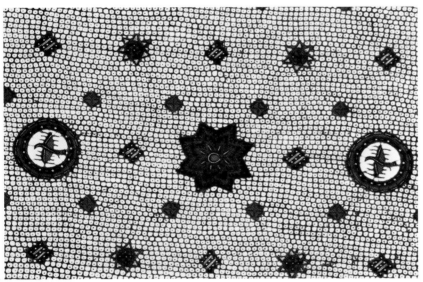

Fig. 138. *Wayang* figure. Central Java.

Fig. 139. *Grinsing* motif on a batik *kain*. Here it forms the background for medallion figures. *Soga* brown, indigo blue, black, and cream. From Central Java. Authors' collection.

variety of traditional patterns. The *sekarjagad* or "flower of the universe" pattern juxtaposes many batik motifs—*grinsing, parang, kawung, truntum,* and flowers—in a jigsaw-puzzle arrangement (see plate 46). The *tambal* motif similarly utilizes many designs but fits them into a framework of rectangles and triangles rather than the amorphous shapes of the *sekarjagad.*

Central Javanese patterns have influenced the motifs of other batik-making centers in Java. The batik of Tasikmalaya in West Java, for example, features *parang* and other classic Jogjakarta-Solo motifs in subtle shades of red, green, and *soga* brown against a yellow background. Nearby Banyumas is noted for similar motifs in light brown *soga* and golden yellow against a blue-black background. Several East Javanese cities, notably Sidoarjo and Mojokerto, also adopted Central Javanese motifs. Sidoarjo batik makers, for example, draw *garuda* and other traditional Solo motifs and dye the cloth in the colors of the north coast—red, blue, and green against a dark brown or black background. Mojokerto batik features Central-Javanese-style *semen* and *peksi* (bird) motifs in blue, brown, and black.

Chinese Influence and the North Coast Style

Central Java and the areas mentioned above have a well-defined style of batik with shared characteristics of design and motif. The north coast of Java from Jakarta to Lasem, although it shows some Central Javanese influence, has also developed its own distinct regional style. While the Jogjakarta-Solo area developed in an inward manner, assimilating foreign influences rather than adopting them directly, the north coast is geographically an open region and its batik centers have been more strongly affected by outside sources.

The most important contribution to the batik of the north coast came from the Chinese. Chinese have been in Indonesia since the Srivijaya period (732–1010) when they came as Buddhist pilgrims, but most of the Chinese immigrated during the seventeenth and eighteenth centuries. These Chinese were merchant-class people from Fujian (Fukien) Province who later came to view Indonesia as their home. In contrast, a subsequent wave of immigrants in the nineteenth century were poor Cantonese who were generally interested in making their fortune and returning to China. The earlier settlers from Fujian had a respect for Chinese and eventually Indonesian culture that was missing among the later immigrants.

Chinese (as well as Dutch) were not allowed to own land, so they were primarily involved in business. In the eighteenth and nineteenth centuries, the Chinese acted as middlemen between the Dutch and the Indonesians, collecting agricultural goods and taxes. Because of this and the superior status accorded the Chinese by the Dutch, relations between Indonesians and Chinese were usually strained. Chinese eventually gained control over much of the economy, beginning with the opium trade, pawn shops, and moneylending. When the Dutch government took over the pawn shops and opium business in the late nineteenth century, the Chinese turned their capital and entrepreneurial skills to organizing native labor.

By the 1890s, the Chinese controlled the import of cambric cloth, and thus came to dominate the batik industry. It is ironic, considering the importance of batik in Javanese culture, that the industry was so quickly taken over by outsiders. Since the Chinese were a closeknit group, they were able to ignore regulations meant to protect the workers, and Javanese batik artisans became like bonded slaves in the batik industry. This situation was denounced by the Dutch government in the late nineteenth and early twentieth centuries, but little changed. In 1911, Javanese batik traders organized a society, the Sarikat Islam, to oppose the Chinese monopoly of batik, but it had little success. Still today, most batik factories are owned by Chinese.

The Chinese were especially powerful along the north coast of Java, where they controlled ricefields, toll roads, and moneylending in the villages. The north coast batik centers were also, with few exceptions, commercial enterprises that were owned by the Chinese. Consequently, all of the batik-making areas on the north coast show strong Chinese influence in their motifs.

REMBANG AND JUANA: In the silk batik industry of Rembang and Juana on the Pasisir Plain, Chinese factory owners employed Javanese *pengobeng*, the itinerant women who were professional waxers, to draw favorite Chinese patterns on batik intended for export. Even the silk fabric for the sarong and selindang was imported from China. An attempt to start a silk industry in Java was made around this time but it never took root.

This silk batik was exported to Bali, Kalimantan, and Sumatra. In Bali, especially, these silk cloths are treasured and worn to religious ceremonies and festivals by those wealthy enough to own them (see plate 47). The silk selindang are often used as *saput,* the waistcloth that completes the Balinese costume and is required for entering temples.

The motifs on these Rembang and Juana sarong and selindang are Chinese in origin. The featured motif on almost all the batik produced in this area is a bird figure known as *luk cuan,* which appears in brown and black against a cream or occasionally green background (see fig. 140). The same motif is found in all other north coast centers as well, in Lasem, Kudus, Semarang, Pekalongan, Tegal, Indramayu, and Cirebon.

Luk cuan birds are variations of the Chinese phoenix. In Chinese legend, the phoenix appears only in times of peace and prosperity; its association with good luck has made it a popular pattern among Chinese people. It is a common decorative motif on Chinese ceramics and costume, especially on garments worn by an empress. The

Fig. 140. *Luk cuan* bird on a silk batik sarong. *Soga* brown, black, and cream. From Rembang, northern Central Java. Tama Art University collection.

mythical creature is a combination of the most beautiful features of many birds, and its long streaming tail and outstretched wings as they are seen on batik are often very Chinese. Sometimes the head and body may be stylized so that only a whirl of feathers dominates the motif.

Another figure associated with good fortune, the Chinese dragon is occasionally borrowed for batik motifs. The dragon is a benevolent figure in Chinese mythology; the traditional Chinese version with a camel's head, stag's antlers, serpent's body, and clawed feet is often modified in local batik designs. Chinese ceramics are the probable source for many batik motifs like the dragon.

LASEM: Lasem, a small town in northern Central Java, is famous for its distinctive batik. Batik was never a large-scale industry in Lasem and all batik produced there was hand-drawn. The Lasem workshops were also controlled by Chinese, and a distinct Chinese-influenced style developed that was popular especially among people from nearby Madura Island and Surabaya. Lasem batik often features *luk cuan* birds against a *semen*-like background of foliage, showing a combination of Central Javanese and Chinese influences. The patterns are characterized by small, delicate motifs in red, green, and gold.

An unusual abstract motif found only in Lasem is *kapal kandas,* which means "ship run aground." In the time of sailing ships it was customary for villagers who helped push a beached ship back to sea to share in some of the wealth on board, so a ship run aground was probably a welcome sight for poor villagers and could have been the inspiration for the motif. This pattern is a repeating series of crescents (the ancient representation of a ship, especially the ship of the dead) in green, brown, and yellow against a cream background (see plate 48). A batik like the *kapal kandas* that features dark motifs against a lighter colored background is always more highly valued for the extra care and work that must go into it. Batik equal to the finest once made in Lasem is rarely seen today because few people there have the skill or are willing to take the time to create such fine work.

INDRAMAYU: Indramayu is a well-known batik center on the northwest coast. Its batik patterns are often similar to those of Lasem, usually featuring *luk cuan* birds against a vine-and-tendril design. Indramayu pieces differ from Lasem batik in that they are more somberly colored and the motifs are generally larger. The Indramayu motifs may appear in black and brown against a cream background or in indigo blue and white only. Along with typical north coast motifs such as the *luk cuan* bird, the cloth may be decorated with dark *citcik* against the light background. These dots, in contrast to the usual white *citcik*, are produced by puncturing the waxed areas so that the dye can enter. The holes are made by a paddle set with many needles.

Cirebon

Cirebon on the north coast is justly famed for its eccentric batik, and the city produces a wider variety of patterns than any other area outside of Jogjakarta-Solo. The Cirebon area, like Central Java, was ruled by two powerful courts, Kanoman and Kesepuhan, and the city is the only batik center along the north coast where many of the motifs developed under an aristocratic influence rather than a commercial one. The palaces of the two courts are separated by only a few miles and can still be seen today. Although the best known motifs of Cirebon were developed for the sultans, they too show strong Chinese influence, reflecting the power of the Chinese in the area. In the late eighteenth century the sultans of Cirebon allowed Chinese to act as their landlords. Apparently the Chinese so ruthlessly took advantage of their power that the people of Cirebon at one point revolted and requested that the Dutch rule them directly.

The best known textiles of Cirebon are cloud-patterned batik in which the surface of the cloth is covered with clouds in four shades of blue set off by glimpses of a red, or occasionally white or light blue, background. The Cirebon style of rendering clouds is derived from Chinese sources. Chinese clouds like those seen on Cirebon batik are curving and asymmetrical and were originally derived from animal forms. *Megomendung,* or "threatening clouds" (see plate 49), have curved edges, while *megomalang* clouds, another Cirebon style, are pointed on the ends.

Megomendung and *megomalang* batik were used as decorations for the royal bedchamber although some sources say the cloths were also worn by the sultan. The sultan did wear a headcloth whose shades of blue and red were similar in color to those on the *megomendung* and that featured a rooster motif surrounded by slender, cloudlike figures. Each *megomendung* and *megomalang* takes several months to complete since the cloth must be dyed and waxed five separate times to achieve the variations in colors on the clouds and to fill in the contrasting background. Traditionally, indigo and *mengkudu* dyes produced the blue and red, but today synthetic dyes are used.

The creation of *megomendung* and *megomalang,* the most famous of Cirebon batik, died out in Cirebon, but fortunately a few batik makers kept the style alive in Jogjakarta. Today the traditional Cirebon patterns are enjoying a revival in popularity. A different style of court batik is still hand-waxed, like all Cirebon batik, in several small villages, especially Trusmi and Kalitengah just outside of Cirebon.

The classic batik made in Cirebon is a unique style that depicts palaces, gardens, and fantastic landscapes populated with a myriad of incredible animals, including dragons, lions with elephant heads, *naga* serpents, and other mythical beasts as well as realistically portrayed deer, elephants, chickens, fish, monkeys, and so on. The arrangement of the scenery and animals is notable; this pictorial style of layout is found only in Cirebon. Several levels of mountains, rocks, pools, and other features are arranged horizontally across the cloth. The importance of landscape in Cirebon batik has a parallel in Chinese art, and the style of depicting mountains, rocks, water, and clouds shows a strong Chinese influence. Because of their paintinglike scenes these batik seem more suitable as wall-hangings than clothing, but they are said to have been worn by the consorts of the sultan.

One traditional pattern features the pavilions, pools, fountains, and walls of a water palace called Sunyaragi. The limestone ruins of Sunyaragi still exist on the outskirts of Cirebon. Local legend says that nine men built it in a day and a night for a Chinese princess. In China, similar gardens were laid out with caves, pools, and grottoes and often incorporated naturally water-sculpted limestone into the scene. On the batik, fish swim in the pools and animals wander through the garden, but at Sunyaragi today, only the empty rock formations remain. Few visitors stop to visit the spot although an old man and a gang of kids delight in taking guests through the ruins (see fig. 141).

The gardens of the palaces of Kanoman and Kesepuhan are also a favorite subject for batik, and these palace motifs are believed by local people to be the oldest Cirebon patterns. In Indonesia, palaces are not grand mansions but a collection of smaller buildings, pavilions, and gardens. On these batik, rock formations and pavilions form a backdrop for animal life both real and imagined. Depicted here are crowned *naga* serpents and carved lions that guard the palaces just as Chinese lions guard temples (see fig. 142). The chariots used by one of the sultans are in the form of a *peksi naga sakti,* a combination of elephant, lion, and bird, and this strange

Fig. 141. Sunyaragi Water Palace motif on a batik *kain*. Blue, brown, black, and cream. From Cirebon, West Java. Tama Art University collection.

Fig. 142. Lions flanking a coral rock formation at Kesepuhan Palace, Cirebon, West Java. This scene is the inspiration for many traditional Cirebon patterns.

figure occasionally appears on batik (see plate 50).

Other Cirebon batik cloths portray animals and rocks in a similar style but without the direct references to historical places. Animals and rocks are sometimes blended together so that an elephant or chicken may appear to be growing from a stone, and just where the beast begins and the rock ends is difficult to say (see fig. 143). Some of the unusual abstract patterns of Cirebon seem to have been inspired by the strange rock formations that are part of the walls of the palaces. Other abstract patterns are like highly stylized flamelike figures; often these motifs are arranged diagonally across the cloth.

Fig. 143. Animals and rocks against the sea on a batik sarong. Blue, brown, black, and cream. From Cirebon, West Java. Authors' collection.

Fig. 144. Realistically drawn animals on a batik sarong. Red, yellow, green, indigo blue, and cream. From Cirebon, West Java. Toyama Kinenkan Foundation collection.

Cirebon batik, especially that using pictorial patterns, is no longer worn as *kain* in the city, but it has become popular in Jakarta. There, officials and businessmen wear shirts cut from fine hand-drawn batik, a type of dress that has become acceptable for formal occasions in Indonesia.

Besides the court-styled batik, with its cloud and scenic patterns, other Cirebon batik was decorated with motifs similar to those of Central Java. Older Cirebon batik may show classic *semen* patterns with *garuda*, the "tree of life," *lar* motifs, and the mystical mountain, Mahameru, all of which are Central Javanese influences.

Other types of Cirebon batik were similar to those made in other cities along the north coast and show typical Chinese influences. *Luk cuan* birds were depicted in their most natural and distinctive style here, and animal figures were portrayed in a realistic manner (see fig. 144). Flowers and vines in red, green, and blue often formed the background for these birds and animals.

Pekalongan

The largest producer of batik on the north coast (and in Java), Pekalongan, also displays a strong Chinese influence in its batik. Not only did the Chinese contribute motifs and own factories in Pekalongan, but they were very much involved in making batik themselves. It is possible to meet

Chinese women who learned to make batik from their mothers and grandmothers. They created batik for themselves, spending months or even years on a single cloth, and the treasured results of such labor are kept as family heirlooms. The Chinese women in Pekalongan and other cities along the north coast once wore batik sarong, a form of dress that was not common among Chinese in other parts of Indonesia.

The earliest influence on Pekalongan batik, as on most of the other north coast batik centers, came from Central Java. The patterns that were restricted to the nobility in Jogjakarta and Solo were never forbidden in Pekalongan (or, for that matter, in other cities outside of Central Java). Thus early Pekalongan batik often features forbidden *larangan* motifs like *parang* and *sawat*. Broken-line *nitik* patterns are also believed to have been drawn on the early Pekalongan batik.

Because of the heavy Chinese involvement in the batik industry in Pekalongan, it is not surprising that many local batik motifs are derived from Chinese sources. The *luk cuan* bird and the use of *banji* backgrounds for floral patterns are two outstanding examples of Chinese influence on Pekalongan batik. But contemporary Pekalongan patterns owe much to the Dutch, and the distinct style of batik that Pekalongan has developed over the past sixty years is the result of a combination of Chinese and Dutch influences.

Despite their long involvement in Indonesia since the late sixteenth century, the Dutch did not have much direct effect on Indonesia's people or arts until the late nineteenth century. Relatively few Dutch actually lived in the country until this time, and Chinese middlemen handled most of their dealings with the Indonesians. The first substantial immigration of Dutch other than soldiers and merchants of the Dutch East India Company took place between 1870 and 1890, and it was at this time that the Dutch became interested in gaining greater control over the Indonesians so that new crops aimed for export could be easily introduced. Generally speaking, the Dutch did not meddle with Indonesian *adat* (traditional law). It was not until the early twentieth century that they became more concerned about the living conditions in their colony, thus instigating social programs aimed at bettering the lot of Indonesians.

At this time the Dutch also began to take a greater interest in Indonesian culture. The Dutch government granted a subsidy to a craft school in 1907 and in 1910 opened some trade schools. Cultural circles were established in Java around 1916 to promote the arts, both European and Indonesian. These circles helped revitalize Javanese dance and music and even established a Javanese cinema. A magazine of cultural affairs, *Djawa,* with articles by Dutch and Indonesians, was published. In 1922, the Dutch started an institute in Bandung to study batik and other textiles, and in 1930 they set up an institute in Jogjakarta to do the same. This institute was the forerunner of the Batik Research Center, established in 1951 and still active in Jogjakarta today.

Priyayi Javanese, many of whom had been educated in Holland, often took part in these cultural activities with the Dutch. The growing sense of nationalism among Indonesian people, combined with the Dutch attention, sparked a renewed interest in traditional arts among these upper-class Javanese, and a general revival in Javanese arts occurred in the early part of this century.

Working against the revitalization of native crafts, however, was the tendency of some educated Indonesians to emulate European ways. Also, cheap imports of printed cloth from Europe and Japan worked against the local batik makers. In fact, in the early twentieth century, the comparatively low price of stamped batik and of the imports had just about driven hand-drawn batik into extinction in Pekalongan, although a few Indonesians and Chinese continued to hand-wax pieces for themselves. At this point, a number of Dutch women who appreciated the artistry of hand-drawn batik began to show an interest in the craft. Like Chinese women, they began to make batik themselves. They encouraged the Javanese women to continue making their traditional hand-drawn batik, and some Dutch organized Javanese batik workers on a commercial basis. This interest, together with the general revival in Javanese arts and crafts, was instrumental in saving hand-drawn work in Pekalongan.

The adoption of European patterns in Pekalongan also began in the early twentieth century. Ev van Zuylen, a Dutch woman, made an important contribution to the design of Pekalongan batik, and she is generally credited with introducing the layout of floral bouquets that became its trademark. A sarong was usually decorated with three of four bouquets and a *tumpal* motif. Birds and butterflies appeared in elaborate displays of roses, tulips, lilies, and other flowers (see fig. 145). The layout of these Pekalongan designs

Fig. 145. Flower bouquet, a product of European influence, on a batik sarong. Light red, deep red, and white. From Pekalongan, northern Central Java. Authors' collection.

is European, although the combination of birds and butterflies with flowers is also a favorite theme. The early works of this type are visually pleasing, but over the years the style has become rigid and unimaginative. European subjects new to batik such as machines, automobiles, and ships also appear on some of the batik made in this period (see figs. 146–48).

Beginning with the Dutch, batik waxers in Pekalongan took up the custom of signing their names to their work. Today the names on the best hand-drawn pieces are often those of Chinese, who are continuing a tradition of fine *tulis* batik. The detailed concentration of fill-in work characteristic of Pekalongan batik is a Chinese contribution to the style. Hundreds of *citcik* dots and fine lines may decorate leaves, flowers, and butterflies. Chinese motifs like *luk cuan* birds are also popular in Pekalongan (see plate 51).

Pekalongan motifs have reflected many influences including Central Javanese, Chinese, Dutch, and even Japanese. As early as 1918, the Japanese began importing unbleached cotton into Java. By 1930, they were active in business in Java and began to control the supply of better-quality cotton. At this time, like the Europeans, they began to import cheap, printed sarong into Java, an action that had a detrimental effect on the local batik industry.

During the World War II Japanese occupation of Java, cloth supplies were cut off to the island. To keep waxers employed, factory owners gave them one piece of cloth and told them to work slowly. The batik of this Java Baru or Hokokai period,* as it is called, displays some virtuoso tjanting work, particularly in Pekalongan, which was already famed for its careful attention to detail. Pekalongan batik makers were quick to pick up new patterns, and the clichéd Japanese patterns of chrysanthemums, fans, and ladies in kimono of that period still appear occasionally on Pekalongan batik.

Pekalongan is famed as a producer of exquisitely fine hand-drawn batik but it is also the major producer of cheap, stamped batik for export. Garish flowered sarongs from Pekalongan can be seen on village women in Thailand, Malaysia, and northern Borneo as well as on the other islands of Indonesia.

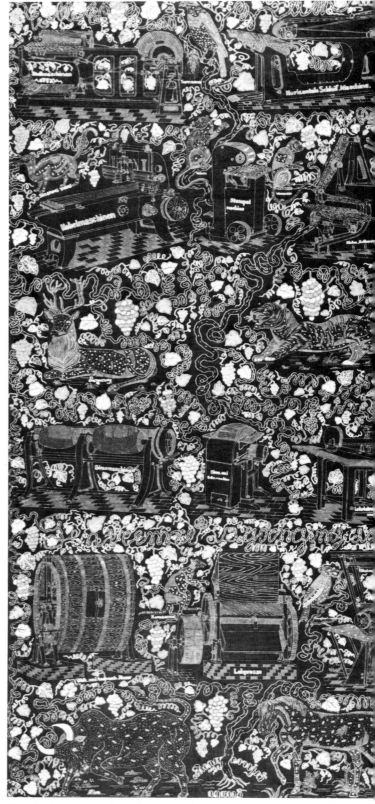

Fig. 146. Batik *kain* using a variety of Dutch names and Dutch machines as motifs. Cotton; indigo blue, *soga* brown, and cream using natural dyes; 202 cm. × 105 cm. Made in the 1930s in Central Java. Tomoyuki Yamanobe collection.

* Yazir Marzuki, N. Tirtaamidjaja, and Benedict R. O'G. Anderson, *Batik: Pola dan Tjorak—Pattern and Design* (Jakarta: Jambatan, 1966), p. 20.

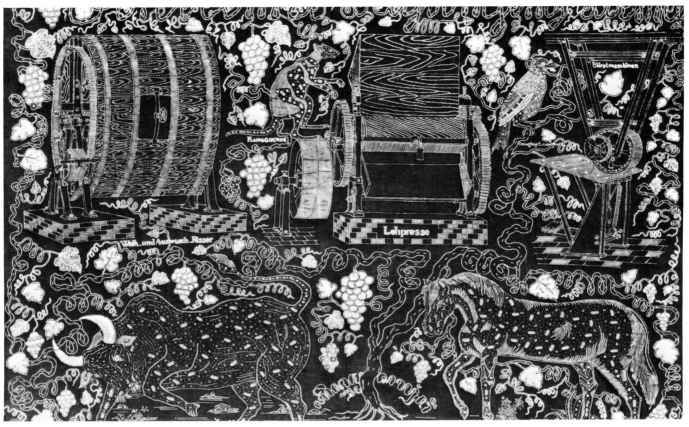

Fig. 147. Detail of figure 146.

Fig. 148. Realistically drawn ships, an example of Dutch influence, on a batik *kain*. *Soga* brown, black, and cream. From Jogjakarta, Central Java. Authors' collection.

Fig. 149. Modern pattern on a batik *kain*. Gold, black, and cream. From Jakarta, West Java. Authors' collection.

Pekalongan, like Solo, is a batik town; its main streets are dotted with batik stores and wax and dye shops, and its outer edges with factories and workshops. Many of the hotels in Pekalongan cater to the batik buyers that flock to the city. Early one morning we were amazed to see a forklift, piled high with cheap batik, come rolling into the courtyard of our hotel. A batik dealer from Kalimantan sorted through the stack of two hundred or more sarong in a short time; a glance at a piece was enough for him to decide if he would take or reject it. The buyers do not even need to leave the hotel; the batik comes to them by peddler, small truck, pedicab, and sometimes, as we saw, by forklift.

Today Pekalongan batik keeps abreast of the latest in Western fashion since batik designed for clothing is exported to Europe and America. In the tradition of the Chinese, Dutch, and Japanese, there are Europeans, Americans, and Australians behind the scenes today, exerting an influence on patterns and colors.

Contemporary Batik

A living craft like batik cannot remain static, and even the traditional batik of Central Java reflects change. The classic motifs, such as *kawung* and *parang*, are not altered, but variations on these themes are continually being created. As patterns rise and fall in popularity, new ones are constantly appearing (see fig. 149).

An excellent place to see the changing tastes in batik is the classical-dance practice held at the palace of Sultan Hamangkubuwana IX in Jogjakarta (see fig. 150). The palace guards still wear *kain soga*, often with large *ceplokkan* patterns of a style that was popular twenty or more years ago. A kris knife tucked into their belt, a batik headcloth, and a high-necked fitted jacket complete their traditional costume. The young men and women that gather to rehearse court dances prefer to wear batik with tiny *kawung* and *parang rusak klitik* motifs, classic patterns that are currently in favor (see plate 52). Con-

Fig. 150. This traditionally dressed young dancer is taking a break during one of the weekly dance practices held at the Sultan's Palace in Jogjakarta, Central Java.

temporary styles are represented by the modern batik tee-shirts and dresses worn by young foreign tourists, and by the shirts of Cirebon batik worn by visitors to Jakarta.

The uses for batik have been diversifying in recent years. The fabric is becoming a favorite material for Western-style clothing worn by Indonesians. Tablecloths, pillow covers, sheets, and curtains are new uses in Java for both stamped and hand-drawn batik.

New motifs are always being adapted to batik. The *pancasila,* for example, an emblem representing the five principles of Indonesian national ideology—belief in god, nationalism, humanism, democracy, and social justice—has become a popular batik pattern (see fig. 151). A vital source of motifs for contemporary batik makers is the textile patterns of other islands of Indonesia, some of which have been adapted to batik with success. These distinctive designs are a rich source of material with a lot of potential for batik, just as Chinese ceramics, the patola

Fig. 151. *Pancasila* motif on a batik *kain. Soga* brown, indigo blue, and black. From Central Java. Tama Art University collection.

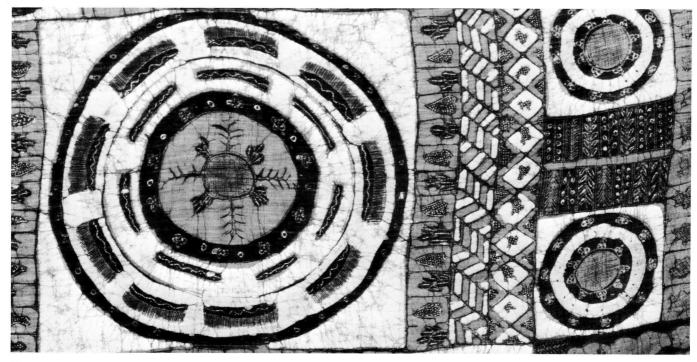

Fig. 152. Modern motif inspired by the Dong-Son-style bronze drums of Alor. Red, black, and white. From Jogja-karta, Central Java. Authors' collection.

cloth, and other outside sources have historically been the inspiration for new patterns. Torajan house motifs and patterns from Sumba and from the ship cloths of Sumatra have been used as a basis for batik patterns, as have motifs from sources other than textiles, such as the bronze Dong-Son-style drums of Alor (see fig. 152). Chinese ceramics are being reexamined by some batik designers and Chinese-style scenes are enjoying a revival.

There has also been a resurgence of interest in fine batik as a symbol of prestige among Javanese, especially among Jakartans, who are, according to batik designers working in Jogja-karta, seeking one-of-a-kind batik when they visit Central Java. Silk has again become a fabric for batik despite the fact that it is very difficult to import, expensive, and requires much skill to wax. Many of the silks being produced show typical north-coast-style motifs of *luk cuan* birds, lotus blossoms, and other Chinese patterns (see fig. 153). They also may have European-inspired motifs such as autumn leaves and grapevines.

Batik techniques are being used to create cloth paintings that depict subjects ranging from *wayang* figures, Indonesian versions of the *Ramayana* epic, and rural scenes to modern abstracts. The artistic value of each painting varies with

the would-be artist and few batik paintings have yet to become more than pleasant decorations. But the standard of batik craftsmanship on the paintings is generally high and the use of dyes is often creative. These new and admittedly commercial uses of batik produce a climate of interest in which, we hope, the more serious forms of hand-drawn batik will be able to grow.

Costume is still the foremost use of batik cloth, and batik as attire is actually spreading throughout Indonesia, where it is often taking the place of local dress. Most of the textiles discussed in this book are primarily traditional clothing for the people who make them. The richness of Indonesian costume is seen in a set of twenty-six stamps issued by the government in the mid-1970s. Although each stamp depicts the costume garments of a different region, the set gives only a partial picture of the variety of national dress. Many of these costumes, however, are no longer worn even on festive days. For better or worse, the women in many outlying regions now prefer a batik from Java. Patterns like the *sawat* or the *parang,* once worn only by the sultans in Central Java, can be seen on girls today in Kupang on Timor and on Samosir Island in Sumatra. Batik is rapidly becoming a symbol, not only of Java, but of all Indonesia.

Fig. 153. Birds and lotus flowers on a contemporary silk batik *kain*. Orange and cream. From Solo, Central Java. Authors' collection.

Bibliography

Adam, Tassilo. "The Art of Batik in Java." *Bulletin of the Needle and Bobbin Club* 18 (1934).

Adams, Marie Jeanne. *System and Meaning in East Sumba Textile Design: A Study in Traditional Indonesian Art.* Cultural Report Series, no. 16. New Haven: Yale University, 1969.

————. "Classic and Eccentric Elements in East Sumba Textiles." *Bulletin of the Needle and Bobbin Club* 55 (1972).

Batik Research Institute. *Batik Manual.* Jogjakarta: Batik Research Institute, 1972.

Birrell, Verla. *The Textile Arts.* New York: Schocken Books, 1973.

Bühler, Alfred. *Materialien zur Kenntnis der Ikattechnik* [Materials for a study of ikat technique]. Leiden: E. F. Brill, 1943.

————. "Primitive Dyeing Methods." *Ciba Review* 68 (1948).

————. "Patola Influences in Southeast Asia." *Journal of Indian Textile History* 4 (1959).

————; Ramseyer, Urs; and Ramseyer-Gygi, Nicole. *Patola und Gringsing.* Basel: Das Museum fur Volkerkunde und Schweizerische Museum fur Volkskunde, 1975–76.

Covarrubias, Miguel. *The Island of Bali.* Kuala Lumpur: Oxford University Press, 1974.

Fitzgerald, C. P. *The Southern Expansion of the Chinese People.* London: Barrie and Jenkins, 1972.

Furnivall, J. S. *Netherlands India: A Study of Plural Economy.* New York: Macmillan, 1944.

Geertz, Clifford. *The Religion of Java.* Chicago and London: University of Chicago Press, 1960.

Gittinger, Dr. Mattiebelle S. "South Sumatran Ship Cloths." *Bulletin of the Needle and Bobbin Club* 57 (1974).

Graber, Oleg. *The Formation of Islamic Art.* New Haven, Conn., and London: Yale University Press, 1973.

Gulati, A. N. *The Patola of Gujurat.* Bombay: Museums Association of India, 1951.

Holt, Claire. *Art in Indonesia: Continuities and Change.* Ithaca, N.Y.: Cornell University Press, 1967.

Jones, David. *Islamic Art: An Introduction.* London: The Halnlym Group, 1974.

Langewis, Laurens, and Wagner, Frits A. *Decorative Art in Indonesian Textiles.* Amsterdam: N. V. Boekhandel en Vitgeverij C. P. J. van der Peet, 1964.

Linton, George E. *The Modern Textile Dictionary.* New York: Duell, Sloan and Pierce, 1963.

Marzuki, Yazir, and Awvy, Fred D. *Namo Buddhaya* [Amida Buddha]. Amsterdam: Indonesian Overseas Bank, n.d.

Marzuki, Yazir; Tirtaamidjaja, N.; and Anderson, Benedict R. O'G. *Batik: Pola dan Tjorak—Pattern and Design.* Jakarta: Jambatan, 1966.

Meuraxa, Dada. *Sejarah Kebudayaan Sumatera* [A cultural history of Sumatra]. Medan, Indonesia: Firma Hasmar, 1974.

Newman, Thelma. *Contemporary Southeast Asian Arts and Crafts.* New York: Crown Publishers, 1977.

Petu, Pater Piet S. V. D. *Nusa Nipa* [Flores]. Ende (Flores), Indonesia: Pertjetakan Arnoldus and Penerbitan Nusa Indah, 1969.

Rouffaer, G. P., and Juinboll, Dr. H. H. *De Batikkunst in Ned. Indie en Haare Geschiendenis* [The art of batik in the Netherland Indies and its development]. Utrecht: Rijks Ethnographisch Museum, 1914.

Simpson, L. E., and Weir, M. *The Weaver's Craft.* 11th ed. Leicester: Dryad Press, 1969.

Sowerby, Arthur de Carle. *Nature in Chinese Art.* New York: John Day, 1940.

Steinmann, Alfred. "The Ship of the Dead in the Textile Art of Indonesia" and "The Ship of the Dead as Represented in the Art of Southeast Asia." *Ciba Review* 52 (1946).

————. "The Art of Batik" and "Batik Work: Its Origin and Spread." *Ciba Review* 58 (1947).

Taber, Barbara, and Anderson, Marilyn. *Backstrap Weaving.* New York: Watson-Guptill Publications, 1975.

Tidball, Harriet. *The Weaver's Book.* New York: Collier Books, 1976.

Trotman, E. R. *Dyeing and Chemical Technology of Textile Fibers.* 4th ed. High Wycombe, England: Charles Griffin, 1970.

Van Der Hoop, A. N. J. Th. a Th. *Indonesische Siermotievan.* [Indonesian ornamental motifs]. Batavia (Jakarta): Koninklijk Bataviaasch Genootscap Van Kunsten en Wetenschappen, 1949.

Vlekke, Bernard H. M. *Nusantara: A History of the East Indian Archipelago.* Cambridge, Mass.: Harvard University Press, 1943.

Von Heime-Geldern, Robert. *Indonesian Art.* Exhibition Catalog. New York: Asia Institute, 1948.

Index

indigo, as dyestuff, 66, 67, 70, 75, 162–63, 180
indigo blue, 66, 158
indigo dyeing
    for batik, 145, 158–60
    for gringsing, 111
    for warp ikat, 65–69, 72
Indigofera tinctoria, 66, 68
indigo paste, 158, 162
indigosol dye, 163
indigo white, 66, 158
Indochina, 143, 145
Indramayu, Java, 145, 178, 179
iron vitriol, as dye ingredient, 158
isen-isen motifs, 170, 172, 174, 176
Islam, 54, 88, 114, 168–69, 175

Jakarta, Java, 145, 178, 182
Jambi, Sumatra, 145
Japan, 103, 109, 143, 168, 184
Java Baru batik, 184
Java Hokokai batik, 184
Java Island
    arts of, 70, 166, 183, 188
    batik of, 143–45, 147, 154, 165–68, 186–88
    Chinese people on, 178, 182
    motifs of, 168–84
    royal courts of, 102, 145, 147, 148, 158, 164, 169, 180
    traditional costume of, 167, 172–74, 188
jilimprang motif, 104, 106, 107, 171
joged (court dance), 169
Jogjakarta, Java
    batik of, 145, 146, 149, 160, 162, 172, 177, 178, 180
    tie-dye of, 122, 123
Juana, Java, 145, 172, 178–79

kabakil technique, 138
Kai Island, 54
kain (length of cloth), 152, 167, 168, 182
kai ne'e motif, 92
kain hoba textile, 91
kain panjang ("long cloth"), 167, 168
kain soga (Central Javanese batik), 152, 186
Kalimantan (Indonesian Borneo), 114, 160, 178
Kalitengah village, Java, 148, 180
Kaliuda village, 82–83, 103
kalumpang nut, as dye ingredient, 68, 69
Kanatang district, Sumba, 83
kanduhu motif, 82
Kanoman Palace, 180
kapal kandas motif, 179
karihu motif, 83
Karo Batak people, 95, 129
    See also Batak people
kawung motif, 156, 169, 171, 172, 175, 177
kebaya (blouse), 167, 168
kekamahaba motif, 85, 87
kelim technique, 79, 91, 139
kembang cenkeh motif, 170
kembang jeruk motif, 170
kembang kelapa motif, 170
kembang lombok motif, 170
kembang pisang motif, 170
kemben (breastcloth), 122, 134, 168, 170
kemiri nut, as dye ingredient, 69, 109
kepala (break in the sarong pattern), 116, 119, 131, 133, 167
Kesepuhan Palace, 180
kimonoed-lady motif, 184
Kisar Island, 54, 91
klowongan stamp, 156
klowong wax, 154, 156, 157, 159
Klungkung, Bali, 103, 120

Korabafu district, Rote, 97
Koran, 168
kris knife, 172
Kröe area, Sumatra, 134, 135, 140
Kudus, Java, 145, 178
Kupang, Timor, 78, 188

lafa'ina textile, 97
Lake Tempe, Sulawesi, 115
Lake Toba, Sumatra, 95
lakon (Javanese myth dramatization), 169
Lamboya district, Sumba, 138
Lampung, Sumatra, 54, 104, 134, 140
larak fruit, as batik washing agent, 162
larangan (forbidden) motifs, 169, 175, 182
Larantuka, Flores, 91
lar motif, 175–76, 182
Lasem, Java, 145, 163, 178, 179
Late Chou culture, influence of, 54, 57, 101, 140
lau pahekung textile, 136–37
lau patola ratu textile, 83
lawo butu textile, 142
lawo gamba textile, 90
lease cords, 61–62, 74
lease sticks, 128, 130
le'do motif, 84
lemak textile, 138
lemon juice, as dye ingredient, 161
Leran, Java, 168
leo motif, 107
Leti Island, 54
lidah api motif, 176
lidi stick (or rod), 130–31, 132, 135, 137, 138
life-force concept, 55, 90, 135
lily motif, 183
lime, as dye ingredient, 66, 67, 68, 71, 158, 159
Lio district, Flores, 55, 88, 89–90 106, 107
lion motif, 82, 87, 180
lizard motif, 82, 90, 91, 92, 138, 139
loba bark, as dyestuff, 68, 69, 70, 71
    See also mordant; *mengkudu* dyeing
lobster motif, 176
Lomblen Island, 57, 91, 106
Lombok Island, 114, 122
longong (sash), 122
lontar palm, leaves of, 64, 85
loom. *See* backstrap loom; hand loom
lotus motif, 141, 172, 188
loyang (batik wax pan), 153
luk cuan motif, 178–79, 182, 184
lukis ("painters"), 143, 150
lung motif, 174
lye water, as dye ingredient, 66, 68, 69, 70, 71, 109, 111

machine motif, 184
Madura Island, 145, 179
Mahabharata epic, 102, 174
Mahameru motif, 182
Majapahit kingdom, 102
makaba motif, 86
Makassar, 86, 87
    See also Ujung Pandang
Malang, Java, 102, 120
Malaysia, 146, 184
    See also Iban Dyak people
male-female polarity of textiles, 95–96
Maluku Islands, 54, 106
mamuli motif, 96
Mandeling Batak people, 95
    See also Batak people
Manggarai people, 134
manggaran motif, 170